PHYSICAL ACTIVITY ASSESSMENT

Lifecourse research in physical activity tracks long-term trends in physical activity behaviours and gives an insight into the link between a physically active lifestyle and later-life health outcomes. However, the complexity of physical activity behaviours, and the analytical issues posed by lifecourse research, present researchers with real challenges in accurately assessing the relationship between lifelong physical activity and health. *Physical Activity Assessment: A Lifecourse Approach* is the first book to approach the assessment of physical activity for health from a lifecourse perspective and provide students and researchers with much-needed guidance on conducting lifecourse studies.

The book provides readers with a thorough grounding in physical activity assessment from across the lifecourse perspective and evaluates current methods of measurement, including comparison studies, criterion methods, subjective assessment methods and physical activity monitors. It then goes on to offer guidance on the optimal measurement techniques of physical activity across the lifecourse, suggesting how data should be collected, analysed and quantified in light of modern technology and global connectivity, and what these methods mean for physical activity guidelines and interventions, and public health outcomes.

Offering a unique and novel combination of theoretical grounding and quantitative research guidance, this is important reading for any students taking modules in physical activity measurement or physical activity and health, and any researchers conducting lifecourse physical activity studies.

Paul Innerd is a Lecturer in Exercise Physiology at the University of Sunderland, UK.

PHYSICAL ACTIVITY ASSESSMENT

A Lifecourse Approach

Paul Innerd

Routledge
Taylor & Francis Group

LONDON AND NEW YORK

First published 2020
by Routledge
2 Park Square, Milton Park, Abingdon, Oxon OX14 4RN

and by Routledge
711 Third Avenue, New York, NY 10017

Routledge is an imprint of the Taylor & Francis Group, an informa business

British Library Cataloguing in Publication Data
A catalogue record for this book is available from the British Library

Library of Congress Cataloging-in-Publication Data
Names: Innerd, Paul, author.
Title: Physical activity assessment : a lifecourse approach / Paul Innerd.
Description: New York : Routledge, 2020. | Includes bibliographical
   references and index. | Summary: "The book provides readers with a
   thorough grounding in physical activity assessment from a lifecourse
   perspective and assesses current methods of measurement, including
   comparison studies, criterion methods, subjective assessment methods
   and physical activity monitors. It then goes on to offer guidance on
   the optimal measurement techniques of physical activity across the
   lifecourse, suggesting how data should be collected, analysed and
   quantified in light of modern technology and global connectivity,
   and what these methods mean for physical activity guidelines and
   interventions, and public health outcomes"— Provided by publisher.
Identifiers: LCCN 2019011072 | ISBN 9781138059986 (hardback) |
   ISBN 9781138059993 (paperback) | ISBN 9781315163260 (ebook)
Subjects: LCSH: Physical fitness—Testing. | Exercise tests. | Accelerometers.
Classification: LCC GV436 .I56 2019 | DDC 613.7—dc23
LC record available at https://lccn.loc.gov/2019011072

ISBN: 978-1-138-05998-6 (hbk)
ISBN: 978-1-138-05999-3 (pbk)
ISBN: 978-1-315-16326-0 (ebk)

Typeset in Bembo
by Swales & Willis Ltd, Exeter Devon, UK

MIX
Paper from responsible sources
FSC   FSC® C013985

Printed in the United Kingdom
by Henry Ling Limited

To my dearest mother and father

CONTENTS

FIGURES

TABLES

INTRODUCTION

Physical activity is essential for health and well-being. Substantial health benefits can be achieved by maintaining a physically active lifestyle, from the very first years of the lifecourse to the very last. Unsurprisingly, large-scale assessments of physical activity are a major focus in all age groups. However, physical activity is notoriously difficult to assess. It is a complex, multi-dimensional behaviour, and it changes progressively with increasing age; across the lifecourse, we generally do less physical activity and carry out different types.

Large-scale assessments of physical activity require carefully chosen measurement methods. A multitude of measurement instruments are available, from short-form questionnaires to body-worn sensors. As technology advances, there is a continuing increase in the use of wrist-worn accelerometer-based activity monitors, commonly called *accelerometers*. Modern accelerometers provide continuous tracking of physical activity capturing long-term changes across the lifecourse. They have been used to produce large data sets in studies such as the National Health and Nutrition Examination Survey (NHANES) and UK Biobank. Accelerometers can be used to produce continuous 24-hour movement data using open-source analytical methods, from which measures of physical activity, sedentary activity and sleep can be obtained.

Lifecourse assessments of physical activity should embrace innovation but maintain adherence to agreed measurement standards. Physical activity questionnaires are cost-effective and easy to administer, but they are subjective and prone to varying degrees of error. Current technologies offer outstanding opportunities in movement measurement; however, there is a need to understand, reproduce and communicate new data derived from them.

Selecting the best method to suite your study aims can be challenging. Yet these decisions are critically important since measurement inconsistencies can render the findings of a study useless. To overcome this, the reader should understand how the device works, the analytical methods used to derive physical activity from sensor data, and how external factors such as the ageing process affect measurement – in short, a guide to assessing physical activity across the lifecourse. Therein lies the aim of this book.

Background

Physical *in*activity is the fourth biggest risk factor for non-communicable disease (NCD) alongside smoking, excess alcohol and bad diet. The first *Lancet Series on Physical Activity* combined physical activity data from 122 countries, revealing an alarming 31% of adults (15 years or older) and 80% of 13–15-year-olds are not physically active enough to maintain health (Hallal et al. 2012). This results in 6% of all deaths, roughly 3.4 million per year, as shown in Figure 0.1.

These estimates are likely to be conservative as most evidence is based on self-reported physical activity levels which are imprecise. Objective measurements allow researchers to assess the optimal physical activity for numerous health outcomes such as type II diabetes, cardiovascular disease and cancers. The features of physical activity are that it reduces with age, is higher in women than men (but higher in boys than girls) and increased in high-income countries. However, the absence of robust trend data presents a major knowledge gap in physical activity surveillance. This is being addressed through continued improvements in objective monitoring of physical activity using new technologies.

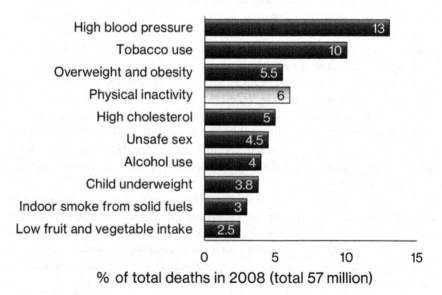

FIGURE 0.1 Leading risk factors for mortality from any cause. Physical *in*activity caused roughly 6% of deaths.

Source: World Health Organization 2011.

The NHANES first implemented accelerometer-based physical activity monitors from 2003 onwards. Since then, the technology of accelerometry has since evolved considerably. Technologies used today, can provide highly detailed acceleration data. These devices, called *raw accelerometers*, provide data from which detailed assessments of physical activity can be obtained from a single device generally worn on the wrist to maximise comfort. The sensor records high-throughput, sub-second-level acceleration data, ranging between 10 and 100 observations per second (Hz). Open-source analytics (openly accessible, at no cost, for use, modification and sharing) such as GGIR (van Hees 2014) can convert a single acceleration signal from a device worn >7 days into measures relating to non-wear time, energy expenditure, physical activity intensity from sedentary, light, moderate to vigorous activity, sedentary behaviours such as sitting, activity types, and even sleep.

NCDs and their risk factors are most effectively tackled throughout the course of people's lives, through healthy behaviours and early diagnosis and treatment. The benefits of healthy behaviours such as physical activity, and the deleterious effects of physical *in*activity, begin before pregnancy, during foetal development, and continue through childhood into adult life and then old age. Thus, it is critical to understand the correlates and determinants of physical activity causing individual levels of physical activity to rise or fall. Objective measurements from wearable sensors represent a feasible way of amassing a robust body of physical activity data. We will explore how this can be done in the following chapters.

Overview

In this book, I present physical activity the behaviour, carried out across the lifecourse, how it changes as we age, why it changes as we age, and the health consequences of physical *in*activity as it is accumulated in varying amounts over time. A lifecourse approach pays special attention to the cumulative detrimental effects of physical *in*activity, from early changes to the cells and systems to the point of diagnosis when disease becomes symptomatic. This improves the design and timing of interventions. After observing how and why physical activity changes across the lifecourse, we will identify ways of obtaining accurate and precise measurements.

We will identify the measurement standards that all measurement methods should meet and learn that the field of accelerometry has not always adhered to these standards. All current measurement methods have distinct strengths and limitations, which are illustrated well using method comparison studies. The use of a measurement method must be preceded by studies which demonstrate validity and reliability in the main study population. The design, statistics and interpretation of method comparison studies are essential to ensure the correct measurement method has been chosen.

Finally, we identify the optimal measurement methods to use across the lifecourse – chiefly, raw accelerometers and their wearable sensors recording 24-hour movement data. However, where early accelerometers came with manufacturer software, such as the ActiGraph GT1M, raw accelerometers are accompanied by less *user-friendly* software. However, a lack of knowledge of computation language is typically all that holds the non-specialist back. Accordingly, an explanation of the often-complex algorithms, how they function and how to use them, and a clear and concise discussion of current, more advanced technologies will render them accessible to the reader.

All this is provided in three parts:

Part I: Physical activity assessment: a lifecourse perspective.

Part II: Current measurement methods used across the lifecourse.

Part III: Optimal measurement of physical activity across the lifecourse.

The field of physical activity measurement is highly multidisciplinary, perhaps due to the scale of the health burden it causes. Within the ten chapters of this book is knowledge from the disciplines of epidemiology, measurement, wearable technology and engineering and data science, which is defined as 'using advanced statistics on large data sets to extract new knowledge and insights'. Incorporating all the aforementioned fields, we will use the lens of a theoretical framework, namely lifecourse epidemiology, to explain how physical activity levels are influenced by biological, behavioural and social factors during gestation, childhood, adolescence and adult life, and across the generations (Kuh et al. 2003).

Chapter 1 highlights lifecourse assessments of physical activity. Physical activity is essential to preserve health and prevent disease, and it is effective at all stages of life. During gestation, maternal activity levels promote conditions conducive to optimal development, in childhood and adolescence it is possible to nurture a period of pronounced physical and psychological change through adequate physical activity, and in adulthood it acts to slow the ageing process and risk of NCDs. Evidence suggests there is a general reduction in activity levels and an increase in sedentary behaviour, yet the extent to which this occurs, if indeed at all, and when it occurs are determined by a multitude of factors, such as self-efficacy, motivation and life events such as parenthood and marriage, and these determinants change as we age. Overall, physical activity over the lifecourse and its determinants is the focus of Chapter 1.

Population surveillance involves the tracking of target populations using methods defined by their practicality and feasibility. Hence, the World Health Organization carries out international activity surveillance using the Global Physical Activity Questionnaire (GPAQ) and has done so in well over 100 countries. Population surveillance facilitates physical activity research from a lifecourse perspective, since surveillance studies follow groups over time. Due to the preference for feasible measurement instruments, either physical activity questionnaires or, more recently, activity monitors are used. Measures used to asses physical activity are typically physiological – activity energy expenditure (AEE), metabolic equivalents (METs) and moderate to vigorous physical activity (MVPA) – or behavioural (activity type, such as sitting, walking or activities of daily living).

Note that both physiological and behavioural physical activity change across the lifecourse; older adults exert more energy during a given movement, whilst the repertoire of activity types synonymous with able-bodied life tends to become more difficult to perform. In Chapter 2, we will examine these common measures related to physical activity measurement and, taking each in turn, look at how they change across the lifecourse.

The theoretical models derived from lifecourse epidemiology track long-term exposures and create an understanding of their cumulative effects on health trajectories and health outcomes. The lifecourse model has been around for some years and is grounded in the understanding that disease in adulthood is the result of repeated insults to health, often brought about by the cumulative effects of many exposures, incidents and behaviours over a long period of time, sometimes starting as far back as infancy. In Chapter 3, we will learn key terms which describe how multiple exposures act and interact to cause disease progression or recession. In addition to this, we will explore the framework of physical activity determinants – in other words, what motivates people to become active, and what causes people to be less active. We will use case studies to help understand the interaction of determinants and significance of key life events in Chapter 3. But what instruments best capture these changes? What factors should you use to inform your choice?

In such large-scale assessments, physical activity is captured routinely with either questionnaires or activity monitors. However, choosing which to use is difficult. A new measurement method should be compared with an existing method of known validity and reliability, preferably a criterion reference. Method comparison studies are essential in determining whether the measurement instrument is valid for the purpose for which it is being used. But they must be well executed. For example, waist-mounted accelerometers may provide valid estimates of time spent in MVPA but not valid estimates of energy expenditure. All current devices and analytical methods are validated as part of a method comparison of validation study. Chapter 4 will show how to interpret method comparison and validation studies and carry them out. After learning how to critique a new measurement method, ensuring its suitability for use in a study, we will look at the measurement instruments that form the backbone of physical activity epidemiology.

The most accurate and precise measures of physical activity tend to be obtained from so-called *criterion methods*. Instruments featuring expensive equipment such as metabolic carts, doubly labelled water and direct observation are too large, expensive or cumbersome for use in large cohorts. Nevertheless, the method comparison studies described in Chapter 4 use criterion methods to determine the criterion validity of a new physical activity questionnaire or activity monitor. Questionnaires can feature large measurement error due to their subjectivity and reliance on memory. Error that becomes too large can lead to erroneous claims being made. We will highlight key steps to minimise measurement error in questionnaires. Physical activity monitors provide objective measures of physical activity. The inclusion of the ActiGraph 7164 in the NHANES 2003–2005 data sweep was seen as a major leap forward. Many other studies followed suit. Current accelerometers have evolved drastically. Raw accelerometers adopted by NHANES and used in the UK Biobank are increasingly suited to large-scale measurement. Nonetheless, many studies use accelerometers and questionnaires to provide objective measures of physical activity and additional context respectively. Chapter 5 will explore the strengths and limitations of current measurement methods.

Physical activity monitors used in epidemiology are largely accelerometer-based. First-generation devices used proprietary manufacturer software and, with limited storage capacity, condensed the acceleration signal into output in non-standardised *activity counts*. Furthermore, placement of the monitor on the hip caused a lot of missing data during device removal. Modern devices are less expensive since they feature no onboard processors to condense the data. Instead, raw data are stored in standardised SI units of gravitational acceleration, *g*-force or simply *g*. Such devices are small, lightweight and designed to be worn continuously. After data are downloaded, they are analysed to provide meaningful measures of physical activity. Placement at the wrist drastically decreases removal by the participant, and the device itself is less expensive since it features no onboard processors which perform proprietary processing, but rather it has the storage space to provide output in standardised SI units of gravitational acceleration: *g*-force. The evolution of activity monitor technology is highlighted in Chapter 6.

Measurement standards indicate that prior to using an accelerometer, the user should understand how it works. This can be difficult as the technology of accelerometry has evolved rapidly. Nevertheless, we can split accelerometry into three parts: hardware, data processing and data analysis. The accelerometer is actually the internal sensor which converts movement by the body into a digitally sampled signal. Depending on the model, acceleration data are processed using one of several approaches. This gives accelerometer output, typically in counts or a form of *g* acceleration. Analytical methods used to derive meaningful measures of physical activity are diverse. Activity intensity can be obtained using accelerometer cut-points developed using a regression algorithm. More advanced methods such as activity type recognition employ machine learning techniques which recognise signature *features* in the acceleration data. Sedentary activities and sleep can be detected using the orientation of the device or arm angle. Chapter 7 discusses the technology of accelerometry, starting with the sensor and hardware, data processing techniques and the analyses which provide measures relating to physical activity.

Thus far, we will have provided an understanding of the utility of lifecourse epidemiology, the instruments which best track long-term trends in physical activity, and the remarkable technology now available at the user's fingertips. However, measurement should be transparent and understandable to all concerned. The huge complexity of raw acceleration data provided by current accelerometers continues to provide endless measurement opportunities, but for the physician, epidemiologist or physiologist looking to implement raw accelerometry in their studies, confusion often occurs when they learn that the processing techniques and analytical methods require an understanding of computational language and the use of powerful software packages such as R or MATLAB. Missing from most texts on the innovations and excitations of what raw accelerometry can achieve is an easy to follow step-by-step guide to allow the non-measurement specialist to collect, process and analyse physical activity. Here you will find it in Chapter 8.

Technology has made many of these advances possible. The large data sets of today and tomorrow will exceed the storage and processing capacity of traditional desktop programmes and require cloud technology. An increasing number of efforts focus on creating accelerometer databases, including the International Children's Accelerometry Database (ICAD) and recent International Activity Monitor Database (IAMD). Many studies have to use web-based resources to store and analyse study data. E-science applications are connected to the internet, so they have increased computing power, storage, data processing and analysis. Typically, with e-science applications come big data. This expanding internet technology is featured in Chapter 9.

Finally, in Chapter 10, we will look at the future of lifecourse physical activity assessment. Undoubtedly, the future is set to look very different, if only due to the technological advances which support bigger data sets and more complex analysis. Some countries have already released 24-hour movement guidelines on physical activity, sedentary behaviour and sleep. Future technologies look set to connect the patient/public, the clinician and researcher with possible real-time monitoring of a wide range of variables from sensor-based technologies.

Defining key terms

The terminology used in the field of physical activity assessment has not always been consistent. Where published definitions exist, care should be taken to use the terms correctly. In some cases, definitions have been updated or expanded. The definition of physical activity itself is an example. However, if scientists are supposed to acquire new knowledge, then this is inevitable and arguably a sign of progress. In other cases, understanding of behaviours such as sedentary behaviour gradually increases in significance as evidence is accrued to a point where standardised definitions are needed to maintain accurate and clear scientific discussion. Other terms slowly work their way into the research lexicon. The term 'accelerometer' is regularly used to describe a particular activity monitor which uses an accelerometer sensor. The use of accelerometers to measure movement-based behaviours is called accelerometry. However, accelerometers are complex devices. This complexity need not confuse the reader. The use of simplified statements does. We will now define the key terms used in this book.

Population surveillance

Population surveillance consists of ongoing scrutiny of a population (general population, study population, target population etc.), generally using methods distinguished by their practicability, uniformity, and frequently their rapidity, rather than by complete accuracy.

Physical activity

The most common definition of physical activity was proposed some years ago (Caspersen, Powell and Christenson 1985): 'any bodily movements produced by skeletal muscles that result in energy expenditure'. Physical activity is a complex behaviour performed in varying amounts and different contexts; both change across the lifecourse. The amount of habitual physical activity fluctuates in response to several determinants, whilst the context in which physical activity takes place changes in response to key life events.

To *quantify* the amount of physical activity carried out, four dimensions are used: (1) mode or type of activity, (2) frequency of performing activity, (3) duration of performing activity and (4) intensity. To understand where in daily life people carry out physical activity, four domains are used to categorise physical activity – occupational, domestic, transportation and leisure time.

Physical activity is also *categorised* according to its four dimensions: (1) mode or type of activity, (2) frequency of performing activity, (3) duration of performing activity and (4) intensity of performing activity. The combination of frequency, duration and intensity is often referred to as the dose or volume of physical activity and reflects the total amount of movement performed within a specific duration.

Four domains are used to categorise physical activity – occupational, domestic, transportation and leisure time. Physical activity can occur in any of these four domains, so the assessment of physical activity should capture each one. For example, where behaviour change is the intended goal, a substitution effect can materialise: an increase in physical activity in one domain (e.g., occupation) may be compensated by decreased activity in another domain (e.g., leisure time).

Sedentary behaviour

Sedentary behaviour (from the Latin *sedere*, 'to sit') refers to any waking activities involving low energy expenditure, commonly <1.5 METs typically while sitting, reclining or lying down. When sedentary behaviour first gained recognition, it lacked a standard definition: the terms sedentary activity and physical *in*activity were initially used interchangeably. However, sedentary behaviour is now distinguished from 'physical *in*activity', defined as an insufficient physical activity level to meet present physical activity recommendations. The Sedentary Behaviour Research Network (SBRN) steering committee developed key definitions, published in 2017 (available at www.sedentarybehaviour.org).

The health consequences caused by inadequate physical activity are independent from those due to sedentary behaviour (Tremblay et al. 2010). Physical *in*activity involves low levels of muscular activity, falling below levels needed to preserve health, whereas prolonged bouts of sedentary behaviour involve very low whole-body movement and near total muscular inactivity.

Researchers aiming to assess all behaviours related to physical activity such as physical inactivity, sitting, sedentary activity and breaks in sedentary time must understand the distinctions between different terms.

Physical inactivity: an insufficient activity level to meet current physical activity guidelines.

Sedentary behaviour: any waking behaviour with an energy expenditure ≤1.5 METs while in a sitting, reclining or lying posture.

Screen time: time spent on screen-related behaviours. These behaviours can be performed while being sedentary or physically active.

Non-screen-based sedentary time: the time spent in sedentary behaviours that do not involve the use of screens.

Epidemiological and experimental investigations of prolonged sedentary activities have prompted calls to update public health physical activity and sedentary behaviour guidelines, namely by providing recommendations on maximal daily sedentary time and explicitly avoiding prolonged bouts of inactivity by breaking up sedentary time. UK, US, Canadian and Australian physical activity guidelines have included statements on reducing sedentary behaviour. Continuously evolving activity surveillance highlighted a shift toward monitoring of the whole 24-hour cycle, including both waking activity and sleep.

Sleep

Sleep is characterised by well-defined behavioural and neurophysiological changes. The onset of sleep involves tiredness, reduced movement and decreased response to external stimuli.

Sleep onset is not an acute event. We gradually progress through three stages of deepening sleep: NREM1 (non-rapid eye movement 1: drowsiness), NREM2 (light sleep), NREM3 (deep sleep or slow wave sleep), then we enter a fourth stage called REM (rapid eye movement) sleep. NREM1 is a transitionary stage from which you are easily roused, for example when falling asleep sat upright in a chair or nodding off then suddenly waking.

Thereafter, NREM2 is accompanied by a slowing of cortical activity, and NREM3 is characterised by low-frequency, higher-voltage brain waves. Hence, NREM3 is also called slow-wave sleep. NREM3 is associated with physiologically restorative processes and cellular repair mechanisms. Approximately 60–90 minutes after sleep onset, the individual enters REM sleep, which features a high level of cortical activity similar to that observed during wakefulness (Kleitman 1957, 1970), hence it is often called paradoxical sleep.

REM sleep is characterised by rapid eye movements and complete muscle atonia (Aserinsky and Kleitman 2003). REM sleep plays an important role in the maintenance of memory and cognitive function (Abbott, Knutson and Zee 2018). During sleep, you transition between NREM and REM over approximately 90–120 minutes (Kleitman 1960). NREM sleep accounts for 75–80% of total sleep time and dominates during the early stages of sleep, whilst later in the sleep period, REM sleep increases (Hishikawa and Shimizu 1995).

Correlates and determinants

Many factors affect the physical activity people carry out. Over the lifecourse, a change in behaviour often correlates with one or more biological, social or economic factors. For example, an increase or decrease in physical activity often correlates with a change in socioeconomic position. Many of these observations are reported from cross-sectional studies. Therefore, we cannot say with certainty that this truly determines how active someone is. The term 'correlates' describes these cross-sectional exposures. We require longitudinal observations to confirm whether an exposure determines how active someone is. The term 'determinant' is reserved specifically for longitudinal associations with physical activity. They are reducible associations that are potentially causal.

Lifecourse epidemiology

Unlike epidemiology, which is a study design, lifecourse epidemiology is a theoretical framework. It has been defined as the study of long-term effects on later health or disease risk of physical or social exposures during gestation, childhood, adolescence, young adulthood and later adult life. We apply lifecourse epidemiology as a framework to build models that explain temporal ordering of exposures and how they interact. This can involve data from birth cohorts, longitudinal studies, or the combination of data from several studies to span stages of the lifecourse we are interested in. This places great importance on the measurement of physical activity producing accurate and reliable results.

Accelerometry

An accelerometer is a sensor which converts physical acceleration into a digitally readable signal. Modern accelerometers are typically very small and use nanotechnology. Acceleration is expressed as gravitational acceleration, or g-force (g). Accelerometer sensors have been used in many different applications in industry and, of course, in physical activity measurement.

In physical activity research, the term 'accelerometer' also refers to a body-worn activity monitor which uses an accelerometer sensor to estimate physical activity. Simplified, it refers to both the sensor and the device itself. Accelerometers quantify acceleration of the body and, from that data, measures of physical activity can be derived. Importantly, we discuss two types of accelerometer. The first accelerometers used in epidemiological research were developed before technology was available to house all necessary components required to store the continuous acceleration data on the device. Consequently, onboard processors filtered and condensed the acceleration data into summary measures called *counts* stored locally on the device (van Hees et al. 2010). Counts are created using brand-specific computational methods considered proprietary to the device manufacturer; they are not standard units of measurement like centimetres, kilograms or kilometres. The use of accelerometer counts attracted much criticism, mainly because they are calculated in different ways depending on the device, so different devices can give different measures of the same activity. This hinders the comparison of data when different accelerometers are used at follow-up or across different studies (Ferrari, Friedenreich and Matthews 2007).

Advances in sensor technology meant that from 2008 onwards accelerometers were made available which do not convert the acceleration data into counts but instead allow the researcher to access unprocessed data in the form of a continuous acceleration signal in *g* which is an SI unit of measurement. This provides complete methodological transparency, greater analytical freedom and the opportunity to carry out 24-hour movement monitoring, typically providing measures of physical activity, sedentary behaviour and sleep from one participant.

In the literature, accelerometers producing counts are often not differentiated from those producing the raw data. Importantly, though, accelerometers giving access to the raw data are called 'raw accelerometers'.

Raw accelerometers

Raw accelerometers are typically worn on the wrist. The decision of the UK Biobank in 2006 to use raw accelerometers to collect movement data in 100,000 adults and the use of raw data in the NHANES study 2008 data sweep marked the swift increase in popularity of this measurement instrument. Raw accelerometers are used in the Pelotas Birth Cohort (van Hees et al. 2014), Whitehall II Study (Sabia et al. 2014), Newcastle 85+ Study (Innerd et al. 2015) and English Longitudinal Study of Ageing (Hamer, Lavoie and Bacon 2014).

In the literature, the only term used consistently to refer to accelerometers which produce counts is 'traditional accelerometer.' To ease understanding, in this book we will use the terms 'raw accelerometry' and 'traditional accelerometry'.

References

Abbott, S. M., K. L. Knutson, and P. C. Zee. 2018. 'Health implications of sleep and circadian rhythm research in 2017', *Lancet Neurol*, 17: 17–18.

Aserinsky, E., and N. Kleitman. 2003. 'Regularly occurring periods of eye motility, and concomitant phenomena, during sleep [1953]', *J Neuropsychiatry Clin Neurosci*, 15: 454–5.

Caspersen, C. J., K. E Powell, and G. M Christenson. 1985. 'Physical activity, exercise and physical fitness: definitions and distinctions for health related research', *Public Health Rep*, 100: 126–31.

Ferrari, P., C. Friedenreich, and C. E. Matthews. 2007. 'The role of measurement error in estimating levels of physical activity', *Am J Epidemiol*, 166: 832–40.

Hallal, P. C., L. B. Andersen, F. C. Bull, R. Guthold, W. Haskell, and U. Ekelund. 2012. 'Global physical activity levels: surveillance progress, pitfalls, and prospects', *Lancet*, 380: 247–57.

Hamer, M., K. L. Lavoie, and S. L. Bacon. 2014. 'Taking up physical activity in later life and healthy ageing: the English longitudinal study of ageing', *Br J Sports Med*, 48: 239–43.

Hishikawa, Y., and T. Shimizu. 1995. 'Physiology of REM sleep, cataplexy, and sleep paralysis', *Adv Neurol*, 67: 245–71.

Innerd, P., M. Catt, J. Collerton, K. Davies, M. Trenell, T. B. Kirkwood, and C. Jagger. 2015. 'A comparison of subjective and objective measures of physical activity from the Newcastle 85+ Study', *Age Ageing*, 44: 691–4.

Kleitman, N. 1957. 'Sleep, wakefulness, and consciousness', *Psychol Bull*, 54: 354–9; discussion 60.

Kleitman, N. 1960. 'The sleep cycle', *Am J Nurs*, 60: 677–9.

Kleitman, N. 1970. 'Study wakefulness. Study the rest-activity cycle. Don't just study sleep', *Int Psychiatry Clin*, 7: 381–4.

Kuh, D., Y. Ben-Shlomo, J. Lynch, J. Hallqvist, and C. Power. 2003. 'Life course epidemiology', *J Epidemiol Community Health*, 57: 778–83.

Sabia, S., V. T. van Hees, M. J. Shipley, M. I. Trenell, G. Hagger-Johnson, A. Elbaz, M. Kivimaki, and A. Singh-Manoux. 2014. 'Association between questionnaire- and accelerometer-assessed physical activity: the role of sociodemographic factors', *Am J Epidemiol*, 179: 781–90.

Tremblay, M. S., R. C. Colley, T. J. Saunders, G. N. Healy, and N. Owen. 2010. 'Physiological and health implications of a sedentary lifestyle', *Appl Physiol Nutr Metab*, 35: 725–40.

van Hees, V. 2014. 'GGIR: raw accelerometer data analysis'. Accessed 10 April 2019. https://cran.r-project.org/web/packages/GGIR/.

van Hees, V. T., Z. Fang, J. Langford, F. Assah, A. Mohammad, I. C. da Silva, M. I. Trenell, T. White, N. J. Wareham, and S. Brage. 2014. 'Autocalibration of accelerometer data for free-living physical activity assessment using local gravity and temperature: an evaluation on four continents', *J Appl Physiol (1985)*, 117: 738–44.

van Hees, V. T., M. Pias, S. Taherian, U. Ekelund, and S. Brage. 2010. 'A method to compare new and traditional accelerometry data in physical activity monitoring'. In *2010 IEEE International Symposium on 'A World of Wireless, Mobile and Multimedia Networks' (WoWMoM)*, 2, 1–6.

World Health Organization. 2011. *Global Status Report on Noncommunicable Diseases 2010*, Geneva, Switzerland: World Health Organization.

PART I

Physical activity assessment

A lifecourse perspective

1

LIFECOURSE ASSESSMENT OF PHYSICAL ACTIVITY

Physical activity has unique, important health benefits. Equally, physical *inactivity* and sedentary behaviour have their own detrimental effects on health. These effects act throughout the whole lifecourse. So let us be clear about what is meant by 'the whole lifecourse'.

The lifecourse begins before birth. Gestational growth and development are influenced by foetal conditions, thus maternal health is critical at this point, and physical activity is a key component of maternal health. In children, physical activity plays an essential role in growth and development, and physical activity levels in childhood and adolescence tend to track into adulthood. Adults categorised as young, middle-aged and older exhibit highly variable physical activity habits which may increase or decrease due to life circumstances. As older age arrives, considered over 60 or 65 years in most literature, lifelong physical activity may have prevented disease from developing. Even after years of relative inactivity, significant health benefits occur in people who become physically active late in life, around their seventies. In those who survive to be very old, commonly over 85 years, health behaviours tend to cluster, with poor health seen in people who have led relatively unhealthy lives and often exceptional health in those who have sustained a healthy lifestyle.

Innumerable, severe NCDs, including stroke, hypertension, type II diabetes and cardiovascular disease (CVD), can be prevented by physical activity and their effects ameliorated once they have developed. These diseases develop gradually across the lifecourse due to cumulative changes in body systems which are curtailed by physical activity but accelerated by inactivity and sedentary behaviour. Generally, physical activity tends to decline as we age. The reasons why people become less active and how to make them more active are not well understood.

To accomplish this, more needs to be known about changes in physical activity behaviour over the lifecourse, the domains of physical activity in which they occur, the characteristics of those whose physical activity declines and the factors associated with such changes. Over the years, studies have increased in size, improved in design and enhanced measurement.

The evidence so far shows that the relationship between physical activity and health changes with age, but more evidence is needed to provide as clear and detailed an image as possible of the mechanisms and interacting factors associated with the physical activity–health relationship. Similarly, the current evidence shows that factors which determine how physically active people are differ from childhood to adulthood and old age. Therefore, we need to know why people become inactive and how to make them more active.

In this chapter, we will:

- Examine the beginnings of physical activity epidemiology, from studies comparing occupational physical activity, to the vast amount of evidence from questionnaires and the technological advances made possible by wearable sensors.
- Describe the trends in physical activity across the whole lifecourse from childhood to older age and the factors affecting how active people are.
- Investigate the changing health benefits of physical activity from gestational development, then childhood to adulthood and in later life.
- Explore the challenges resulting from an ageing population, focus on the concept of health ageing and the role that physical activity plays.

A journey into physical activity assessment in lifecourse epidemiology starts with an examination of the beginnings of physical activity epidemiology itself.

Physical activity epidemiology: setting the scene

Pick up any textbook on physical activity and health and you will likely read about the seminal work of pioneering epidemiologist Professor Jeremy Morris in the 1950s. Motivated by his observation that heart disease seemed to be sweeping the UK, Morris compared the occupational physical activity of workers on London's double-decker buses, and in a larger study, workers of the British postal service. Morris found that bus conductors, who spent the day standing and walking while collecting passenger fares, experienced under half the number of heart attacks compared to bus drivers, who were seated for their working day. Morris replicated his findings when comparing postal carriers who cycled or walked to deliver mail with office workers in the postal service, revealing higher rates of heart disease in the inactive office staff and more deaths from heart disease (Morris et al. 1953). Similar studies were carried out in the US (Paffenbarger 1972; Paffenbarger et al. 1970).

Comparisons of occupational physical activity published through the 1950s to 1970s sparked an interest in physical activity epidemiology (Heady, Morris and Raffle 1956; Morris 1960; Morris et al. 1966). However, the claims that occupational comparisons demonstrated that physical activity is beneficial to health were met with scepticism, particularly from the medical community, who were acutely aware of the multifactorial aetiology of coronary heart disease.

Furthermore, occupational classifications are complicated by those in active roles transferring to inactive roles and by the unknown activities carried out in leisure time, outside of work. Defining the intensity and volume of physical activity to examine dose–response relationships needed a measurement method that was cheap and easy to administer.

Researchers quickly adopted physical activity questionnaires. Morris and colleagues carried out a study of UK civil servants (n=16,682) and reported that vigorous physical activity done in their leisure time such as keeping fit, gardening and stair climbing conferred the greatest protection from heart disease for the cohort. The results confirmed an association between vigorous physical activity and a lowered risk of cardiac disease (Morris et al. 1980). The main attraction of questionnaires is the ease with which they can be applied to large population samples. Perhaps the largest prospective cohort study investigating cardiovascular disease is the Framingham Heart Study.

Based in the town of Framingham, Massachusetts, USA, evidence from the Framingham Heart Study shed the first light on the relationship between CVD and lifestyle exposures such as physical *in*activity and smoking (Kannel and Shurtleff 1973). The coronary risk factors clearly identified in early Framingham papers sparked interest in the aetiology of the disease (Dawber and Kannel 1966), which was reported in subsequent studies (McKee et al. 1971). Initially, the study employed the Framingham Exercise & Physical Activity Questionnaire (Kannel and Sorlie 1979), but it recently added objective monitoring of physical activity (Spartano et al. 2017).

The first cohort study to focus primarily on physical activity and its effects on health was the Harvard Alumni Study (n=50,000). Data were collected on the lifestyle and health of male Harvard college graduates in 1962, 1966, 1977, 1988 and 1993, at which point 11,894 men remained in the study. Combining participant social, psychological and medical histories resulted in many reports on the benefits of physical activity in reducing stroke (Lee and Paffenbarger 1998), heart disease and all-cause mortality (Paffenbarger, Wing and Hyde 1978; Lee and Paffenbarger 1992). The study also drew attention to the amount of physical activity needed and the notable effects of physical *in*activity, namely activity levels resulting in <2000 kcal/week, which in one study resulted in a 64% increased risk of heart attack (Paffenbarger et al. 1986). Note that the improved quality of evidence was only made possible due to the use of improved methods to assess physical activity.

A large number of epidemiological studies employing physical activity questionnaires published during and prior to the study show that NCDs are closely linked to lifestyle, in particular tobacco use (Wolf et al. 1988), excess alcohol consumption (Friedman and Kimball 1986), bad diet and physical *in*activity (Powell et al. 1987). Several evidence-based consensus reports prompted the development of guidelines, thus supporting the promotion of a physically active lifestyle to improve public health, and prompted efforts by the USA (US Department of Health and Human Services 2008), Canada (Warburton et al. 2007) and the UK (Department of Health 2011) to produce guidelines on physical activity.

As the number of studies including physical activity measurements increased, so did the number of different questionnaires included in them. However, the number of different physical activity questionnaires in use meant data from studies were not comparable. We will discuss the scale of the problem and provide recommendations to improve the quality of data from questionnaires in Chapter 5. However, a limitation inherent to all self-report methods is that their subjectivity alone creates varying amounts of measurement error.

The evidence on which physical activity guidelines were based was obtained using several different questionnaires across studies, each with varying degrees of precision and feasibility. Few had been validated against a gold standard measure (Lamonte and Ainsworth 2001). Combined, this makes the interpretation of dose response difficult to carry out. The only solution is to use an objective instrument, namely a physical activity monitor. However, many of these devices remain prohibitively expensive for use in epidemiology. Particular devices which are cost-effective, comfortable to wear and used in large-scale studies are highlighted in this book and feature continually throughout.

The first large-scale, longitudinal studies to feature physical activity monitors include NHANES 2003–2004 (Clark et al. 2011) and EPIC-Norfolk 2006–2010 (Wijndaele et al. 2011). Due to technological limitations of devices at the time, the available activity monitors, such as the waist-worn ActiGraph GT1M, had to be removed before bed to prevent discomfort. Early devices focused on capturing bouts of physical activity intensity during the day, such as MVPA. Even in people who are vigorously active for >30 minutes per day, the remainder of their time could be spent carrying out unhealthy activities which cancel out the beneficial effects of physical activity, such as sedentary activities.

Sedentary behaviour is now recognised as an independent risk factor for NCDs. Studies show that interventions increasing physical activity levels can also result in an increase in sedentary behaviour (Dos Santos et al. 2018), which counteracts the beneficial effects of increased physical activity. Initially, associations between TV viewing time and sitting were highlighted as estimates of sedentary behaviour (Ekelund et al. 2006). However, with improved measurement instruments, namely physical activity monitors, an evidence base is now established from which guidelines on sedentary behaviour can be based. Emphasis is placed on limiting recreational screen time to no more than 2 hours per day – lower levels are associated with additional health benefits and avoiding prolonged sitting time (Tremblay et al. 2011).

Since accelerometers were first implemented in the NHANES, the methodological gap between accuracy and feasibility has continually narrowed. Modern accelerometer-based activity monitors such as the GENEActiv, Axivity and ActiGraph GT3X+ record continuous acceleration data over 7 days. These waterproof devices do not have to be removed before showering, bathing or bed-time. Wrist-worn accelerometers are designed to be worn continuously for 24 hours per day, 7 days per week. Users can obtain measurements of activity intensity, activity type and sedentary activity from a single acceleration signal using open-source (no financial cost) analytical packages (Innerd, Harrison and Coulson 2018). Since measurement methods are now available which capture the whole 24-hour movement cycle, attention has now focused on considering what should be done in that remaining time.

Only one third of adults typically meet traditional physical activity guidelines (Mudd et al. 2008). Clearly, guidance on activity during the whole day is more helpful. Accelerometers have uncovered new relationships between physical activity, sedentary behaviour and sleep. For example, unhealthy behaviours such as low physical activity, reduced sleep and sedentary activity tend to cluster in people who have other unhealthy characteristics (e.g., obesity) (Cassidy et al. 2017). Combined, these findings highlight the needs for a combined approach to guidelines on physical activity and sedentary behaviour and sleep.

Mounting evidence from studies using wrist-worn raw accelerometers have resulted in 24-hour movement guidelines. These guidelines represent a sensible evolution of public health guidelines whereby optimal health is framed within the balance of movement behaviours across the whole day, while respecting personal preferences. Guidelines are needed for children (Tremblay et al. 2016), young adults, middle-aged adults and older adults to facilitate a lifecourse approach to physical activity epidemiology and successfully (i) track movement patterns over the lifecourse, (ii) identify determinants and correlates that cause them to change and (iii) understand why these factors change at different stages of the lifecourse.

Physical activity has specific health effects at each stage of the lifecourse. However, as shown in Figure 1.1, physical activity declines as we age. This is not only due to the ageing process itself, but also various external factors, such as socio-economic status and the occurrence of key life events.

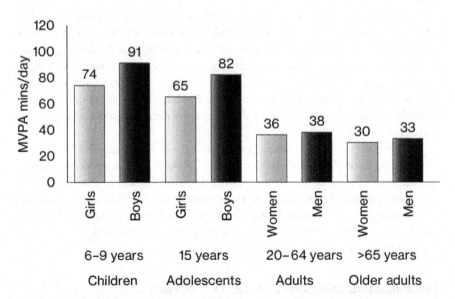

FIGURE 1.1   Physical activity across the lifecourse assessed by accelerometer. Accelerometer-assessed MVPA (minutes/day) from the Norwegian surveillance system (n = 8309) in male and female children, adolescents, adults and older adults.

Source: Rossi and Calogiuri (2018).

We will ask why some people are active and why some are not in Chapter 3. Before looking at what causes changes in physical activity, we must understand the changing relationship between physical activity and health that occurs from our first to our final years.

Physical activity and health over the lifecourse

The stages of the human lifecourse can be categorised according to age. The stages of *gestation* (<0 years), *childhood* (0–12 years) and *adolescence* (13–17 years) are characterised by growth and development, and *early adulthood* (18–35 years), *middle-age* (45–65 years) *old age* (65–85 years) and *very old* (80+ years) by the process of ageing. The body is constantly changing under the influence of genes and environmental factors. Therefore, each stage sees a different response to the effects of physical activity.

Gestation

The effects of lifestyle on individual health are shaped not only by the person's behaviours but also by their mother's. Maternal health before and during gestation influences disease risk in later life. The period of gestation involves in utero foetal development from conception to birth. Gestational conditions have a marked effect on health in childhood and later life, such as susceptibility to develop NCDs.

Diseases that affect pregnant women but are not caused by pregnancy are called intercurrent diseases. One example is gestational diabetes, which is linked to being overweight, physical inactivity and poor diet. Increases in body fat during gestation are typically caused by maternal overnutrition – an increasingly common occurrence during pregnancy. Maternal overnutrition occurs when energy consumed in the diet exceeds energy expended through physical activity. The importance of energy expenditure through moderate physical activity is increasingly recognised for optimal foetal development.

Overnutrition not only leads to gestational diabetes and obesity but also, in the offspring, increases the risk of insulin resistance, diabetes and cardiovascular changes in adulthood (Yeung et al. 2010). Overnutrition is also linked to macrosomia – a baby significantly larger than normal. Macrosomia is also linked to adult obesity and metabolic syndrome. Maternal health directly influences foetal health, which in turn has a substantial influence on the biological programming responsible for individual susceptibility to risk factors in later life.

Childhood and adolescence (0–12, 13–17 years)

Childhood and adolescence are marked by significant growth and development. The process of growth and development is influenced by behaviours such as nutritional status and, of course, physical activity. Adequate physical activity is essential for promoting healthy growth and development.

The prevalence of obesity in children and adolescents is increasing. The short-term effects of this include increased blood pressure, lipid dysregulation and elevated blood glucose. Obesity in childhood and adolescence tends to track into adulthood, leading to serious NCDs such as type II diabetes, CVD and several cancers (Eisenmann 2004). Low levels of physical activity are also associated with slow musculoskeletal development and poor mental health (Reilly 2005). Common problems include emotional disorders such as anxiety and depression and behavioural disorders such as substance abuse and eating disorders.

Early Adulthood (18–35 years)

Maintaining a healthy lifestyle during early adulthood is essential to reduce NCD risk in later life. Since lifestyle habits can become temporarily fixed in adulthood, it can be a time when increased exposures to damaging factors such as physical inactivity start to accumulate. Unhealthy exposures can act at any time, depending on lifestyle choices, and if prolonged, for example, long-term physical *in*activity from the ages of 21 to 30 years can trigger the biological changes of disease progression, though it may be some years until the disease becomes symptomatic.

Middle Adulthood (45–65 years)

Middle adulthood or *middle age* is of increasing interest due to the fact that the body is no longer 'young', but is neither 'old', although it is typically when the body starts to show signs of ageing. In some cases, middle-aged adults have spent several years carrying out relatively stable lifestyle habits. Specifically, the long-term effects of a physical *in*activity and sedentary lifestyles start to affect health in middle age. Some adults already have serious conditions such as heart disease by their forties or fifties. Risk of heart attack climbs after age 55 for women and after age 45 for men; ~10% of all heart attacks in men occur before age 45 years (Wei et al. 2015). Thus, physical activity is important to prevent any onset of NCD-related changes, for example, according to data from the Framingham Heart Study, to significantly lower vascular stiffness (Andersson et al. 2015).

From mid-life, variation in physical function and health across adults continues to increase whilst the effects of physical activity and inactivity/sedentary behaviour exert positive and negative effects respectively. Lifestyle behaviours are more psychologically fixed, making behaviour change more challenging. This may be why middle-aged adults in the NHANES tended to adopt overall healthy or unhealthy lifestyles, where the clustering of several healthy behaviours tended to be reported together, including healthy eating, higher vitamin intake and higher step-count (Choi and Ainsworth 2016). Physical activity has been associated with higher ratings of perceived health and well-being (Niemela et al. 2019), perhaps making this a period of increased sensitivity to changes associated with ageing.

Overall, adults demonstrate a gradual reduction in physical activity, due in part to diminished physical function associated with the ageing process. The Newcastle Thousand Families Birth Cohort (Spence 1947), which followed up participants aged 49–51 years, showed that adult lifestyle and biological risk markers are the most important determinants of cardiovascular health and conditions such as hypertension, insulin resistance, weight gain and obesity (Lamont et al. 2000). However, health throughout adult life can be maintained through the combination of key lifestyle factors such as physical activity, healthy diet, avoidance of tobacco and alcohol, and the management of psychological stressors. Good health can be maintained well into later years.

Old age (65–80 years)

In adults aged 65–85 years living in 'Western' society, the additional life years resulting from increasing longevity coincide with reduced risk of NCD-related disability. This is due mainly to early diagnosis and treatment rendering conditions less disabling (Christensen et al. 2009). However, these health gains are largely due to advances in long-term pharmacological therapies which are costly and not financially sustainable. Thus, better lifestyle interventions which increase physical activity are needed to prevent and treat the NCDs occurring in old age.

In older age, health shows marked variability. Some people remain remarkably healthy whilst others have multiple comorbidities. A healthy lifestyle results in well-preserved physical and psychological function, whereas the accumulated effects of repeated negative health exposures throughout life are by now typically symptomatic. Age interactions with physical activity are reported for some NCDs, namely a decrease in arthritis risk and diabetes for those aged under 65 years, and reduced risk of chronic lung disease, stroke and myocardial infarction (Okely and Gale 2016). The detrimental effects of lifestyle combine with the biological consequences of ageing, meaning that NCDs often start to impact quality of life from around age 60 years.

Ageing is to some extent genetically predetermined, but largely due to lifestyle (Kirkwood 2017). Physical activity shows health benefits across the whole lifecourse. Curtailment of the ageing process occurs with a physically active childhood; healthy lifestyle exposures in early life can slow the ageing process and alter susceptibility to NCDs later in life. The health benefits of physical activity have been observed right up to the ninth decade, at the other end of the lifecourse (Menai et al. 2017).

Very old (80+ years)

In ageing research, adults in the 80–90 years age group are often referred to as the 'old old' or 'very old'. The first longitudinal study to objectively monitor physical activity in the very old recruited adults aged 85 years and was called the Newcastle 85+ Study (Innerd et al. 2015). The 85+ age demographic are of great interest, firstly because they are the fastest-growing age demographic in the Western world, and secondly because despite the large healthcare costs linked to old age, relatively little was known about adults aged over 85 years until evidence started to emerge in 2007 (Collerton et al. 2007).

In the very old, a strong relationship is reported between lifestyle factors such as physical activity and diet and healthy ageing (Adamson et al. 2009). Healthy ageing is defined as low prevalence of chronic diseases, autonomy in activities of daily living, and low functional impairment or disability (Lara et al. 2013). Efforts to increase healthy ageing depend heavily on a detailed understanding of the biological nature of ageing itself. This biological understanding is most effectively achieved by long-term tracking of health trajectories into older age based on the lifecourse nature of the ageing process and its amenability to positive lifestyle change.

A striking feature of biological ageing is its marked variability between individuals. In the very old, some individuals preserve remarkably high levels of health and functional ability. However, understanding the sources of variability in health from a lifecourse perspective is essential to identify the keys to healthy ageing in this age demographic.

Oldest old (>90 years)

The number of people aged 90 years and older in the US is predicted to quadruple from 2010 to 2050 (Rozing, Kirkwood and Westendorp 2017). Adults living past age 90 years, referred to as the 'oldest old', typically have multiple comorbidities and are prescribed ≥6 medications (Paganini-Hill, Kawas and Corrada 2016). Since this age group only recently became large enough to involve in research, evidence is emerging. The oldest old are currently underrepresented in research. Therefore, an understanding of healthy exposures, such as to physical activity across the lifecourse, is necessary to inform effective interventions in very old adults.

Consequences of ageing and senescence

Across the lifecourse, all aspects of human physiology undergo alterations to some degree. Ageing is characterised by a number of changes in molecular signatures that eventually lead to detrimental alterations in metabolism and reduced physiological function. However, these alterations are cumulative and only begin to negatively affect physiology towards the later stages of life. The decline in function that occurs with age is termed senescence (Kirkwood 2017). Ageing and senescence are shown in Figure 1.2. Thus, it is ageing and senescence that eventually lead to the development of morbidity and mortality. However, note that the ageing process is amenable to physical activity.

As ageing occurs, cumulative damage is seen on a cellular and tissue level. Metabolic and hormonal changes ultimately lead to reduced insulin sensitivity,

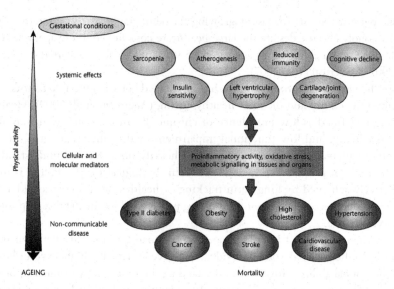

FIGURE 1.2 The effects of physical activity on ageing and senescence. The ageing process can be slowed significantly in response to physical activity.

impaired blood glucose control and a reduced capacity to utilise adipose tissue as fuel. There is an increase in systolic blood pressure across the lifecourse, with a mid-life acceleration generally seen in the fourth decade. Blood vessel walls lose elasticity and, due to changes in blood lipid profiles, become susceptible to athero-genesis. The process of atheroma (reversible accumulation of degenerative material in the inner layer of the artery wall) activates an immune response that results in the release of pro-inflammatory cytokines which, if left untreated, can cause an eventual blockage of blood vessels leading to total occlusion and a heart attack or stroke.

Pathological changes in the heart involve hypertrophic enlargement of the myocardium, particularly in the left ventricle, causing a reduction in end diastolic volume and ejection fraction (Hardy, Lawlor and Kuh 2015). A reduction in the number of cells in the sinoatrial node has been described, as well as the degeneration of cardiac muscle cells, which combined often result in cardiac arrhythmias.

In the immune system, morphological changes occur in the thymus gland, causing a gradual reduction in glandular mass. This results in reduced T-lymphocyte sub-populations and a decrease in antibody titres. Peristaltic contractions in the digestive tract reduce, whilst gastric secretions can be diminished by up to 25% by age 60 (Boyum et al. 1996). The cells lining the gut are amongst the most proliferative of the body, making them susceptible to mutations and the possible formation of a malignancy.

The mass of the brain declines slowly but progressively, causing an estimated ≥11% decrease in brain size by age 65; this ultimately results in cognitive decline (Fjell et al. 2013). This loss of brain mass is generally brought about not by a loss of neurons but by a degradation of the nerve cell body and synaptic regions where nerve impulses are passed to neighbouring cells. The balance between bone synthesis and degradation changes due to a shift in hormonal, metabolic and behavioural inputs results in net loss in bone matrix, often causing osteopenia and osteoporosis. Cartilage cells degenerate, reducing cushioning from compression forces in the joints. Over time, this can result in inflammation, tissue damage and, in many cases, symptoms of osteoarthritis.

Physical activity and healthy ageing

There is plasticity to the ageing process, with strong evidence showing that it can be attenuated by healthy behaviours such as physical activity. The probability of successful ageing is higher with increasing physical activity. Raw accelerometer-derived MVPA collected during the Whitehall II Study (n=3749) shows continued benefits from the amount of physical activity performance, but 40–60 minutes/day MVPA is where the optimal dose response appears to lie (Menai et al. 2017). Ageing and senescence are not dependent solely on the passage of time but are inextricably linked to two factors: genetics and lifestyle. Genetics account for approximately 25% of the variability in age-ing, whilst the remaining 75% is due to lifestyle – including physical activity (Franco et al. 2007). Ageing can therefore be modified in such a way that an individual's genet-ically determined susceptibility to chronic disease can be improved. The preservation of health and prevention of chronic disease in later life is known as healthy ageing.

Healthy ageing is a multidimensional phenotype consisting of adequate physical function, preserved cognition and effective social interaction (Franco et al. 2009). More broadly, it is a concept promoted by the WHO that considers the ability of people of all ages to live a healthy, safe and socially inclusive lifestyle. It recognises key factors which have a major effect on health and well-being in later life, includ-ing physical activity, inactivity and sedentary behaviour. Healthy ageing embraces a lifecourse approach that recognises the impact early life experiences have on the way in which population groups age (Franco et al. 2009). It is essential to prevent the accumulation of age-related cellular and organ system damage before a patho-logical state is reached. From a lifecourse perspective, old age represents a stage where physical activity can curtail any negative effects of biological, behavioural, social and psychological exposures occurring in earlier life.

Challenges of ageing populations

Lifespan is increasing dramatically and shows no signs of slowing. Since 1990, the global life expectancy has more than doubled, reaching 70 years. Some countries with the highest life expectancy from birth, include Canada (~82 years) Australia (~83 years), Japan (~84 years), UK (~81 years) and the US (~79 years) (Rozing, Kirkwood and Westendorp 2017). Most children born after the year 2000 will celebrate their 100th birthday. In fact, if you are now around 20 years old and female, you have a 1 in 4 chance of seeing your 100th birthday; if you are male, your chances are 1 in 5.

Before 1950, much of the gain in life expectancy was due to large reductions in childhood mortality due mostly to communicable diseases. An interplay between improved healthcare, higher incomes, better nutrition, education and sanitation reduced this threat. After 1950, improvements in lifespan became increasingly due to the postponement of mortality at older age through slowing of the ageing process (Lee et al. 2012). Improvements in housing conditions and public transport, changing social policies and greater socioeconomic opportunity have contributed to this ever-expanding longevity.

The rapid expansion of the very old age demographic provides opportunities to investigate the factors influencing health in this age group. These insights are important not only to improve current understanding of the ageing process itself but also to apply a lifecourse approach and track the timing and duration of positive and negative health exposures, such as physical activity and sedentary behaviour, and better understand the accumulative effects of different types and amounts of these behaviours (Vaupel 2010). Old age is still associated with the development of NCDs and the debility which accompanies them. However, growing research reveals that a growing number of older adults show remarkably preserved quality of life despite the presence of NCD.

The postponement of mortality in developed countries has resulted in a marked change in the age structure of their populations – specifically, the emergence of the very old. In fact, the fastest-growing age demographic are currently adults aged over 85 years. A major consequence of this demographic shift is the overwhelming burden placed on health services, which, at current rates, render many services unsustainable. With continually expanding lifespan and rapidly growing numbers of individuals needing long-term treatment plans, a burden is being placed on the healthcare system which is simply not sustainable. The improvement of health in very old age depends heavily on lifelong exposures to health-preserving behaviours such as physical activity.

The global burden of NCDs is largely due to changes in contemporary lifestyles. Contemporary threats to health are complex, progressive and require tracking over time. NCDs progress in different ways at different rates and are dependent on a multitude of risk factors. A collection of studies investigated long-term health trajectories from childhood to adulthood and old age, through birth cohorts (da Silva et al. 2014), population surveys, longitudinal studies and ageing research. Each stage of the lifecourse has its own distinct set of correlates and determinants. More evidence is needed to clarify these. More evidence is also needed to understand the timing of exposures and outcomes. Physical activity is considered one of the four biggest risk factors for NCDs. However, physical activity changes across the lifecourse. Accurate assessments of physical activity and the consequences of physical inactivity are needed to develop successful age group-specific behaviour change interventions.

Physical activity changes in response to the ageing process. This has direct consequences for the assessment of physical activity. The decline in physical function typically seen in older age makes physical activity in older adults characteristically different from both a movement (shorter duration activities, more sitting, and activities around the home) and physiological (more low-intensity activity but a greater relative energy expenditure) perspective. Therefore, a lifecourse approach to physical activity assessment should consider the consequences of ageing, alterations in human biology over time, and the measurement consequences caused by a decline in physical function: In what ways do these factors affect the choice of assessment method?

Summary

In this chapter, we examined the evidence on physical activity and health from the first evidence linking physical activity and health using simple comparisons of occupational physical activity. Firstly physical activity questionnaires and then physical activity monitors have featured in large-scale epidemiological research. Evidence on physical activity exposure–health relationships shows strong relationships, but has important knowledge gaps such as how physical activity changes across the lifecourse and why. These gaps can be addressed by carrying out long-term activity monitoring, but tackling this requires the use of accurate yet feasible measurement methods.

The key points of Chapter 1 are:

- The lifecourse is segmented into stages. From a lifecourse perspective, these are gestation, childhood, adolescence, young adulthood, middle age, older adulthood, the very old and the oldest old. An individual's risk of developing NCDs is accumulated throughout their lifecourse, at different stages and around key life events.
- Physical activity demonstrates health benefits throughout the whole lifecourse, from childhood to older age.
- The determinants of physical activity change across the lifecourse, typically revolving around key life events.
- To identify how to make people more active, it is necessary to understand the determinants which act at each life stage.
- Evidence gaps require accurate and precise measurements tracking secular trends in physical activity. The use of wrist-worn raw accelerometers is a feasible option. Improved assessments of physical activity will lead to a better understanding of determinants at each stage of the lifecourse.

References

Adamson, A. J., J. Collerton, K. Davies, E. Foster, C. Jagger, E. Stamp, J. C. Mathers, and T. Kirkwood. 2009. 'Nutrition in advanced age: dietary assessment in the Newcastle 85+ Study', *Eur J Clin Nutr*, 63 Suppl 1: S6–18.

Andersson, C., A. Lyass, M. G. Larson, N. L. Spartano, J. A. Vita, E. J. Benjamin, J. M. Murabito, D. W. Esliger, S. J. Blease, N. M. Hamburg, G. F. Mitchell, and R. S. Vasan. 2015. 'Physical activity measured by accelerometry and its associations with cardiac structure and vascular function in young and middle-aged adults', *J Am Heart Assoc*, 4: e001528.

Boyum, A., P. Wiik, E. Gustavsson, O. P. Veiby, J. Reseland, A. H. Haugen, and P. K. Opstad. 1996. 'The effect of strenuous exercise, calorie deficiency and sleep deprivation on white blood cells, plasma immunoglobulins and cytokines', *Scand J Immunol*, 43: 228–35.

Cassidy, S., J. Y. Chau, M. Catt, A. Bauman, and M. I. Trenell. 2017. 'Low physical activity, high television viewing and poor sleep duration cluster in overweight and obese adults; a cross-sectional study of 398,984 participants from the UK Biobank', *Int J Behav Nutr Phys Act*, 14: 57.

Choi, J. E., and B. E. Ainsworth. 2016. 'Associations of food consumption, serum vitamins and metabolic syndrome risk with physical activity level in middle-aged adults: the National Health and Nutrition Examination Survey (NHANES) 2005–2006', *Public Health Nutr*, 19: 1674–83.

Christensen, K., G. Doblhammer, R. Rau, and J. W. Vaupel. 2009. 'Ageing populations: the challenges ahead', *Lancet*, 374: 1196–208.

Clark, B. K., G. N. Healy, E. A. Winkler, P. A. Gardiner, T. Sugiyama, D. W. Dunstan, C. E. Matthews, and N. Owen. 2011. 'Relationship of television time with accelerometer-derived sedentary time: NHANES', *Med Sci Sports Exerc*, 43: 822–8.

Collerton, J., K. Barrass, J. Bond, M. Eccles, C. Jagger, O. James, C. Martin-Ruiz, L. Robinson, T. von Zglinicki, and T. Kirkwood. 2007. 'The Newcastle 85+ Study: biological, clinical and psychosocial factors associated with healthy ageing: study protocol', *BMC Geriatr*, 7: 14.

da Silva, I. C., V. T. van Hees, V. V. Ramires, A. G. Knuth, R. M. Bielemann, U. Ekelund, S. Brage, and P. C. Hallal. 2014. 'Physical activity levels in three Brazilian birth cohorts as assessed with raw triaxial wrist accelerometry', *Int J Epidemiol*, 43: 1959–68.

Dawber, T. R., and W. B. Kannel. 1966. 'The Framingham study: an epidemiological approach to coronary heart disease', *Circulation*, 34: 553–5.

Department of Health. 2011. *Start Active, Stay Active: A Report on Physical Activity for Health from the Four Home Countries' Chief Medical Officers*, London: Department of Health, Physical Activity, Health Improvement and Protection.

Dos Santos, C. E. S., S. W. Manta, G. P. Maximiano, S. C. Confortin, T. R. B. Benedetti, E. d'Orsi, and C. R. Rech. 2018. 'Accelerometer-measured physical activity and sedentary behavior: a cross-sectional study of Brazilian older adults', *J Phys Act Health*, 15: 811–18.

Eisenmann, J. C. 2004. 'Physical activity and cardiovascular disease risk factors in children and adolescents: an overview', *Can J Cardiol*, 20: 295–301.

Ekelund, U., S. Brage, K. Froberg, M. Harro, S. A. Anderssen, L. B. Sardinha, C. Riddoch, and L. B. Andersen. 2006. 'TV viewing and physical activity are independently associated with metabolic risk in children: the European Youth Heart Study', *PLOS Med*, 3: e488.

Fjell, A. M., L. T. Westlye, H. Grydeland, I. Amlien, T. Espeseth, I. Reinvang, N. Raz, D. Holland, A. M. Dale, and K. B. Walhovd. 2013. 'Critical ages in the life-course of the adult brain: nonlinear subcortical aging', *Neurobiol Aging*, 34: 2239–47.

Franco, O. H., K. Karnik, G. Osborne, J. M. Ordovas, M. Catt, and F. van der Ouderaa. 2009. 'Changing course in ageing research: the healthy ageing phenotype', *Maturitas*, 63: 13–19.

Franco, O. H., T. B. Kirkwood, J. R. Powell, M. Catt, J. Goodwin, J. M. Ordovas, and F. van der Ouderaa. 2007. 'Ten commandments for the future of ageing research in the UK: a vision for action', *BMC Geriatr*, 7: 10.

Friedman, L. A., and A. W. Kimball. 1986. 'Coronary heart disease mortality and alcohol consumption in Framingham', *Am J Epidemiol*, 124: 481–9.

Hardy, R., D. A. Lawlor, and D. Kuh. 2015. 'A life course approach to cardiovascular aging', *Future Cardiol*, 11: 101–13.

Heady, J. A., J. N. Morris, and P. A. Raffle. 1956. 'Physique of London busmen; epidemiology of uniforms', *Lancet*, 271: 569–70.

Innerd, P., M. Catt, J. Collerton, K. Davies, M. Trenell, T. B. Kirkwood, and C. Jagger. 2015. 'A comparison of subjective and objective measures of physical activity from the Newcastle 85+ Study', *Age Ageing*, 44: 691–4.

Innerd, P., R. Harrison, and M. Coulson. 2018. 'Using open source accelerometer analysis to assess physical activity and sedentary behaviour in overweight and obese adults', *BMC Public Health*, 18: 543.

Kannel, W. B., and D. Shurtleff. 1973. 'The Framingham Study: cigarettes and the development of intermittent claudication', *Geriatrics*, 28: 61–8.

Kannel, W. B., and P. Sorlie. 1979. 'Some health benefits of physical activity: the Framingham Study', *Arch Intern Med*, 139: 857–61.

Kirkwood, T. B. L. 2017. 'Why and how are we living longer?', *Exp Physiol*, 102: 1067–74.

Lamont, D., L. Parker, M. White, N. Unwin, S. M. A. Bennett, M. Cohen, D. Richardson, H. O. Dickinson, A. Adamson, K. G. M. Alberti, and A. W. Craft. 2000. 'Risk of cardiovascular disease measured by carotid intima-media thickness at age 49–51: lifecourse study', *BMJ*, 320: 273–8.

Lamonte, M. J., and B. E. Ainsworth. 2001. 'Quantifying energy expenditure and physical activity in the context of dose response', *Med Sci Sports Exerc*, 33: S370–8; discussion S419–20.

Lara, J., A. Godfrey, E. Evans, B. Heaven, L. J. Brown, E. Barron, L. Rochester, T. D. Meyer, and J. C. Mathers. 2013. 'Towards measurement of the healthy ageing phenotype in lifestyle-based intervention studies', *Maturitas*, 76: 189–99.

Lee, I. M., and R. S. Paffenbarger, Jr. 1992. 'Change in body weight and longevity', *JAMA*, 268: 2045–9.

Lee, I. M., and R. S. Paffenbarger, Jr. 1998. 'Physical activity and stroke incidence: the Harvard Alumni Health Study', *Stroke*, 29: 2049–54.

Lee, I. M., E. J. Shiroma, F. Lobelo, P. Puska, S. N. Blair, and P. T. Katzmarzyk. 2012. 'Effect of physical inactivity on major non-communicable diseases worldwide: an analysis of burden of disease and life expectancy', *Lancet*, 380: 219–29.

McKee, P. A., W. P. Castelli, P. M. McNamara, and W. B. Kannel. 1971. 'The natural history of congestive heart failure: the Framingham study', *N Engl J Med*, 285: 1441–6.

Menai, M., V. T. van Hees, A. Elbaz, M. Kivimaki, A. Singh-Manoux, and S. Sabia. 2017. 'Accelerometer assessed moderate-to-vigorous physical activity and successful ageing: results from the Whitehall II Study', *Sci Rep*, 8: 45772.

Morris, J. N. 1960. 'Epidemiology and cardiovascular disease of middle age. I', *Mod Concepts Cardiovasc Dis*, 29: 625–32.

Morris, J. N., M. G. Everitt, R. Pollard, S. P. Chave, and A. M. Semmence. 1980. 'Vigorous exercise in leisure-time: protection against coronary heart disease', *Lancet*, 2: 1207–10.

Morris, J. N., J. A. Heady, P. A. Raffle, C. G. Roberts, and J. W. Parks. 1953. 'Coronary heart-disease and physical activity of work', *Lancet*, 265: 1111–20; concl.

Morris, J. N., A. Kagan, D. C. Pattison, and M. J. Gardner. 1966. 'Incidence and prediction of ischaemic heart-disease in London busmen', *Lancet*, 2: 553–9.

Mudd, L. M., A. P. Rafferty, M. J. Reeves, and J. M. Pivarnik. 2008. 'Physical activity recommendations: an alternative approach using energy expenditure', *Med Sci Sports Exerc*, 40: 1757–63.

Niemela, M. S., M. Kangas, R. J. Ahola, J. P. Auvinen, A. M. Leinonen, T. H. Tammelin, E. S. Vaaramo, S. M. Keinanen-Kiukaanniemi, R. I. Korpelainen, and T. J. Jamsa. 2019. 'Dose-response relation of self-reported and accelerometer-measured physical activity to perceived health in middle age-the Northern Finland Birth Cohort 1966 Study', *BMC Public Health*, 19: 21.

Okely, J. A., and C. R. Gale. 2016. 'Well-being and chronic disease incidence: The English Longitudinal Study of Ageing', *Psychosom Med*, 78: 335–44.

Paffenbarger, R. S., Jr. 1972. 'Factors predisposing to fatal stroke in longshoremen', *Prev Med*, 1: 522–8.

Paffenbarger, R. S., Jr., R. T. Hyde, C. C. Hsieh, and A. L. Wing. 1986. 'Physical activity, other life-style patterns, cardiovascular disease and longevity', *Acta Med Scand Suppl*, 711: 85–91.

Paffenbarger, R. S., Jr., M. E. Laughlin, A. S. Gima, and R. A. Black. 1970. 'Work activity of longshoremen as related to death from coronary heart disease and stroke', *N Engl J Med*, 282: 1109–14.

Paffenbarger, R. S., Jr., A. L. Wing, and R. T. Hyde. 1978. 'Physical activity as an index of heart attack risk in college alumni', *Am J Epidemiol*, 108: 161–75.

Paganini-Hill, A., C. H. Kawas, and M. M. Corrada. 2016. 'Lifestyle factors and dementia in the oldest-old: the 90+ Study', *Alzheimer Dis Assoc Disord*, 30: 21–6.

Powell, K. E., P. D. Thompson, C. J. Caspersen, and J. S. Kendrick. 1987. 'Physical activity and the incidence of coronary heart disease', *Annu Rev Public Health*, 8: 253–87.

Reilly, J. J. 2005. 'Physical activity and obesity in childhood and adolescence', *Lancet*, 366: 268–9.

Rossi, A., and G. Calogiuri. 2018. 'Patterns and correlates of physical activity in adult Norwegians: a forecasted evolution up to 2025 based on machine learning approach', *BMC Public Health*, 18: 913.

Rozing, M. P., T. B. L. Kirkwood, and R. G. J. Westendorp. 2017. 'Is there evidence for a limit to human lifespan?', *Nature*, 546: e11–12.

Spartano, N. L., M. D. Stevenson, V. Xanthakis, M. G. Larson, C. Andersson, J. M. Murabito, and R. S. Vasan. 2017. 'Associations of objective physical activity with insulin sensitivity and circulating adipokine profile: the Framingham Heart Study', *Clin Obes*, 7: 59–69.

Spence, J. C. 1947 'Thousand Families Study – The Red Spot Story'. Accessed 1 April 2019. https://research.ncl.ac.uk/plerg/Research/1000F/1000history.htm.

Tremblay, M. S., V. Carson, J. P. Chaput, S. Connor Gorber, T. Dinh, M. Duggan, G. Faulkner, C. E. Gray, R. Gruber, K. Janson, I. Janssen, P. T. Katzmarzyk, M. E. Kho, A. E. Latimer-Cheung, C. LeBlanc, A. D. Okely, T. Olds, R. R. Pate, A. Phillips, V. J. Poitras, S. Rodenburg, M. Sampson, T. J. Saunders, J. A. Stone, G. Stratton, S. K. Weiss, and L. Zehr. 2016. 'Canadian 24-hour movement guidelines for children and youth: an integration of physical activity, sedentary behaviour, and sleep', *Appl Physiol Nutr Metab*, 41: S311–27.

Tremblay, M. S., A. G. Leblanc, I. Janssen, M. E. Kho, A. Hicks, K. Murumets, R. C. Colley, and M. Duggan. 2011. 'Canadian sedentary behaviour guidelines for children and youth', *Appl Physiol Nutr Metab*, 36: 59-64; 65–71.

US Department of Health and Human Services. 2008. 'Physical activity'. Accessed 10 April 2019. www.health.gov/PAGuidelines.

Vaupel, J. W. 2010. 'Biodemography of human ageing', *Nature*, 464: 536–42.

Warburton, D. E., P. T. Katzmarzyk, R. E. Rhodes, and R. J. Shephard. 2007. 'Evidence-informed physical activity guidelines for Canadian adults', *Can J Public Health*, 98 Suppl 2: S16–68.

Wei, G. S., S. A. Coady, J. P. Reis, M. R. Carnethon, J. Coresh, R. B. D'Agostino, D. C. Goff, D. R. Jacobs, E. Selvin, and C. S. Fox. 2015. 'Duration and degree of weight gain and incident diabetes in younger versus middle-aged black and white adults: ARIC, CARDIA, and the Framingham Heart Study', *Diabetes Care*, 38: 2042–9.

Wijndaele, K., S. Brage, H. Besson, K. T. Khaw, S. J. Sharp, R. Luben, N. J. Wareham, and U. Ekelund. 2011. 'Television viewing time independently predicts all-cause and cardiovascular mortality: the EPIC Norfolk study', *Int J Epidemiol*, 40: 150–9.

Wolf, P. A., R. B. D'Agostino, W. B. Kannel, R. Bonita, and A. J. Belanger. 1988. 'Cigarette smoking as a risk factor for stroke: the Framingham Study', *JAMA*, 259: 1025–9.

Yeung, E., F. Hu, C. Solomon, L. Chen, G. Louis, E. Schisterman, W. Willett, and C. Zhang. 2010. 'Life course weight characteristics and the risk of gestational diabetes', *Diabetologia*, 53: 668–78.

2
POPULATION-BASED SURVEILLANCE

A wealth of evidence shows pronounced health-enhancing effects of physical activity at all ages. Conversely, physical *in*activity and sedentary behaviour have distinct and independent detrimental effects on health. We know that physical inactivity is a global health burden, the fourth biggest risk factor for NCD, yet only around a third of adults carry out enough to maintain good health. Gaining greater insights into the long-term trajectories of these behaviours is made possible through the use of accurate and feasible accelerometer-based activity monitors which provide continuous monitoring that captures the whole 24-hour movement cycle. The devices are being used in large-scale cohort studies and also population-based surveillance, both of which involve large numbers of participants.

Physical activity assessment in population surveillance has improved dramatically. The implementation of physical activity questionnaires in the 1990s provided the first global evidence. However, questionnaires are subjective, often resulting in large measurement error. The current use of small, wearable activity monitors represents a huge leap forward and allows us to carry out large-scale, long-term tracking of activity levels at all stages of the lifecourse.

The evidence so far shows the relationship between physical activity and health changes with age, but more evidence is needed to provide as clear and detailed an image as possible of the mechanisms and interacting factors associated with the physical activity–health relationship. Similarly, the current evidence shows that factors which determine how physically active people are differ from childhood to adulthood and old age. Therefore, we need to know why people become inactive and how to make them more active.

However, new technologies must be implemented carefully. To obtain valid and reliable measurements, we must understand how measurements are obtained, how measurement instruments such as accelerometer-based devices work and what factors affect the data derived from them.

In this chapter, we will:

- Examine the evidence on global trends in physical activity which is mainly based on questionnaire data and identify the opportunities wearable technologies bring.
- Define physical activity and discuss the measurements used to assess physical activity including physical activity-related energy expenditure (PAEE), METs, MVPA and activity type.
- Explore the measurement of movement-related behaviours now included in studies carrying out 24-hour activity monitoring such as sedentary behaviour and sleep.
- Investigate measurement methods available to track physical activity- and movement-related behaviours across the lifecourse using a single accelerometer.

Physical activity surveillance suffers from knowledge gaps due to the reliance on questionnaire data in studies. However, modern accelerometer-based activity monitors are primed for use on a global scale. To understand where contributions to the field need to be made, it is essential to understand which measurements best address those knowledge gaps.

Global physical activity surveillance

Public health surveillance is the continuous collection, analysis and interpretation of health-related data needed to preserve or improve public health. Surveillance systems examine long-term trends in public health and explore changes in health and disease frequency.

The pioneering epidemiological work done in the 1950s showing robust associations between physical activity and substantial risk of heart disease and heart attack appeared in one of the world's oldest, most prestigious and best-known general medical journals, *The Lancet* (Morris et al. 1953). However, physical activity would not appear in *The Lancet* again until roughly 50 years later, when the 2012 *Lancet Series on Physical Activity* (Lee et al. 2012) was published.

Surveillance of physical activity in populations was first undertaken using questionnaires as these are relatively inexpensive compared to objective measurement techniques. The development of a set of standardised questionnaires in 1990, the International Physical Activity Questionnaires (IPAQ), would go on to be used in 122 countries representing roughly 89% of the world's population (Bauman et al. 2009). Amassing evidence on this scale resulted in physical activity receiving high-level attention.

Nevertheless, evidence gaps identified in the 2012 *Lancet* series are due at least in part to the limitations of the questionnaires in physical activity surveillance, the IPAQ and Global Physical Activity Questionnaire (GPAQ). Monitoring trends in physical activity over time presents several challenges. Data collection should be done in the same manner over time. Even slight changes in survey questions or data collection procedures can alter findings and challenge the interpretation and comparison of data across different time-points. Advances in technology have presented potential solutions to these issues. Modern accelerometers produce movement data in standardised units of measurement (SI) which can be pooled from different data sets. Increasingly, accelerometer-based monitoring is used in addition to or in place of questionnaires.

Data from surveillance systems must be meaningful and interpretable for policy makers so that answers can be produced to questions such as 'How physically active is a population?', 'How inactive or sedentary is a population?', 'To what extent do certain determinants affect physical activity levels?' and 'Have meaningful improvements to activity levels resulted from particular interventions?' Therefore, a number of different measurements have been used to answer these questions. It is important to understand the origins, definitions and potential applications of these measurements.

Measurements used to assess physical activity

The first principle of measurement is: the measurand must be correctly and unambiguously defined (Stevens 1946). The popular definition 'any bodily movement produced by skeletal muscles that result in energy expenditure' suggests movement and energy expenditure as key terms (Caspersen, Powell and Christenson 1985). A later definition, 'behaviour that involves human movement, resulting in physiological attributes including increased energy expenditure and improved physical fitness' (Chong et al. 1998), includes additional terminology which aids interpretation. The additional term 'behaviour' captures physiological, psychological and environmental aspects of physical activity, and the term 'movement' is beneficial due to the added complexity caused by related behaviours of physical *in*activity and sedentary behaviour: All forms relate back to the notion of physical activity as the variable presence of human movement which involves the expenditure of energy, or in the case of sedentary behaviour, very low levels of human movement.

To quantify the amount of physical activity carried out, four dimensions are used: (1) mode or type of activity, (2) frequency of performing activity, (3) duration of performing activity and (4) intensity. The combination of frequency, duration, and intensity is often referred to as the dose or volume of physical activity and reflects the total amount of movement performed within a specific time period. Table 2.1 defines each of the four dimensions.

Different types of physical activity exert different metabolic demands and elicit variable physiological effects, and therefore varying health benefits. Activities of daily living (ADLs) include all activities that are part of normal daily living which are important for self-care and quality of life. ADLs tend to differ according to age: children develop the ability to perform more, whereas older adults gradually lose the ability to perform as many. For example, younger children often require help from adults to perform ADLs as they have not yet developed the neuromuscular coordination needed to perform them independently. Older adults who experience

TABLE 2.1 Dimensions of physical activity.

Dimension	Definition and context
Mode or type	Specific activity performed (e.g. walking, gardening, cycling). Mode can also be defined in the context of physiological and biomechanical demands/types (e.g. aerobic versus anaerobic activity, resistance or strength training, balance and stability training).
Frequency	Number of sessions per day or per week. In the context of health promoting physical activity, frequency is often qualified as number of sessions (bouts) ≥10 min in duration/length.
Duration	Time (minutes or hours) of the activity bout during a specified time frame (e.g. day, week, year, past month).
Intensity	Rate of energy expenditure. Intensity is an indicator of the metabolic demand of an activity. It can be objectively quantified with physiological measures (e.g. oxygen consumption, heart rate, respiratory exchange ratio), subjectively assessed by perceptual characteristics (e.g. rating of perceived exertion, walk-and-talk test), or quantified by body movement (e.g. stepping rate, three-dimensional body accelerations).

cognitive decline or a reduction in functional capacity may lose the ability to perform more difficult activities unless they remain physically active. Healthy ageing involves the ability to perform the activity types necessary for good quality of life (walking, showering, bathing, food preparation etc.).

The frequency, duration and intensity of physical activity predict the magnitude of any related health benefits. Health-enhancing effects of physical activity only occur above a particular threshold of frequency, duration and intensity. Therefore, a common measurement aim is to estimate the duration and frequency of MVPA carried out. Conversely, the frequency and duration of sedentary activities such as sitting are now of equal interest.

Accelerometers can be used to capture all four dimensions. Wrist-worn devices can be used to collect continuous acceleration data. Several analytical methods exist which provide estimated activity type, intensity, frequency and duration. Capturing the frequency, duration, intensity and type of activity with one assessment tool also allows the combination of activity intensity-related measures with activity type identifiers. For example, sedentary activities, such as sitting or watching TV, can offset the health benefits of moderate to vigorous intensities of activity if carried out for too long. However, it remains unclear how much sedentary behaviour must take place to offset the effects of physical activity. Obtaining concurrent estimates of activity intensity and activity type helps researchers shed light on this evidence gap for the first time.

Physical activity can occur in any of these four domains, so the assessment of physical activity should capture each one. For example, where behaviour change is the intended goal, a substitution effect can materialise: an increase in physical activity in one domain (e.g., occupation) may be compensated by decreased activity in another domain (e.g., leisure time).

Lifecourse assessments of physical activity, combined with the monitoring of participant characteristics, provide greater insights into why people carry out more or less physical activity and how to make people more active. It is essential to understand when and where in daily life people carry out their physical activity. Four domains are used to categorise physical activity in this way: occupational, domestic, transportation and leisure time (Table 2.2).

Good measurements rely on an understanding of the phenomenon being measured: the measurand. This is particularly important when attempting to assess physical activity across the whole lifecourse, where differences across all dimensions and domains occur on an individual level.

Typically, studies investigating the activity–health relationship are motivated to carry out assessments of physical activity to investigate (i) the types of activities carried out or identify differences in how they are carried out and (ii) the metabolic changes during or in response to physical activity. For example, research in Parkinson's Disease, characterised by movement or motor symptoms, carries out gait assessment, detects movement irregularities (behavioural) (Godfrey et al. 2016), and also determines changes in energy expenditure due to treatments for Parkinson's (physiological)

TABLE 2.2 Domains of physical activity.

Domain	Contextual definition or examples
Occupational	Work-related: involving manual labour tasks, walking, carrying or lifting objects
Domestic	Housework, yard work, child care, chores, self-care, shopping, incidental
Transportation/utilitarian	Purpose of going somewhere: walking, bicycling, climbing/descending stairs to public transportation, standing while riding transportation
Leisure time	Discretionary or recreational activities: sports, hobbies, exercise, volunteer work

(Jorgensen et al. 2012). Research into type II diabetes, characterised by dysregulated metabolism, measures energy expenditure (Luke et al. 2011) but also determines changes in walking duration due to physical activity interventions (behavioural) (Valentiner et al. 2017). Despite their multiplicity, all measures relating to physical activity can be categorised as either physiological or behavioural. Figure 2.1 shows these two sectors of physical activity.

We are typically interested in the behaviour (the activity type) and/or physiology (relating to metabolism, energy expenditure and activity intensity). The choice of methods used to assess physical activity is determined by the aim to measure behavioural outcomes in studies focusing on the types of activity performed, or physiological outcomes in studies focusing on the metabolic consequences of physical activity. Once the measure is chosen, it is extrapolated to units of measurement to assess the relationship between physical activity and health outcomes.

Physical activity questionnaires such as the IPAQ and GPAQ provide both physiological and behavioural measures of physical activity. However, innovations in wearable sensor technological give researchers the option to use accelerometers to obtain objective measures of physical activity. In fact, all of the measures used to assess physical activity can be obtained from a single acceleration signal at little to no cost. We will explain how to do so in Chapter 8, but first we must ensure we understand the following measures and how they change across the lifecourse: PAEE, physical activity intensity, MVPA, sedentary behaviour and activity type.

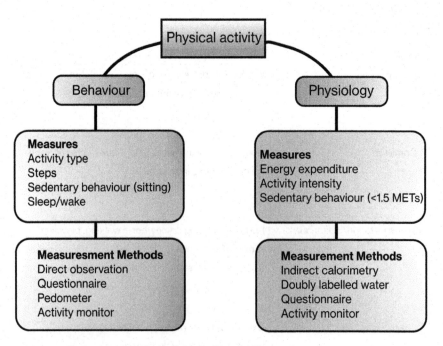

FIGURE 2.1 Behavioural and physiological measures.

Physical activity-related energy expenditure

Physical activity is commonly assessed via the extrapolation of units of energy expenditure. Human energy expenditure consists of three components (Figure 2.2): basal metabolic rate (BMR), thermic effect of food, and energy expended during physical activity, called either physical activity-related energy expenditure or activity-related energy expenditure (AEE) (Passmore and Durnin 1955).

BMR is the energy expended when an individual is lying at complete rest in the morning after sleep in the post-absorptive state. In individuals with sedentary occupations, the basal metabolic rate accounts for approximately 60% of the total daily energy expenditure and is predicted by lean body mass within humans and across the lifecourse. Resting energy expenditure is typically within 10% of the BMR and is measured in subjects at complete rest in the post-absorptive state. The thermic effect of food is the increase in energy expenditure associated with digestion, absorption and storage of food, and accounts for approximately 10% of the total daily energy expenditure.

During physical activity there is an increase in energy expenditure above resting levels, and the rate of energy expenditure is directly linked to the intensity of the physical activity and the duration: very intense exercise can cause an increase in energy expenditure by 20–30 times what it is at rest (Passmore and Durnin 1955). PAEE is therefore the most variable portion of total daily energy expenditure. Daily PAEE equals the sum of all the different physical activities performed on a given day. Energy expenditure during ambulatory physical activity increases directly with the mass of the body being moved. For this reason, energy expenditure is sometimes expressed relative to body mass as kilocalories per kilogram of body mass per minute ($kcal \cdot kg^{-1} \cdot min^{-1}$).

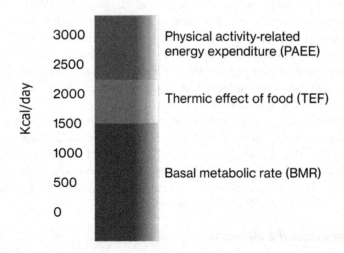

FIGURE 2.2 The components of total daily energy expenditure. Resting energy expenditure, the thermic effect of food and physical activity-related energy expenditure make up the total amount of energy expended daily.

Source: Levine et al. (2001).

Kilocalories

Human energy expenditure is often quantified using units called calories of kilocalories (kcals). Kilocalories provide useful insights mainly from a physiological perspective, so you will find kcals used in physiology lab experiments more often than large-scale surveillance studies. Physical activity surveillance currently requires the ranking of large numbers of individuals. Nevertheless, it is necessary to understand the principle of energy expenditure in kcals. Although most accurately measured using indirect calorimetry, the rate at which technology advances means it could well become a measurement of interest for wearable technologies.

By definition, 1 calorie is the amount of heat energy needed to raise the temperature of 1 gram of water by 1 degree Celsius (Durnin and Brockway 1959), and the equivalent is true of kcals (1000 calories). Despite being replaced by kilojoules (kj) in the SI system (1 kcal = 4.1 kj), kcals are still in use when measuring energy expenditure and also energy consumption in foods.

Due to the involvement of oxygen in the metabolism of energy during physical activity, energy expenditure in kcals can be estimated by directly measuring or estimating oxygen consumption. However, many prediction equations are used that were developed some years ago and feature several assumptions (Durnin 1982). Oxygen consumption at rest is defined as 3.5 ml/kg/min (Heil et al. 1995). Therefore, a 70 kg individual would consume roughly 250 ml/kg/min at rest. Thus, to walk at 4 mph (250 ml/min × 4) would require 1L/minute of oxygen, and to do so for 30 minutes would consume 30L of oxygen (1L/min × 30). One litre of oxygen consumed is roughly equal to 5 kcal of energy. So the energy cost of this 30-minute walk would be ~150 kcals.

Energy expenditure expressed in kcals and categorised as PAEE is a useful measurement to obtain when attempting to assess secular trends in physical activity (Westerterp and Plasqui 2004). However, measurement instruments such as wearable activity monitors are unable to provide the necessary accuracy and precision and strength of evidence needed to inform behaviour change interventions. Modern accelerometers (van Hees et al. 2011) can provide the objective measurement of PAEE on a cost-effective basis.

Undeniably, daily energy expenditure has decreased due to factors such as the widespread use of labour-saving devices. A positive energy balance is independently linked to NCD. Numerous public health efforts utilise principles of energy balance to promote healthy lifestyles – that is, promoting a sensible intake of energy from food and expenditure of energy from physical activity. Therefore, the measurement of PAEE is of great interest.

Changes across the lifecourse

An important health goal is to maintain adequate daily PAEE across the whole lifecourse. PAEE in children is associated with reduced overweight and obesity (Goran et al. 1997) and improved physical fitness (Dencker et al. 2010). Ageing typically results in gradually reduced PAEE. Additionally, BMR is reduced as ageing occurs. However, preserved PAEE can slow any decline in health due to the ageing process.

In middle age (40–60 years), a higher thermic effect of exercise (TEE) has been observed in women due to higher physical activity levels (Tooze et al. 2007), associated with reduced progression toward metabolic dysregulation, and better body composition (Ekelund et al. 2005). Nevertheless, since the determinants of physical activity change at advancing stages of the lifecourse, PAEE in older adults is highly variable. However, studies report that, depending on occupational physical activity, socioeconomic status and existing health status, PAEE in many individuals is seen to rise.

Older adults (aged 70–82 years) are highly heterogeneous in terms of both physical function and BMR. PAEE tends to decline across the lifecourse, with lowest levels seen in old age. Although PAEE is primarily determined by physical activity, it also depends on other individual characteristics, such as age and body composition. Age affects PAEE due to the loss of skeletal muscle mass, deterioration in muscle oxidation capacity and reduced cardiovascular efficiency. These changes result in altered energy utilisation, with a relative increase in energy needed to carry out the same activity type. This makes PAEE estimation across the lifecourse into old age challenging.

The energy expended during physical activity serves as a good indicator of the expected health benefits. For example, a large amount of energy expended through regular physical activity suggests that the functions of the cardiovascular system, neuromuscular system and metabolic health are being preserved.

Lifecourse research typically involves the large-scale, long-term surveillance of physical activity. Physical activity guidelines describe health benefits from physical activity occurring at moderate-intensity activity performed for 150 minutes/week. Therefore, attempting to monitor population levels of PAEE in kcals is of little value. For this reason, obtaining individual point estimates of PAEE in kcals, although possible in laboratory studies (Brandes et al. 2012), is of little value and is unlikely to generalise well to full-scale real-world studies. Instead, the energy cost of physical activity is often used to categorise individuals as active/non-active, low-activity, moderate-activity or high-activity, or estimate how long individuals spend sedentary, carrying out light-intensity activity, and moderate to vigorous activity.

Therefore, intensity categories are used to more easily determine how intensely and how long physical activity is carried out for. This assists in the measurement, interpretation and communication of important evidence. The intensity of physical activity, when measured using an instrument, is commonly expressed in units of metabolic energy expenditure called METs.

Metabolic equivalents

The acronym MET stands for metabolic equivalent or metabolic equivalent of task. One MET represents a VO_2 of 3.5 ml.kg^{-1}.min^{-1}, and acts as a proxy value for resting metabolic rate (RMR). Physical activity intensity is separated into categories, each with a MET range: sedentary behaviour (1.0–1.5 METs), light-intensity (1.6–2.9 METs), moderate-intensity (3–5.9 METs) and vigorous-intensity (>6 METs) (Table 2.3). METs represent an easy way of assessing the amount of time spent carrying out sedentary, light-, moderate- and vigorous-intensity activities. However, assumptions associated with MET values limit their use across the lifecourse.

TABLE 2.3 The Compendium of Physical Activities, featuring selected activities classified as sedentary, light-, moderate- and vigorous-intensity. Named activities are assigned a MET value to reflect the intensity of the activity and estimated energy expenditure.

Code	METs heading	METs	Description
	Sedentary activities (≤1.5 METs)		
07010	inactivity quiet	1.0	lying quietly, watching television
07070	inactivity quiet	1.0	reclining - reading
11580	occupation	1.5	sitting meetings, general, and/or with talking involved,
	Light-intensity activities (1.6–2.9 METs)		
05070	home activities	1.8	ironing
17151	walking	2.0	walking, less than 2.0 mph, level, strolling, very slow
17180	walking	2.9	walking, 2.5 mph (4 km/h)
	Moderate-intensity activities (3–5.9 METs)		
17133	walking	4.0	stair climbing, slow pace
05140	home activities	4.0	sweeping garage, sidewalk or outside of house
11820	occupation	5.0	walking, 3.5 mph carrying objects 25 to 49 lbs
	Vigorous-intensity activities (≥6 METs)		
12010	running	6.0	jog/walk combination
11550	occupation	9.0	shovelling, heavy (more than 16 lbs/minute
11250	occupation	17.0	forestry, axe chopping, very fast

One MET is the rate of energy expenditure while lying supine at rest and is based on an oxygen uptake of 3.5 ml/km of body weight per minute (3.5 ml.kg^{-1}.min^{-1}). Therefore, physical activity costing 2 METs requires twice the resting metabolism or 7 ml.kg^{-1}.min^{-1} and 3 METs requires 10.5 ml.kg^{-1}. min^{-1}. Physical activities that require more intense physical effort have higher METs. For example, leisure biking at a speed of 5.5 mph has an energy expenditure of 3.5 METs, and competitive mountain bike racing has an energy expenditure of 14 METs.

The Compendium of Physical Activities is a comprehensive list of physical activities each with an assigned MET value to use as a reference for quantifying the intensity of physical activity (Ainsworth et al. 2011). The Compendium of Physical Activities was developed for use in epidemiologic studies to standardise the assignment of MET intensities in physical activity questionnaires.

Adult Compendium activities are classified by a five-digit code that identifies the category (heading) as the first two digits and type (description) of activity as the last three digits, for example:

Code	Heading	Description
01010	01 – Bicycling	010 – 010 – Bicycling, < 10 mph, bicycling

Note that the Compendium was not developed to determine the energy cost of activities at the individual level but rather to provide a classification system that standardises MET intensities used in survey research. METs are commonly used to classify physical activity intensity derived from accelerometer data into sedentary, light-intensity, moderate-intensity and vigorous-intensity (Kozey et al. 2010). Typically, the magnitude of acceleration reflects the movement intensity of the body. In turn, this approach is used to insert accelerometer cut-offs into the data, thereby providing objective estimates of time spent in each physical activity intensity threshold.

Changes across the lifecourse

METs are based on the assumption that a VO$_2$ of 3.5 ml.kg^{-1}.min^{-1} represents RMR, or 1 MET. However, RMR varies by age, weight, height, sex and lean body mass. Inevitably, this raises concerns about the suitability of METs as an indicator of the energy cost of physical activity. Some studies show that these factors, such as adiposity, confound the use of METs (Tompuri 2015). Studies show that measured RMR in older (>75 years) women is roughly 2.6 ml.kg^{-1}.min^{-1} (Smith et al. 2015). Therefore, methods relying on assumptions regarding RMR are not currently suitable to make precise assessments of time spent carrying out sedentary, light, moderate or vigorous physical activity intensity.

However, many studies look at the effects of light-intensity activity, which is typically carried out for longer bouts as part of daily activities – activity under the cut-point of <1.5 - 3 METs. Several studies report that health benefits can be derived from habitual low-level physical activity, particularly in older age groups (Fuzeki, Engeroff and Banzer 2017). However, low-level activity is hard to capture in very old adults, who move less vigorously and less often. Studies have combined intensity categories (sedentary and light, moderate and vigorous) to successfully determine whether very old people are carrying out regular low-level physical activity, which, for healthy ageing, is a more important goal than reaching a certain intensity threshold.

Moderate to vigorous physical activity

Optimal health benefits from physical activity occur during moderate to vigorous physical activity. Unsurprisingly, MVPA is one of the most commonly used measurements in physical activity epidemiology. Typically expressed in minutes/day, MVPA determines the proportion of a population active enough to maintain health, >30 minutes/day, though it makes no difference how it is accumulated just as long as it is (Saint-Maurice et al. 2018) and is used in studies aiming to compare several measurements over time to determine the magnitude of any changes in physical activity levels.

Large-scale cohort studies using accelerometers regularly express physical activity as MVPA, from the first time NHANES used an accelerometer (Troiano et al. 2008), and it is still common in current NHANES papers and recent publications from Pelotas birth cohorts (da Silva et al. 2014) and Whitehall II (Menai et al. 2017). Physical activity guidelines focused solely on MVPA, and although public guidelines have evolved, it remains an important feature, since it is effective but simple to achieve (WHO 2010). Since the first epidemiological studies used accelerometer-based activity monitors, MVPA remains a preferred way to report physical activity.

Changes across the lifecourse

Age can cause uncertainty about the accuracy of MVPA derived from accelerometers. Typically, a cut-point approach is taken of values such as >2000 counts/minute for count-based output or >100 mg for raw accelerometer output. Several systematic reviews (Gorman et al. 2014; Taraldsen et al. 2012; Murphy 2009) report that an astonishing number of accelerometer cut-points exist for older adults for count-based accelerometer data, expressed in counts/minute. This raises serious concerns about the comparability of data across the studies. However, cut-points for older adults based on raw accelerometer output are hard to find, although 70 mg at the wrist produces high classification accuracy in adults aged >65 years (Innerd and University of Newcastle upon Tyne Institute for Ageing 2015).

The problem associated with estimating MVPA from body movement detected by an accelerometer is that older adults do not perform as vigorous movements to elicit a physiological response characteristic to MVPA (Miller et al. 2010). Specific age-related alterations responsible for this include decreased muscle activation, heart rate, lactate, respiratory exchange ratio, oxygen consumption (VO_2), ventilation and rating of perceived exertion (RPE) (LaRoche et al. 2018). Notably, this makes MVPA in older adults difficult to assess without age-specific cut-points. However, machine learning algorithms have been developed which measure

MVPA via a completely different analytical approach. This method, using pattern recognition, is most popular when classifying activity type.

Classification of activity type

The measurement of time spent carrying out certain types of physical activity adds useful contextualisation to the evidence. The detection of activity types facilitates an understanding of how physical activity is accumulated throughout the day. Walking is perhaps the most popular type of physical activity. It is easy to incorporate into daily life, and some adolescents meet targets for walking by simply walking to school (Alexander et al. 2005). Similarly, a number of adults meet physical activity guidelines by simply walking for roughly 30 minutes per day (Besser and Dannenberg 2005).

Much less is known about the types of activity which feature in normal daily life. Obvious activities such as walking and sitting are common. However, the types of activity carried out change across adulthood and are far more varied than physical activity intensity. Identifying the time spent carrying out activity types such as sitting, standing, walking and running demonstrates which activities feature consistently across the lifecourse and which rise and fall. Identification of this behavioural component of physical activity is important to determine the social, psychological and biological factors which influence the types of physical activity we carry out: the determinants of physical activity.

Changes across the lifecourse

As children, we develop the ability to carry out a wider range of activities with increasing age. Throughout childhood there is an ordered pattern of development observable across most children. Biological mechanisms largely underpin this progression as large muscle groups develop which support ambulatory movement to activities involving fine motor coordination such as those involved in self-care. Typically, by age 2 years, a child can hold a glass securely; at age 3, children can feed themselves; by age 4 they can use the toilet independently, and thereafter can bathe and dress with only little parental supervision.

In adulthood, daily activities vary due to differences in occupation, leisure time choices and the level of health awareness of the individual. Individuals and groups may be more receptive to health-promoting interventions around the times of key life transitions, such as those which occur due to employment, marriage, parenthood and retirement. However, it is currently unclear which lifestyle transitions are most important and what factors are associated with changes in physical activity at these times.

In old age, functional capacity, and therefore physical activity, is most variable. Older adults spend significantly less time walking (Hovell et al. 1989). Just as there is an ordered pattern of development in activities in childhood, there is an ordered regression of activities due to the ageing process, which causes most individuals to experience a diminished ability to carry out activities involving bigger muscle groups and major physical effort, prolonged periods of energy expenditure and cardiovascular function, or in the later stages of life, activities involving fine motor skills and manual dexterity.

The ability to carry out the range of activities required to function independently in daily life, so-called activities of daily living, have long been seen as essential measures of disability in ageing studies and in clinical practice to assess care needs. However, as people age, they lose the ability to perform certain activities. There is an order or hierarchy to the way these activities are gradually lost. Basic Activities of Daily Living (BADLs), for instance personal care activities of feeding, bathing and toileting, are physically challenging only in that they require dexterity and coordination. Instrumental Activities of Daily Living (IADLs) such as shopping, cooking and doing housework require more physical effort. Older adults find walking long distances, shopping and housework harder to carry out. These BADLs are lost first. The activities that remain in older life are IADLs, those necessary for self-care (Kingston et al. 2012). However, adults who are most physically active in later life tend to preserve the ability to carry out most, if not all ADLs.

To track this loss of ability to perform certain activities, questionnaires are often used which require study participants to recall their activity habits retrospectively. The subjective nature of this assessment method renders it susceptible to recall bias (difficulty in recalling past activities) and response bias (difficulty interpreting certain questions), which are made worse with age. However, raw accelerometers now use machine learning algorithms to classify activity types. We will explore these advanced, yet fascinating, machine learning techniques and how they can detect activity types such as walking, running, lying down and sitting in Chapter 8.

Sitting is an activity type classed as sedentary which, due to the increase in desk-based occupations, is a major contributor to sedentary behaviour. It is not uncommon for some people to spend half their waking day sitting, with relatively idle muscles. Such prolonged sedentary behaviour causes unique detrimental changes to health but also unique opportunities to intervene. Thus, a growing number of activity monitors can detect sitting and sedentary activities.

Sedentary behaviour

Jerry Morris' famous comparison of bus drivers and bus conductors was ahead of its time in more ways than one. The bus drivers of his study spent their working day in an activity that was slowly growing, whereas today it is discussed in terms of an epidemic: sitting. No wonder one of his colleagues paid tribute to him in a justifiably glowing catalogue of his scientific achievements (Paffenbarger, Blair and Lee 2001). From Morris' 1950s work, society has witnessed the growth of physically *in*active lifestyles: the disappearance of occupational physical activity, the introduction of labour-saving devices and electronic forms of entertainment and internet connectivity, and continued reductions in the need to carry out even low levels of physical activity have resulted in long periods of time sitting becoming a common feature of many people's lives.

Progressively decreasing levels of physical activity and increasing amounts of sedentary behaviour have caused researchers to investigate the effects, not only of low levels of physical activity, but also the now ubiquitous sedentary activities, such as sitting and TV viewing (Clark et al. 2011).

Opportunities for sedentary behaviour are becoming increasingly common: sedentary activities, such as sitting, are now ubiquitous in modern life. Prolonged bouts of sitting occur in numerous settings, such as during transportation, at work, at home and in leisure time. In fact, objective estimates indicate adults spend roughly 8–10 hours per day of their waking time in sedentary activities (Matthews et al. 2008; Clark et al. 2011). Mounting evidence demonstrates that sedentary behaviour is a serious health concern (Stamatakis et al. 2018). The health consequences caused by inadequate physical activity are independent from those due to sedentary behaviour (Tremblay et al. 2010). Sedentary behaviour is different from physical *in*activity. Conceptualising sedentary behaviour as distinct from a lack of physical activity is essential for three reasons: (i) inactivity is low levels of movement, whereas sedentary behaviour is the absence of movement, (ii) the physiological responses of sedentary behaviour distinct and (iii) the measurement of sedentary behaviour is carried out using instruments developed specifically for that purpose (Tremblay et al. 2010). Furthermore, the mechanisms through which sedentary activity acts to exert its health-damaging effects are independent from those of simply not being physically active.

Physical *in*activity involves low levels of muscular activity, falling below levels needed to preserve health, whereas prolonged bouts of sedentary behaviour involve very low whole-body movement and near total muscular inactivity. Sedentary physiology or inactivity physiology is a relatively new concept which refers to a distinct set of consequences which are specific to sedentary activity and different from a lack of physical activity. Initial findings came from bed rest studies where individuals were confined to conditions of sedentary behaviour for a defined period (Gretebeck et al. 1995). The physiology of sedentary activity centres on the fact that sedentary behaviours involve near complete inactivation of skeletal muscle and the metabolic and neuroendocrine mechanisms which muscles contract. Therefore, the health consequences of sedentary behaviour are linked to the response of body organs and tissues to misuse (Ekblom-Bak, Hellenius and Ekblom 2010). This includes reduced aerobic capacity, muscular atrophy and metabolic dysregulation. Recent evidence shows that prolonged and reoccurring bouts of sedentary activity are associated with risk of developing chronic diseases such as type II diabetes (Lamb et al. 2016), cardiovascular diseases (Whitaker et al. 2019), osteoporosis (Chastin et al. 2014), depression (Vallance et al. 2011), and with premature death (Matthews et al. 2016)

Changes across the lifecourse

Sedentary behaviour is thought to be alarmingly high across the whole lifecourse. Studies have reported children spending roughly 8 hours being sedentary per day

(Verloigne et al. 2013). Despite the current guidelines which recommend ≤2 hours/day of leisure screen time, some children could spend over 2 hours/day in front of TVs and computers (Stierlin et al. 2015).

Sedentary behaviour in adults typically increases across the lifecourse. Reductions in MVPA are shown to be modest compared to reductions in light-intensity activity and increased sedentary behaviour from youth to middle age (Pettee Gabriel et al. 2018) and adulthood to old age (>63 years) (Dos Santos et al. 2018). However, it should be noted that the majority of studies are using count-based accelerometers and sedentary activity cut-points. Firstly, activity counts are summarised over a specified time frame or epoch, for example 15 seconds (Yildirim et al. 2011). Thus, any movement lasting under 15 seconds is likely to be missing from the data. Furthermore, the measurement of sedentary activity in minutes/day using cut-points does not typically result in accurate reliable data. When the use of 1-second, 10-second and 15-second epochs with sedentary cut-points up to <200 counts/minute was compared, time spent in sedentary behaviour disagreed by up to 2 hours 4 minutes/day (Aguilar-Farias, Brown and Peeters 2014). Although the limitations of activity counts cannot be overcome, using raw accelerometer data and analysing the accelerometer output using more advanced analytical methods is strongly recommended.

Raw accelerometers allow analysis of the full unprocessed acceleration signal. This is essential when attempting to detect behaviours which feature low-level, short-duration movement. Sedentary activity can be measured using more effective analytics than cut-points, such as pattern recognition. A systematic review of accelerometer methods used to measure sedentary behaviour reported that pattern recognition techniques provide the most valid estimates of sedentary time (Heesch et al. 2018). We will see how these analytics work in Chapter 7 and directly apply them in Chapter 8.

Estimates of sedentary behaviour and physical activity need to be derived from a single acceleration signal. A novel study derived estimates of sedentary behaviour, sitting and MVPA from raw accelerometer data by simply reanalysing the data using different analytical methods (Innerd, Harrison and Coulson 2018). Epidemiological studies should aim to adopt the same approach to accurately detect any overspill of behaviours, for example if an intervention increases physical activity but sedentary behaviour decreases concomitantly.

Frameworks for public health and chronic disease prevention initially focused on the higher end of the activity level spectrum, then physical activity surveillance systems utilising improved measurement instruments started to capture the lower end of the activity spectrum, namely sedentary activities. Continuously evolving activity surveillance highlighted a shift toward monitoring of the whole 24-hour cycle, including both waking activity and sleep.

Sleep

Over 24 hours, we are either physically active (standing, walking, running), sedentary (sitting, reclining, lying down) or asleep. Physical activity, sedentary behaviour and sleep are interrelated activities. An individual's drive to sleep is influenced mostly by the environment around them, specifically the light/dark cycle – one of several external cues called *zeitgebers* (time givers).

In dim-lit conditions or darkness, sleep-promoting hormones, primarily melatonin, are released. Melatonin promotes tiredness and increases the drive to sleep Photosensitive retinal ganglion cells in the eyes are in direct neuronal link via the retinohypothalamic tract to a small cluster of cells (approximately 20,000) called the suprachiasmatic nucleus (SCN), or master clock (Saper, Scammell and Lu 2005). The SCN is situated bilaterally in the hypothalamus. The name 'master clock' refers to the control exerted by the SCN over peripheral cellular oscillators or clock genes. Clock genes influence the fluctuating pattern of physiological processes throughout the duration of the circadian rhythm. Most endogenous processes fluctuate throughout the 24-hour sleep/wake cycle. With each hour of wakefulness there is a decrease in wake-promoting hormones such as orexin (also called hypocretin) which gradually increases the drive to sleep. Therefore, the prior length of time spent awake causes variation in sleep drive and sleep onset latency (time taken to fall asleep).

Short sleep, like physical *in*activity and sedentary behaviour, has increased to near epidemic proportions. Chronic short sleep, variously defined as ≤5 hours, <5.5 hours, or <6 hours per night, is reported by nearly a third of adults (Willetts et al. 2018). Much like physical *in*activity, inadequate sleep is associated with type II diabetes obesity, cardiovascular disease and neurodegenerative disorders.

Sleep plays a critical role in the preservation of physiological and cognitive function. The sleep/wake cycle is accompanied by fluctuations in body temperature and endogenous levels of circulating hormones, including cortisol, melatonin, growth hormone, prolactin, epinephrine/norepinephrine and various cytokines, including some T-lymphocyte populations (Spiegel, Sheridan and van Cauter 2002), interleukins and TNF-α (Abedelmalek et al. 2013).

Blood glucose levels are tightly regulated during sleep to maintain euglycaemic conditions in the fasted sleep state. Experimentally induced sleep restriction of 4 hours in bed over 4 days followed by 2 days of recovery sleep resulted in a 40% reduction in glucose tolerance at the 6 day time-point (van Cauter et al. 1994). Short sleep is also associated with an imbalance in endocrine appetite regulators, specifically an increase in the appetite-stimulating hormone ghrelin and reduction in the satiety hormone leptin (Chaput et al. 2007). Interestingly, this hormonal imbalance results in increased appetite, consumption of food, and a preference for calorie-rich, high-carbohydrate foods (Spiegel et al. 2004).

The NHANES examined the incidence of type II diabetes over a period of 8–10 years, adjusting for alcohol consumption, ethnicity, marital status and age. Participants who reported sleeping <5 hours per night had an increased risk of developing type II diabetes (odds ratio of 1.47) (Liu, Hay and Faught 2013)

There is an extensive body of evidence linking short or disrupted sleep with increased cardiovascular risk. Results from the Whitehall II Study show significantly greater risk of cardiovascular disease in people regularly sleeping <5 hours per night (Ferrie et al. 2007). Cross-sectional studies demonstrate that 7–8 hours of sleep is associated with the lowest risk of cardiovascular disease (Buxton and Marcelli 2010).

Short or poor-quality sleep can be caused by increasingly hectic lifestyles, often causing people to sacrifice sleep, more specifically because of exposure to blue light from computer screens causing circadian rhythm dysregulation, or by one of many sleep-related complaints, ranging from common disorders such as insomnia and sleep apnoea to a spectrum of sleep disorders of complex and varied aetiology.

Sleep disorders

Over 70 sleep disorders are described in the most recent edition of the *International Classification of Sleep Disorders (ICSD-3)* (AASM 2014). Sleep disorders are broadly categorised into two groups, (i) dyssomnias, which are disorders that involve insomnia or result in excessive sleepiness, and (ii) parasomnias, which are a range of sleep disorders that cause disruption to sleep, e.g. night terrors, but do not cause excessive sleepiness. Many sleep disorders occur in the idiopathic form or in association with intrinsic (poor mental health) or extrinsic (caffeine consumption) factors. Due to their complex neurophysiological and behavioural symptomatology, many sleep disorders can only be diagnosed using polysomnography (PSG), which measures cortical and biophysiological changes (Williams and Karacan 1985). Disordered sleep poses a serious risk to health, as many sleep disorders are associated with an increased risk of cognitive decline and chronic diseases such as type II diabetes, obesity and cardiovascular disease. The most common sleep disorders are insomnia and sleep apnoea.

Insomnia is defined as difficulty initiating and maintaining a duration or quality of sleep that does not result in the impairment of daytime function (AASM 2014). Chronic insomnia is associated with reduced metabolic function and the development of obesity and type II diabetes (Vgontzas et al. 2009b). Compared to controls, patients with insomnia have increased cerebral glucose when awake and when asleep (Seelig et al. 2013), increased sympathetic nervous activity (Vgontzas et al. 2009a), and higher levels of adrenocorticotropic hormones and circulating cortisol (Spiegelhalder et al. 2011). Pharmacological therapies are often used despite notable side effects and a lack of evidence for their efficacy (Silber 2005). Cognitive behavioural therapy has proven effective in tackling cognitions that cause insomnia, and has shown efficacy in 50–70% of adults (Morin et al. 2006). However, the measurement of intervention efficacy in the home setting has proven challenging, as many studies use sleep diaries, which are unreliable as the perception of sleep in people with insomnia is commonly distorted (Tang and Harvey 2004). Accelerometers are an objective alternative. However, a widely cited review by Chambers and colleagues showed that the mean error of early traditional accelerometers and sleep diaries did not significantly differ (Chambers 1994). Insomnia-specific accelerometer algorithms reduce measurement error (Lichstein et al. 2006). However, this precludes the use of these algorithms in people without insomnia and people with other common sleep disorders such as sleep apnoea.

Sleep apnoea is characterised by recurrent closures of the airway (apnoeas), resulting in reduced oxyhaemoglobin, causing sympathetic nervous activation, which rouses the patient to wakefulness or into lighter stages of sleep (Afzelius 1981). Sequelae include excessive daytime sleepiness, difficulty concentrating and reduced quality of life (Dutt et al. 2013). Moderate to severe sleep apnoea increases an individual's risk of insulin resistance (Strohl 1996), dyslipidaemia (Minoguchi et al. 2006), cardiovascular disease (Marin et al. 2005) and all-cause mortality (Gami et al. 2005). Obesity increases the risk of developing sleep apnoea due to the weight of subcutaneous fat on the airways when lying supine (Kawaguchi et al. 2011). Sleep apnoea is responsive to continuous positive airway pressure (CPAP), and weight loss where the individual is overweight or obese (Chirinos et al. 2014). Although sleep questionnaires have differentiated normal sleep and sleep apnoea (Johns 1993), conflicting results are often reported, as sleep quality is often misperceived (Walter et al. 2002). Traditional accelerometers have differentiated healthy sleepers from people with sleep apnoea (Elbaz et al. 2002). However, many devices fail to detect the postural changes associated with apnoeas (Middelkoop et al. 1995), which can number >100/hour, so, with increasing severity of sleep apnoea, the accuracy of accelerometry generally decreases (Elbaz et al. 2002).

It is noteworthy that the recent 2014 update of the ICSD features *short sleeper* as a proposed sleep disorder. The essential feature of the short sleeper is described as 'sleeping less than is expected for a person of that age or gender' (AASM 2014). Epidemiological evidence associates short sleep – variously defined as ≤5 hours to <7.5 hours – with chronic fatigue, depression and an increased risk of chronic disease in old age (Xi et al. 2014). There has been a marked increase in the prevalence of short sleep in Westernised, technology-dependent societies. Knutsen and colleagues report a significant increase in the number of short sleepers between 1975 and 2006 amongst full-time workers (Knutson et al. 2010). Changes in endocrine activity and metabolic function caused by a sleep disorder or chronic short sleep is the first stage in the progression toward the development of chronic disease.

As is the case in physical activity epidemiology, a limitation of epidemiological studies monitoring sleep is that many use sleep diaries or questionnaires. However, the objective measurement of sleep is difficult to carry out, as accelerometers perform poorly in people with short or disrupted sleep. As ageing occurs, changes in sleep duration and efficiency are described, with over half of adults experiencing sleep problems by the age of 65 years.

Changes across the lifecourse

Sleep undergoes a pronounced change across the adult lifecourse. Several PSG studies show well-defined changes in sleep duration and sleep architecture. Sleep duration reduces, with an estimated loss of approximately 10 minutes per decade (Monjan 2010), and becomes more fragmented, with an increased number of awakenings during the night. NREM3 decreases by approximately 2% per decade, whilst REM sleep diminishes more subtly, reaching a plateau by age 60 (van Cauter et al. 1998). As a result, more time is spent in the lighter sleep stages NREM1 and NREM2, making sleep less restorative. Ageing is associated with an increase in sleep complaints affecting over 50% of adults aged >60 years (Ancoli-Israel 2009) from approximately 30% of middle-aged adults (Grandner et al. 2010). People over 65 years show higher rates of primary sleep disorders such as insomnia and sleep apnoea (Vitiello 2007)

The underpinning reasons for diminished sleep quality in the elderly are poorly understood. Sleep appears to be redistributed from one consolidated nighttime episode to shorter, fragmented nighttime sleep with more frequent daytime naps (Goldman et al. 2008). This may be attributable in changes in the control mechanisms of sleep and the circadian rhythm. The circadian rhythm become less robust with age as the SCN shows a diminished responsiveness to external zeitgeibers, mainly the light/dark cycle, that entrain the circadian rhythm (Copinschi and van Cauter 1994). The circadian rhythm often becomes phase-advanced or phase-delayed (Jean-Louis et al. 2000). Phase advancement is characterised by earlier time in bed (e.g. 8 pm) due to an inability to stay awake and early morning wakefulness (e.g. 4 am) with an inability to go back to sleep (Moldofsky, Musisi and Phillipson 1986). This is likely to be caused by a slowing or quickening of the circadian pacemaker (Moore-Ede, Czeisler and Richardson 1983).

Advanced technologies, namely accelerometers, today are capable of carrying out large-scale surveillance of activity spanning the whole activity spectrum, including physical activity, sedentary behaviour and sleep. As equipment costs continue to fall to affordable levels and efforts are directed at making complex analytical methods more user-friendly, these devices are set to see widespread application. Already, studies are reporting that time spent in sleep, sedentary behaviour and physical activity are co-dependent. To simplify: spending too much or too little time on one behaviour means the person cannot engage in another.

Summary

In this chapter, we identified the physiological and behavioural measures used in physical activity monitoring, namely PAEE, METs, MVPA and activity type. Modern raw accelerometers provide greater analytical freedom and the opportunity to derive measurements relating to the parts of the day someone is not active. Sedentary behaviour is an independent risk factor separate from physical *in*activity. Similarly, there is growing interest in sleep assessment since, over a 24-hour cycle, we are typically either physically active, sedentary or sleeping. Thus, these behaviours are interrelated.

The key points of Chapter 2 are:

- Population surveillance has evolved from questionnaire-based assessments of physical activity to comprehensive assessments from wearable sensors combining physical activity intensity, activity types, sedentary behaviour and sleep.
- Lifecourse changes in physical activity from a physiological perspective are occasionally obtained by measuring PAEE or METs, but most commonly activity intensity, typically focusing on MVPA.

- Activity type classification of common activities such as sitting, walking and particularly ADLs provides important information as to how physical activity is accumulated and how ageing can cause a reduction in physical function and certain activity types.
- Sedentary behaviour is pervasive in modern life. Accurate and reliable, long-term assessments of sedentary behaviour are needed to identify key correlates and determinants.
- Physical activity, sedentary behaviour and sleep are interrelated activities. Sleep is critically important for health, therefore long-term assessments of physical activity should include sedentary behaviour and sleep where possible.

References

AASM. 2014. *International Classification of Sleep Disorders, Third Edition (ICSD-3)*, Darien, IL: American Academy of Sleep Medicine.

Abedelmalek, S., N. Souissi, H. Chtourou, M. Denguezli, C. Aouichaoui, M. Ajina, A. Aloui, M. Dogui, S. Haddouk, and Z. Tabka. 2013. 'Effects of partial sleep deprivation on pro-inflammatory cytokines, growth hormone, and steroid hormone concentrations during repeated brief sprint interval exercise', *Chronobiol Int*, 30: 502–9.

Afzelius, L. E. 1981. Obstructive sleep apnea, *N Engl J Med*, 305: 1472.

Aguilar-Farias, N., W. J. Brown, and G. M. Peeters. 2014. 'ActiGraph GT3X+ cut-points for identifying sedentary behaviour in older adults in free-living environments', *J Sci Med Sport*, 17: 293–9.

Ainsworth, B. E., W. L. Haskell, S. D., Herrmann, N. Meckes, D. R. Bassett, Jr, C. Tudor-Locke, J. L. Greer, J. Vezina, M. C. Whitt-Glover, and A. S. Leon. 2011. '2011 Compendium of physical activities: a second update of codes and MET values', *Med Sci Sports Exerc*, 43: 1575–81.

Alexander, L. M., J. Inchley, J. Todd, D. Currie, A. R. Cooper, and C. Currie. 2005. 'The broader impact of walking to school among adolescents: seven day accelerometry based study', *BMJ*, 331: 1061–2.

Ancoli-Israel, S. 2009. 'Sleep and its disorders in aging populations', *Sleep Med*, 10 Suppl 1: S7–11.

Bauman, A., F. Bull, T. Chey, C. L. Craig, B. E. Ainsworth, J. F. Sallis, H. R. Bowles, M. Hagstromer, M. Sjostrom, and M. Pratt. 2009. 'The International Prevalence Study on Physical Activity: results from 20 countries', *Int J Behav Nutr Phys Act*, 6: 21.

Besser, L. M., and A. L. Dannenberg. 2005. 'Walking to public transit: steps to help meet physical activity recommendations', *Am J Prev Med*, 29: 273–80.

Brandes, M., V. T. van Hees, V. Hannover, and S. Brage. 2012. 'Estimating energy expenditure from raw accelerometry in three types of locomotion', *Med Sci Sports Exerc*, 44: 2235–42.

Buxton, O. M., and E. Marcelli. 2010. 'Short and long sleep are positively associated with obesity, diabetes, hypertension, and cardiovascular disease among adults in the United States', *Soc Sci Med*, 71: 1027–36.

Caspersen, C. J., K. E. Powell, and G. M. Christenson. 1985. 'Physical activity, exercise and physical fitness: definitions and distinctions for health related research', *Public Health Rep*, 100: 126–31.

Chambers, M. J. 1994. 'Actigraphy and insomnia: a closer look. Part 1', *Sleep*, 17: 405–8; discussion 408–10.

Chaput, J. P., J. P. Despres, C. Bouchard, and A. Tremblay. 2007. 'Short sleep duration is associated with reduced leptin levels and increased adiposity: results from the Quebec Family Study', *Obesity (Silver Spring)*, 15: 253–61.

Chastin, S. F., O. Mandrichenko, J. L. Helbostadt, and D. A. Skelton. 2014. 'Associations between objectively-measured sedentary behaviour and physical activity with bone mineral density in adults and older adults, the NHANES study', *Bone*, 64: 254–62.

Chirinos, J. A., I. Gurubhagavatula, K. Teff, D. J. Rader, T. A. Wadden, R. Townsend, G. D. Foster, G. Maislin, H. Saif, P. Broderick, J. Chittams, A. L. Hanlon, and A. I. Pack. 2014. 'CPAP, weight loss, or both for obstructive sleep apnea', *N Engl J Med*, 370: 2265–75.

Chong, Y., R. J. Klein, C. Plepys, and R. Troiano. 1998. 'Operational definitions for year 2000 objectives: Priority Area 1, physical activity and fitness', *Healthy People 2000 Stat Notes*, 1–17.

Clark, B. K., G. N. Healy, E. A. Winkler, P. A. Gardiner, T. Sugiyama, D. W. Dunstan, C. E. Matthews, and N. Owen. 2011. 'Relationship of television time with accelerometer-derived sedentary time: NHANES', *Med Sci Sports Exerc*, 43: 822–8.

Copinschi, G., and E. van Cauter. 1994. 'Pituitary hormone secretion in aging: roles of circadian rhythmicity and sleep', *Eur J Endocrinol*, 131: 441–2.

da Silva, I. C., V. T. van Hees, V. V. Ramires, A. G. Knuth, R. M. Bielemann, U. Ekelund, S. Brage, and P. C. Hallal. 2014. 'Physical activity levels in three Brazilian birth cohorts as assessed with raw triaxial wrist accelerometry', *Int J Epidemiol*, 43: 1959–68.

Dencker, M., A. Bugge, B. Hermansen, and L. B. Andersen. 2010. 'Objectively measured daily physical activity related to aerobic fitness in young children', *J Sports Sci*, 28: 139–45.

Dos Santos, C. E. S., S. W. Manta, G. P. Maximiano, S. C., Confortin, T. R. B. Benedetti, E. D'Orsi, and C. R. Rech. 2018. 'Accelerometer-measured physical activity and sedentary behavior: a cross-sectional study of Brazilian older adults', *J Phys Act Health*, 15: 811–18.

Durnin, J. V. 1982. 'Energy consumption and its measurement in physical activity', *Ann Clin Res*, 14 Suppl 34: 6–11.

Durnin, J. V., and J. M. Brockway. 1959. 'Determination of the total daily energy expenditure in man by indirect calorimetry: assessment of the accuracy of a modern technique', *Br J Nutr*, 13: 41–53.

Dutt, N., A. K. Janmeja, P. R. Mohapatra, and A. K. Singh. 2013. 'Quality of life impairment in patients of obstructive sleep apnea and its relation with the severity of disease', *Lung India*, 30: 289–94.

Ekblom-Bak, E., M. L. Hellenius, and B. Ekblom. 2010. 'Are we facing a new paradigm of inactivity physiology?', *Br J Sports Med*, 44: 834–5.

Ekelund, U., S. Brage, P. W. Franks, S. Hennings, S. Emms, and N. J. Wareham. 2005. 'Physical activity energy expenditure predicts progression toward the metabolic syndrome independently of aerobic fitness in middle-aged healthy Caucasians: the Medical Research Council Ely Study', *Diabetes Care*, 28: 1195–200.

Elbaz, M., G. M. Roue, F. Lofaso, and M. A. Quera Salva. 2002. 'Utility of actigraphy in the diagnosis of obstructive sleep apnea', *Sleep*, 25: 527–31.

Ferrie, J. E., M. J. Shipley, F. P. Cappuccio, E. Brunner, M. A. Miller, M. Kumari, and M. G. Marmot. 2007. 'A prospective study of change in sleep duration: associations with mortality in the Whitehall II cohort', *Sleep*, 30: 1659–66.

Fuzeki, E., T. Engeroff, and W. Banzer. 2017. 'Health benefits of light-intensity physical activity: a systematic review of accelerometer data of the National Health and Nutrition Examination Survey (NHANES)', *Sports Med*, 47: 1769–93.

Gami, A. S., D. E. Howard, E. J. Olson, and V. K. Somers. 2005. 'Day–night pattern of sudden death in obstructive sleep apnea', *N Engl J Med*, 352: 1206–14.

Godfrey, A., A. Bourke, S. Del Din, R. Morris, A. Hickey, J. L. Helbostad, and L. Rochester. 2016. 'Towards holistic free-living assessment in Parkinson's disease: unification of gait and fall algorithms with a single accelerometer', *Conf Proc IEEE Eng Med Biol Soc*, 651–654.

Goldman, S. E., M. Hall, R. Boudreau, K. A. Matthews, J. A. Cauley, S. Ancoli-Israel, K. L. Stone, S. M. Rubin, S. Satterfield, E. M. Simonsick, and A. B. Newman. 2008. 'Association between nighttime sleep and napping in older adults', *Sleep*, 31: 733–40.

Goran, M. I., G. Hunter, T. R. Nagy, and R. Johnson. 1997. 'Physical activity related energy expenditure and fat mass in young children', *Int J Obes Relat Metab Disord*, 21: 171–8.

Gorman, E., H. M. Hanson, P. H. Yang, K. M. Khan, T. Liu-Ambrose, and M. C. Ashe. 2014. 'Accelerometry analysis of physical activity and sedentary behavior in older adults: a systematic review and data analysis', *Eur Rev Aging Phys Act*, 11: 35–49.

Grandner, M. A., N. P. Patel, P. R. Gehrman, M. L. Perlis, and A. I. Pack. 2010. 'Problems associated with short sleep: bridging the gap between laboratory and epidemiological studies', *Sleep Med Rev*, 14: 239–47.

Gretebeck, R. J., D. A. Schoeller, E. K. Gibson, and H. W. Lane. 1995. 'Energy expenditure during antiorthostatic bed rest (simulated microgravity)', *J Appl Physiol*, 78: 2207–11.

Heesch, K. C., R. L. Hill, N. Aguilar-Farias, J. G. Z. van Uffelen, and T. Pavey. 2018. 'Validity of objective methods for measuring sedentary behaviour in older adults: a systematic review', *Int J Behav Nutr Phys Act*, 15: 119.

Heil, D. P., P. S. Freedson, L. E. Ahlquist, J. Price, and J. M. Rippe. 1995. 'Nonexercise regression models to estimate peak oxygen consumption', *Med Sci Sports Exerc*, 27: 599–606.

Hovell, M. F., J. F. Sallis, C. R. Hofstetter, V. M. Spry, P. Faucher, and C. J. Caspersen. 1989.' Identifying correlates of walking for exercise: an epidemiologic prerequisite for physical activity promotion', *Prev Med*, 18: 856–66.

Innerd, P., and University of Newcastle upon Tyne Institute for Ageing. 2015. *Assessment of Physical Activity and Sleep Using Raw Accelerometry*, Newcastle upon Tyne, UK: Newcastle University.

Innerd, P., R. Harrison, and M. Coulson. 2018. 'Using open source accelerometer analysis to assess physical activity and sedentary behaviour in overweight and obese adults', *BMC Public Health*, 18: 543.

Jean-Louis, G., D. F. Kripke, S. Ancoli-Israel, M. R. Klauber, R. S. Sepulveda, M. A. Mowen, J. D. Assmus, and R. D. Langer. 2000. 'Circadian sleep, illumination, and activity patterns in women: influences of aging and time reference', *Physiol Behav*, 68: 347–52.

Johns, M. W. 1993. 'Daytime sleepiness, snoring, and obstructive sleep apnea: the Epworth Sleepiness Scale', *Chest*, 103: 30–6.

Jorgensen, H. U., L. Werdelin, A. Lokkegaard, K. R. Westerterp, and L. Simonsen. 2012. 'Free-living energy expenditure reduced after deep brain stimulation surgery for Parkinson's disease', *Clin Physiol Funct Imaging*, 32: 214–20.

Kawaguchi, Y., S. Fukumoto, M. Inaba, H. Koyama, T. Shoji, S. Shoji, and Y. Nishizawa. 2011. 'Different impacts of neck circumference and visceral obesity on the severity of obstructive sleep apnea syndrome', *Obesity (Silver Spring)*, 19: 276–82.

Kingston, A., J. Collerton, K. Davies, J. Bond, L. Robinson, and C. Jagger. 2012. 'Losing the ability in activities of daily living in the oldest old: a hierarchic disability scale from the Newcastle 85+ Study', *PLOS ONE*, 7: e31665.

Knutson, K. L., E. van Cauter, P. J. Rathouz, T. Deleire, and D. S. Lauderdale. 2010. 'Trends in the prevalence of short sleepers in the USA: 1975–2006', *Sleep*, 33: 37–45.

Kozey, S. L., K. Lyden, C. A. Howe, J. W. Staudenmayer, and P. S. Freedson. 2010. 'Accelerometer output and MET values of common physical activities', *Med Sci Sports Exerc*, 42: 1776–84.

Lamb, M. J., K. Westgate, S. Brage, U. Ekelund, G. H. Long, S. J. Griffin, R. K. Simmons, and A. J. Cooper. 2016. 'Prospective associations between sedentary time, physical activity, fitness and cardiometabolic risk factors in people with type 2 diabetes', *Diabetologia*, 59: 110–20.

LaRoche, D. P., E. L. Melanson, M. P., Baumgartner, B. Bozzuto, V. M. Libby, and B. N. Marshall. 2018. 'Physiological determinants of walking effort in older adults: should they be targets for physical activity intervention?', *Geroscience*, 40: 305–15.

Lee, I. M., E. J. Shiroma, F. Lobelo, P. Puska, S. N. Blair, and P. T. Katzmarzyk. 2012. 'Effect of physical inactivity on major non-communicable diseases worldwide: an analysis of burden of disease and life expectancy', *Lancet*, 380: 219–29.

Levine, J., E. L. Melanson, K. R. Westerterp, and J. O. Hill. 2001. 'Measurement of the components of nonexercise activity thermogenesis', *Am J Physiol Endocrinol Metab*, 281: E670–5.

Lichstein, K. L., K. C. Stone, J. Donaldson, S. D. Nau, J. P. Soeffing, D. Murray, K. W. Lester, and R. N. Aguillard. 2006. 'Actigraphy validation with insomnia', *Sleep*, 29: 232–9.

Liu, J., J. Hay, and B. E. Faught. 2013. 'The association of sleep disorder, obesity status, and diabetes mellitus among US adults – the NHANES 2009–2010 Survey results', *Int J Endocrinol*, 2013: 234129.

Luke, A., P. Bovet, T. E. Forrester, E. V. Lambert, J. Plange-Rhule, D. A. Schoeller, L. R., Dugas, R. A. Durazo-Arvizu, D. Shoham, R. S. Cooper, S. Brage, U. Ekelund, and N. P. Steyn. 2011. 'Protocol for the modeling the epidemiologic transition study: a longitudinal observational study of energy balance and change in body weight, diabetes and cardiovascular disease risk', *BMC Public Health*, 11: 927.

Marin, J. M., S. J. Carrizo, E. Vicente, and A. G. Agusti. 2005. 'Long-term cardiovascular outcomes in men with obstructive sleep apnoea-hypopnoea with or without treatment with continuous positive airway pressure: an observational study', *Lancet*, 365: 1046–53.

Matthews, C. E., K. Y. Chen, P. S. Freedson, M. S. Buchowski, B. M. Beech, R. R. Pate, and R. P. Troiano. 2008. Amount of time spent in sedentary behaviors in the United States, 2003–2004, *Am J Epidemiol*, 167: 875–81.

Matthews, C. E., S. K. Keadle, R. P. Troiano, L. Kahle, A. Koster, R. Brychta, D. van Domelen, P. Caserotti, K. Y. Chen, T. B. Harris, and D. Berrigan. 2016. 'Accelerometer-measured dose-response for physical activity, sedentary time, and mortality in US adults', *Am J Clin Nutr*, 104: 1424–32.

Menai, M., V. T. van Hees, A. Elbaz, M. Kivimaki, A. Singh-Manoux, and S. Sabia. 2017. 'Accelerometer assessed moderate-to-vigorous physical activity and successful ageing: results from the Whitehall II Study', *Sci Rep*, 8: 45772.

Middelkoop, H. A., A. Knuistingh Neven, J. J. van Hilten, C. W. Ruwhof, and H. A. Kamphuisen. 1995. 'Wrist actigraphic assessment of sleep in 116 community based subjects suspected of obstructive sleep apnoea syndrome', *Thorax*, 50: 284–9.

Miller, N. E., S. J. Strath, A. M. Swartz, and S. E. Cashin. 2010. 'Estimating absolute and relative physical activity intensity across age via accelerometry in adults', *J Aging Phys Act*, 18: 158–70.

Minoguchi, K., T. Yokoe, A. Tanaka, S. Ohta, T. Hirano, G. Yoshino, C. P. O'Donnell, and M. Adachi. 2006. 'Association between lipid peroxidation and inflammation in obstructive sleep apnoea', *Eur Respir J*, 28: 378–85.

Moldofsky, H., S. Musisi, and E. A. Phillipson. 1986. 'Treatment of a case of advanced sleep phase syndrome by phase advance chronotherapy', *Sleep*, 9: 61–5.

Monjan, A. A. 2010. 'Perspective on sleep and aging', *Front Neurol*, 1: 124.

Moore-Ede, M. C., C. A. Czeisler, and G. S. Richardson. 1983. 'Circadian timekeeping in health and disease. Part 1: basic properties of circadian pacemakers', *N Engl J Med*, 309: 469–76.

Morin, C. M., R. R. Bootzin, D. J. Buysse, J. D. Edinger, C. A. Espie, and K. L. Lichstein. 2006. 'Psychological and behavioral treatment of insomnia: update of the recent evidence (1998–2004)', *Sleep*, 29: 1398–414.

Morris, J. N., J. A. Heady, P. A. Raffle, C. G. Roberts, and J. W. Parks. 1953. 'Coronary heart-disease and physical activity of work', *Lancet*, 265: 1053–7; contd.

Murphy, S. L. 2009. 'Review of physical activity measurement using accelerometers in older adults: considerations for research design and conduct', *Prev Med*, 48: 108–14.

Paffenbarger, R. S., Jr., S. N. Blair, and I. M. Lee. 2001. 'A history of physical activity, cardiovascular health and longevity: the scientific contributions of Jeremy N Morris, DSc, DPH, FRCP', *Int J Epidemiol*, 30: 1184–92.

Passmore, R., and J. V. Durnin. 1955. 'Human energy expenditure', *Physiol Rev*, 35: 801–40.

Pettee Gabriel, K., S. Sidney, D. R. Jacobs, Jr., K. M. Whitaker, M. R. Carnethon, C. E. Lewis, P. J. Schreiner, R. I. Malkani, J. M. Shikany, J. P. Reis, and B. Sternfeld. 2018. 'Ten-year changes in accelerometer-based physical activity and sedentary time during midlife: the CARDIA Study', *Am J Epidemiol*, 187: 2145–50.

Saint-Maurice, P. F., R. P. Troiano, C. E. Matthews, and W. E. Kraus. 2018. 'Moderate-to-vigorous physical activity and all-cause mortality: do bouts matter?', *J Am Heart Assoc*, 7: e03713.

Saper, C. B., T. E. Scammell, and J. Lu. 2005. 'Hypothalamic regulation of sleep and circadian rhythms', *Nature*, 437: 1257–63.

Seelig, E., U. Keller, M. Klarhofer, K. Scheffler, S. Brand, E. Holsboer-Trachsler, M. Hatzinger, and S. Bilz. 2013. 'Neuroendocrine regulation and metabolism of glucose and lipids in primary chronic insomnia: a prospective case-control study', *PLOS ONE*, 8: e61780.

Silber, M. H. 2005. 'Clinical practice: chronic insomnia', *N Engl J Med*, 353: 803–10.

Smith, A. E., R. Eston, G. D. Tempest, B. Norton, and G. Parfitt. 2015. 'Patterning of physiological and affective responses in older active adults during a maximal graded exercise test and self-selected exercise', *Eur J Appl Physiol*, 115: 1855–66.

Spiegel, K., J. F. Sheridan, and E. van Cauter. 2002. 'Effect of sleep deprivation on response to immunization', *JAMA*, 288: 1471–2.

Spiegel, K., E. Tasali, P. Penev, and E. van Cauter. 2004. 'Brief communication: Sleep curtailment in healthy young men is associated with decreased leptin levels, elevated ghrelin levels, and increased hunger and appetite', *Ann Intern Med*, 141: 846–50.

Spiegelhalder, K., L. Fuchs, J. Ladwig, S. D. Kyle, C. Nissen, U. Voderholzer, B. Feige, and D. Riemann. 2011. 'Heart rate and heart rate variability in subjectively reported insomnia', *J Sleep Res*, 20: 137–45.

Stamatakis, E., U. Ekelund, D. Ding, M. Hamer, A. E. Bauman, and I. M. Lee. 2018. 'Is the time right for quantitative public health guidelines on sitting? A narrative review of sedentary behaviour research paradigms and findings', *Br J Sports Med*, 53.

Stevens, S. S. 1946. 'On the theory of scales of measurement', *Science*, 103: 677–80.

Stierlin, A. S., S. De Lepeleere, G. Cardon, P. Dargent-Molina, B. Hoffmann, M. H. Murphy, A. Kennedy, G. O'Donoghue, S. F. Chastin, and M. De Craemer. 2015. 'A systematic review of determinants of sedentary behaviour in youth: a DEDIPAC-study', *Int J Behav Nutr Phys Act*, 12: 133.

Strohl, K. P. 1996. 'Diabetes and sleep apnea', *Sleep*, 19: S225–8.

Tang, N. K., and A. G. Harvey. 2004. 'Correcting distorted perception of sleep in insomnia: a novel behavioural experiment?', *Behav Res Ther*, 42: 27–39.

Taraldsen, K., S. F. Chastin, I. Riphagen, B. Vereijken, and J. L. Helbostad. 2012. 'Physical activity monitoring by use of accelerometer-based body-worn sensors in older adults: a systematic literature review of current knowledge and applications', *Maturitas*, 71: 13–19.

Tompuri, T. T. 2015. 'Metabolic equivalents of task are confounded by adiposity, which disturbs objective measurement of physical activity', *Front Physiol*, 6: 226.

Tooze, J. A., D. A. Schoeller, A. F. Subar, V. Kipnis, A. Schatzkin, and R. P. Troiano. 2007. 'Total daily energy expenditure among middle-aged men and women: the OPEN Study', *Am J Clin Nutr*, 86: 382–7.

Tremblay, M. S., R. C. Colley, T. J. Saunders, G. N. Healy, and N. Owen. 2010. 'Physiological and health implications of a sedentary lifestyle', *Appl Physiol Nutr Metab*, 35: 725–40.

Troiano, R. P., D. Berrigan, K. W. Dodd, L. C. Masse, T. Tilert, and M. McDowell. 2008. 'Physical activity in the United States measured by accelerometer', *Med Sci Sports Exerc*, 40: 181–8.

Valentiner, L. S., M. Ried-Larsen, K. Karstoft, C. F. Brinklov, C. Brons, R. O. Nielsen, R. Christensen, J. S. Nielsen, A. A. Vaag, B. K. Pedersen, and H. Langberg. 2017. 'Long-term effect of smartphone-delivered Interval Walking Training on physical activity in patients with type 2 diabetes: protocol for a parallel group single-blinded randomised controlled trial', *BMJ Open*, 7: e014036.

Vallance, J. K., E. A. Winkler, P. A. Gardiner, G. N. Healy, B. M. Lynch, and N. Owen. 2011. 'Associations of objectively-assessed physical activity and sedentary time with depression: NHANES (2005–2006)', *Prev Med*, 53: 284–8.

van Cauter, E., L. Plat, R. Leproult, and G. Copinschi. 1998. 'Alterations of circadian rhythmicity and sleep in aging: endocrine consequences', *Horm Res*, 49: 147–52.

van Cauter, E. V., K. S. Polonsky, J. D. Blackman, D. Roland, J. Sturis, M. M. Byrne, and A. J. Scheen. 1994. 'Abnormal temporal patterns of glucose tolerance in obesity: relationship to sleep-related growth hormone secretion and circadian cortisol rhythmicity', *J Clin Endocrinol Metab*, 79: 1797–805.

van Hees, V. T., F. Renstrom, A. Wright, A. Gradmark, M. Catt, K. Y. Chen, M. Lof, L. Bluck, J. Pomeroy, N. J. Wareham, U. Ekelund, S. Brage, and P. W. Franks. 2011. 'Estimation of daily energy expenditure in pregnant and non-pregnant women using a wrist-worn tri-axial accelerometer', *PLOS ONE*, 6: e22922.

Verloigne, M., W. van Lippevelde, L. Maes, M. Yildirim, M. Chinapaw, Y. Manios, O. Androutsos, E. Kovacs, B. Bringolf-Isler, J. Brug, and I. De Bourdeaudhuij. 2013. 'Self-reported TV and computer time do not represent accelerometer-derived total sedentary time in 10 to 12-year-olds', *Eur J Public Health*, 23: 30–2.

Vgontzas, A. N., D. Liao, E. O. Bixler, G. P. Chrousos, and A. Vela-Bueno. 2009a. 'Insomnia with objective short sleep duration is associated with a high risk for hypertension', *Sleep*, 32: 491–7.

Vgontzas, A. N., D. Liao, S. Pejovic, S. Calhoun, M. Karataraki, and E. O. Bixler. 2009b. 'Insomnia with objective short sleep duration is associated with type 2 diabetes: a population-based study', *Diabetes Care*, 32: 1980–5.

Vitiello, M. V. 2007. 'Growing old should not mean sleeping poorly: recognizing and properly treating sleep disorders in older adults', *J Am Geriatr Soc*, 55: 1882–3.

Walter, T. J., N. Foldvary, E. Mascha, D. Dinner, and J. Golish. 2002. 'Comparison of Epworth Sleepiness Scale scores by patients with obstructive sleep apnea and their bed partners', *Sleep Med*, 3: 29–32.

Westerterp, K. R., and G. Plasqui. 2004. 'Physical activity and human energy expenditure', *Curr Opin Clin Nutr Metab Care*, 7: 607–13.

Whitaker, K. M., K. Pettee Gabriel, M. P. Buman, M. A. Pereira, D. R. Jacobs, Jr., J. P. Reis, B. B. Gibbs, M. R. Carnethon, J. Staudenmayer, S. Sidney, and B. Sternfeld. 2019. 'Associations of accelerometer-measured sedentary time and physical activity with prospectively assessed cardiometabolic risk factors: the CARDIA Study', *J Am Heart Assoc*, 8: e010212.

WHO. 2010. *Global Recommendations on Physical Activity for Health*, Geneva, Switzerland: World Health Organization.

Willetts, M., S. Hollowell, L. Aslett, C. Holmes, and A. Doherty. 2018. 'Statistical machine learning of sleep and physical activity phenotypes from sensor data in 96,220 UK Biobank participants', *Sci Rep*, 8: 7961.

Williams, R. L., and I. Karacan. 1985. 'Recent developments in the diagnosis and treatment of sleep disorders', *Hosp Community Psychiatry*, 36: 951–7.

Xi, B., D. He, M. Zhang, J. Xue, and D. Zhou. 2014. 'Short sleep duration predicts risk of metabolic syndrome: a systematic review and meta-analysis', *Sleep Med Rev*, 18: 293–7.

Yildirim, M., M. Verloigne, I. De Bourdeaudhuij, O. Androutsos, Y. Manios, R. Felso, E. Kovacs, A. Doessegger, B. Bringolf-Isler, S. J. Te Velde, J. Brug, and M. J. Chinapaw. 2011. 'Study protocol of physical activity and sedentary behaviour measurement among schoolchildren by accelerometry – cross-sectional survey as part of the ENERGY-Project', *BMC Public Health*, 11: 182.

3

PHYSICAL ACTIVITY IN LIFECOURSE EPIDEMIOLOGY

The theoretical models derived from lifecourse epidemiology track exposures across the lifecourse and create an understanding of their accumulative effects on health trajectories and health outcomes. This model has been around for some years. The understanding is that disease in adulthood is often brought about by the cumulative effects of many exposures, incidents and behaviours, over a long period of time, starting as far back as infancy – accumulative risk, critical and sensitive periods. What makes people active and what motivates people to be active is therefore presented in this chapter. But what instruments best capture these changes? What factors should you use to inform your choice? How does physical activity change as we age and how does it affect measurement?

A lifecourse approach often involves repeated measurements over several time-points within a study and the comparison of data from several studies. Therefore, careful attention should be paid to the chosen measurement method. This requires accurate and precise measurements which, until recently, have been difficult to obtain. The use of accelerometers in lifecourse research represents a methodo-logically advanced, cost-effective solution. Although the use of raw data and open-source analytical methods creates a host of new opportunities, processing and then analysing the raw data can prove challenging for the non-expert. However, in Chapter 8 we will go through the process, step by step, from data collection and processing to analysis, leaving you equipped with the skills to carry out repeated assessments and interpret cross-study comparisons.

NCDs develop over the long term, in response to a number of exposures that can interact, increase the pace of disease onset or act differently depending on embedded risk that is persistent. Risk factors such as physical *in*activity exert their effects over the long term. Lifecourse epidemiology nicely defines the point of exposure onset to when it takes effect as the induction period, and the time between disease initiation and the point of detection and diagnosis as the latency period. This approach allows us to build and test theoretical models that suggest pathways linking exposures across the lifecourse to later life health outcomes; in this case, it answers the question, 'Why do people become more physically active, and when?'

In this chapter, we will:

- Introduce the concept of lifecourse epidemiology and the theoretical framework it represents.
- Describe the tracking of exposures from childhood to old age and examine how these exposures are combined to explain the trajectory of disease onset.
- Define key models, including causal pathways and disease progression, to demonstrate how the lifecourse framework helps elucidate the occurrence of NCD and thus its prevention.
- Explore ways of using the wealth of longitudinal, biological and social data which is part of existing cohort studies, and the assimilation of cohorts from different studies to increase the size of samples and provide previously unobtainable evidence to exploit measurement opportunities presented later in the book.

The chance to answer long-standing questions about why people become active and stay active is possible by incorporating modern accelerometer technology into lifecourse epidemiology. Providing a comprehensive guide of how to do that requires that we look at the lifecourse approach.

Lifecourse epidemiology: a theoretical framework

NCDs such as coronary heart disease, type II diabetes and cancer are largely the result of common preventable lifestyle risk factors such as smoking, poor diet and physical *in*activity. These risk factors act detrimentally at all stages of life: during gestation (affecting foetal development and gene expression), childhood (affecting growth and development), adulthood (disrupting normal physiology) and old age (exacerbating damage from ageing). Therefore, a person's disease risk depends on when risk factors occur, how long they last and how they interact. This gives important clues as to the aetiology of the disease and indicates that NCDs can be prevented and controlled at multiple stages of the lifecourse.

A lifecourse approach seeks to understand disease development by considering the earliest stages of life, during foetal development, through to the final stages of life, at the end of the lifespan: from beginning to end. The evidence resulting from this approach is critically important, not only because of growing healthcare costs – the treatment of NCDs globally makes up half of these – but also due to the growing number of older adults who are at the greatest risk. Roughly 30% of adults aged 30–35 years have at least one NCD or disability, ~50% of those aged 50–55 years, ~80% of those aged 70–75 years, and of adults aged over 90 years, few are free of disease and disability (Fox 1998). Adults aged 85 years and over are the fastest-growing age demographic (Collerton et al. 2009). Concurrent increases in global NCDs and lifespan are taking place due to improvements in healthcare systems rendering NCDs less disabling.

Lifecourse epidemiology is different from a longitudinal study: the first is a theoretical framework, the second is a study design (Jaeschke et al. 2017). A lifecourse approach involves tracking exposures from childhood to old age, to study the long-term effects on health and disease. Biological, behavioural, psychological and social factors operate and interact across the lifecourse to influence disease risk. Risk factors are influenced by various correlates and determinants which change at each stage of the lifecourse. This provides an understanding of the causal pathways of a disease, which may take decades to develop and feature certain timepoints where interventions would provide the greatest possible results. Lifecourse epidemiology is used to build and test theoretical models that suggest pathways linking exposures across the lifecourse to later life health outcomes: it answers the question, 'Whose behaviour changes, when, and why?'(Corder, Ogilvie and van Sluijs 2009).

The field of epidemiology is one of the more recent to embrace a lifecourse approach. Other interdisciplinary areas such as developmental science place emphasis on psychological and biological processes from conception to death. Epidemiologists took an interest in response to studies demonstrating the importance of conditions during foetal development, such as undernutrition or overnutrition in utero, having a negative impact on the 'biological programming' and therefore the structure and function of tissues and organs. Effects may not become apparent until much later in life (latency), although gestational conditions continue to exist for some individuals (persistency) (Sayer and Cooper 2005). A lifecourse approach combines this and other models based on relationships between lifestyle and NCD development in childhood and adulthood.

A distinct strength of lifecourse epidemiology is the motivation to combine different approaches of assessing risk. It considers the influence of biological programming in utero jointly with risk factors and protective processes that operate in early life, such as childhood and adolescence, and later life. Also, it integrates biological and social processes. The interaction of biological and social factors functions over the lifecourse, from gestation to old age, to influence health in adult life. Socioeconomic status is a well-established determinant of physical activity (Kouvonen et al. 2012). Similarly, lifecourse epidemiology can involve the use of data from one study over several timepoints or the pooling of data from different studies. Longitudinal study designs provide new insights into long-term health trajectories, often in previously unexplored populations which are difficult to detect using other study designs. Few longitudinal studies cover the entire lifecourse, therefore findings from different studies can be combined to formulate comprehensive evidence from a lifecourse perspective.

A lifecourse approach involves the identification of early markers of risk, and in turn provides a comprehensive understanding of causal mechanisms and pathways. The identification of causal pathways is a key theme of epidemiology. Diseases are typically multifactorial in nature. NCDs occur after exposures have acted with sufficient severity over time. Understanding causal pathways is essential in the development of lifestyle interventions aimed at preventing disease.

Relatively modest interventions in early life can have a large effect on disease risk in later life. A reduced risk trajectory in response to early intervention is shown in Figure 3.1 (solid line), whereas later interventions have less of an effect on risk (dotted line). In old age, some years may have passed during which repeated risk exposures have occurred, causing damage to accumulate that limits the body's capacity to respond, for example to repair cellular damage or restore metabolic function. Early life interventions require long-term investment, but lead to worthwhile reductions in disease risk. Thus, lifecourse epidemiology is more effective at preventing NCDs than shorter-term population screening programmes which use a more simplified approach of identifying markers of disease risk and developing interventions for either prevention or treatment.

Exposures, determinants and risk all change across the lifecourse, and often interact. Therefore, lifecourse epidemiology is not a rigid framework, but rather a flexible, adaptable one. Most concepts in the framework can be categorised in accordance with their timing and duration, and three categories have been well described (Fox 1998). First, there are the concepts referring to causal pathways over time, where exposures accumulate causing damage to body systems which become less able to repair as they age (accumulation, chain of risk, trajectory). Second, there are concepts referring to the timing of causal actions (birth cohorts, critical and sensitive periods). Third, there are concepts tracking disease progression involving induction and latency periods.

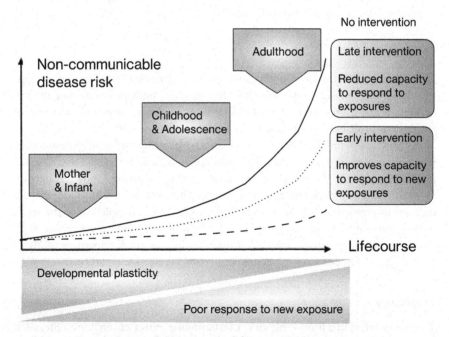

FIGURE 3.1 Accumulation of risk across the lifecourse. Risk increases across the lifecourse as a result of declining developmental plasticity and accumulating effects of inadequate responses to new challenges to health. Risk begins to accumulate early in life, but is most damaging late in life.

Causal pathways over time

Accumulation of risk

The accumulation of risk occurs where exposures gradually accumulate over time, increasing risk, and resulting in illness and injury. A strength of lifecourse epidemiology is the ability to assess the extent of damage on biological systems. This damage gradually increases as the duration and severity of exposures increase and as the inevitable process of ageing occurs, resulting in senescence and reduced ability of body systems to repair. Exposures can act independently of one another, occurring at any point in life, or cluster if they are associated with a particular behavioural, psychological or social factor, such as socioeconomic status.

Prolonged daily physical *in*activity causes cumulative damage over time. Say an individual is not active enough for good health through spending long periods inactive in leisure time, but does walk a short distance to work. The occurrence of too much sedentary behaviour, which is an independent risk factor, increases the amount of damage that would occur. In our example, the person may be promoted to a sedentary, desk-based job. Further, too little sleep can increase the total damage. Let us say that in settling into their new job role, a person spends time working late into the evening on a laptop. The accumulation of different types of exposures related to physical activity occurring over time results in damage to body systems, and unless behaviours are changed, causes the development of NCD.

Chains of risk

Here, the occurrence of one exposure or an experience in life causes damage which leads to another exposure and then another, perhaps continuing in successive events. Each exposure can be deterministic, occurring as a direct result of another, or probabilistic, increasing the probability of another.

A reduction in physical activity is associated with a reduction in sleep duration. A new project at work may last several months involving long hours, and resulting in a person sleeping less. This sleep loss may cause a gradual reduction in physical activity, for example having less leisure time in which to play sport. Over several months, the decrease in physical activity may cause weight gain. After completion of the work project, the individual, having gained weight, may have less energy and remain inactive and slowly gain more weight, eventually leading to the development of NCD such as type II diabetes.

Trajectory

Trajectory refers to a long-term view of a particular aspect of someone's life, such as long-term measurement of physical activity. Typically, there is a recommended trajectory around which all people vary. In this case of physical activity, this would be recommended guidelines of 150 minutes/week of MVPA. A change in trajectory can be caused by specific life events such as marriage, parenthood or a change in socioeconomic status. Changes resulting from these life events are typically referred to as transitions.

Timing of causal actions

Birth cohort

Birth cohorts use the year of birth to locate a population in time. This allows the investigation of factors at specific points in time and how they influence disease occurrence. Typically, birth cohorts collect large amounts of information, including biological, behavioural, psychological and socioeconomic outcomes. Behaviours such as physical *in*activity exert detrimental effects which occur over a period of years, therefore a comprehensive understanding of how to tackle these effects requires long-term tracking of health and disease. Furthermore, the determinants of physical activity change over time. Comparisons between generations enable epidemiologists to not only track temporal changes, but also social change and the reasons behind it, to inform government policy.

Critical and sensitive periods

Particular attention is paid to the timing of an exposure: during particularly vulnerable phases of life, typically early development, irreversible changes in body systems can occur which have implications for long-term health. The basic critical period model, also known as biological programming or as a latency model, underlies the foetal origins of adult disease hypothesis.

Exposures in early life often interact with later life exposures, thereby increasing the risk of NCD in later life (Salinas-Miranda et al. 2017). For example, high birthweight is linked to an increased risk of obesity, diabetes, metabolic syndrome and cardiovascular disease later in life. Babies of high birthweight are often born to mothers who have developed gestational diabetes, typically caused by excess energy intake during pregnancy. Glucose is the main nutrient that controls growth during gestation. Therefore, mothers with gestational diabetes who have elevated blood glucose are more likely to have a baby of high birthweight.

Biological embedding describes how extrinsic factors experienced at key life stages are inscribed into an individual's physical and mental functions. For example, undergoing early life adversity is associated with molecular changes that become biologically embedded in disrupted physiology. This appears to involve neurobiological or psychobiological mediators of the early social environments acting on child development and lifecourse health.

Mediators and modifiers

Mediating factors influence the relationship between exposure and disease. For example, evidence from the International Accelerometry Database showed that the existing relationship between low birthweight and reduced physical activity was mediated by central adiposity (Hildebrand et al. 2015). Lifecourse epidemiology provides a temporal framework which distinguishes between mediating factors, following the exposure chronologically, and confounding factors, occurring before the exposure, interfering with any understanding of causal effects. Modifying factors typically increase or decrease the relationship between exposure and disease.

Resilience, susceptibility and vulnerability

Resilience describes the positive way an individual reacts in response to adverse events. Increased resilience typically results in less damaging effects on health outcomes. For example, emotional resilience reduces the damaging effects of negative psychological factors. Susceptibility describes the likelihood that an exposure eventually results in disease. Often, susceptibility is used to describe occasions where exposures have become embodied over time and development of disease results from a final exposure. In epidemiology, susceptibility changes over time and is commonly used interchangeably with the term 'vulnerability' to describe a largely similar process.

Embodiment

This describes the way in which risk factors which occur across the lifecourse are 'embedded' into a person's anatomy or physiology. Embodiment is most specific to growth and development occurring in childhood. Childhood environments interact with genetic regulation to generate gradients in health and human development across the lifecourse.

Biological embedding is the process by which experience gets under the skin and alters human biology and development. Systematic differences in experience in different social environments lead to different biological and developmental outcomes. These in turn influence health, well-being, learning or behaviour over the lifecourse.

Disease progression: induction and latency

Induction and latency periods

The induction period is the point of exposure and disease initiation, but not detection. This phase is when damage accumulates. Latency period refers to the period between disease initiation and detection, characterised by the onset of symptoms of the disease and diagnosis by a medical professional (Baird et al. 2017).

When the interval between induction and detection is lengthy, the linkage between the two is more difficult to infer. Lifecourse epidemiologists have a particular interest in causal relations with long induction periods. If an exposure has a long induction or latent period, its public health importance may vary according to when in the lifecourse the individual is exposed. Often, it is difficult to observe the

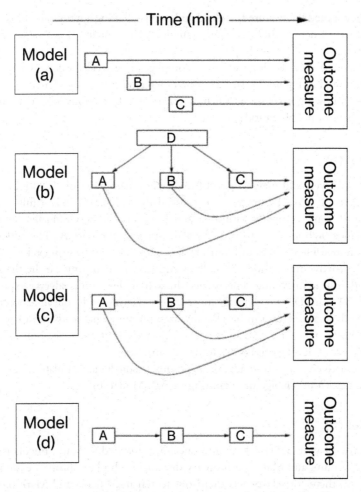

FIGURE 3.2 Lifecourse models of risk. Adverse exposures damage biological systems, with risks being either cumulative or independent. Model (a) independent, Model (b) clustered, Model (c) accumulation, Model (d) trigger effect.

Source: Kuh (2013).

time of disease initiation, and this creates difficulties in determining the differences between induction and latent periods.

Modifying factors alter the strength of association between an exposure and disease. Identifying the modifying factors of a disease sheds light on the nature of the causal process (Green and Popham 2017). For example, NCD due to being physically inactive is made worse by physical inactivity with prolonged periods of sedentary behaviour. Interactions across exposures inevitably occur and are common features of lifecourse processes, such as being physically inactive and having poor sleep. The assessment of exposures which interact is the source of much debate in epidemiology, and they should be measured, assessed and evaluated using appropriate measurement instruments where possible. A good example of this in action is the measurement of both physical activity and sleep using a single wrist-worn accelerometer.

Lifecourse epidemiology involves complex theoretical models. These models are illustrated in Figure 3.2 and described thereafter using case scenarios.

The following cases show just how tremendously relevant lifecourse theory is to the lives of people in today's society.

Model (a)

Dom, a 24-year-old male of good health, has a part-time job. The job involves low levels of stress. Dom cycles to work daily. He moves into a full-time post within the same company with managerial responsibilities. Gradually, he starts to experience high levels of stress. This is the adverse exposure A. The added stress causes noticeable changes in Dom's health. Dom decides to stop cycling to work in order to save time, and because he is entitled to a company car, he then drives to work instead of cycling. This reduces his activity levels: it is adverse exposure B. By age 34 years, Dom is spending more time socialising with colleagues after work. This leads to an increase in his alcohol consumption. This is adverse exposure C. Individually, exposures A, B and C (stress, inactivity and excess alcohol) all increase Dom's risk of developing NCDs (outcome measure).

Alternatively, lifecourse adverse exposures gradually accumulate in association with a significant change or event (Figure 3.2, Model (b)).

Model (b)

Nicola, a 39-year-old female of good health, is married to Mark. Nicola is a stay-at-home mum, and Mark is a property developer who buys properties and either renovates them for sale or lets them out to tenants. Nicola and Mark have two children aged 4 years and 8 years. An unexpected fall in house prices leaves Mark without a job and the couple in financial distress: adverse exposure D, which triggers subsequent chains of events. Nicola tries to find work as a means of financial support, but after a year of looking, she is not successful. Nicola develops depression (adverse exposure A), placing strain on the marriage, and both Mark and Nicola decide to divorce (adverse exposure B). Nicola always finds solace in walking the dog, and finds long walks in the countryside help her depression at first. However, after the divorce, Nicola is forced to rehome her dog and quickly becomes sedentary (adverse exposure C). Collectively, exposures A, B and C were triggered by exposure D. Nicola experiences continued depression and a sedentary lifestyle, and a decade later she develops type II diabetes (outcome measure).

A chain of risk model refers to a sequence of linked exposures that raise disease risk because one bad experience or exposure tends to lead to another and then another. Different types of chains can confer increased or decreased risk. Social, biological and psychological chains of risk are possible, and involve 'mediating factors' and often 'modifying factors'. The sequential links are probabilistic rather than deterministic. It is possible to conceive of two different types of chains of risk. Earlier exposures have no effect on disease risk without the final link in the chain that precipitates disease onset (Figure 3.2, Model (c)).

Model (c)

Sara, a 33-year-old female of good health, is engaged to Ben. They have no children. Both Sara and Ben have good jobs and enjoy a good standard of living. Ben's job involves him spending a lot of time away from home. When Ben is away from home, Sara takes up long bike rides to occupy her mind and lift her mood. She meets a group of cyclists who ask her to join them. One of the group, Nick, becomes friendly with Sara. Eventually the friendship grows into something romantic, causing Sara constant anxiety (adverse exposure A). Sara feels guilty and ruminates on the matter a lot. One day when she is out, 2 days before Ben is due home, when cycling alone she falls and breaks her ankle (adverse exposure B). She is kept in hospital for surgery. Ben arrives home a day early, rushes to hospital and arrives to find Nick sitting comforting Sara by her bed (adverse exposure C). Ben turns and leaves and cuts off all contact with Sara. Six months later, Sara is left with severe depression which does not seem to respond to any medication (outcome measure).

Such a 'trigger effect' (Figure 3.2, Model (d)) describes the situation when it is only the final link in the chain that has a marked effect on disease risk.

Model (d)

Alan is a 55-year-old male, a keen golfer and of good health. Alan has a son called Mike. Alan decides to take early retirement, being financially secure, and he looks forward to spending more time with his son. However, Alan finds that he and Mike do not spend more time together, causing him to worry about making the most of the time he previously spent working. Alan is unhappy about this, but does not tell his son. Increasingly, Alan is left feeling lonely (adverse exposure A). He starts playing golf less often, and starts to spend more time dining out with friends and eating processed foods instead of preparing meals for himself or his family, who are now in another country. Alan eventually stops playing golf and becomes sedentary (adverse exposure B). Over the next 5 years, Alan gains weight and becomes obese (adverse exposure C, the trigger effect). A year later, Alan suffers a heart attack and passes away (outcome measure).

Lifecourse epidemiology is a response to the limitations of previous etiological models of chronic disease. Here we have the opportunity to follow trajectories over time. A trajectory provides a long-term view of one dimension of an individual's lifecourse. These may be social states (such as work, marriage and socioeconomic status), psychological states (such as depression), physiological states (such as lung function) or behavioural states (such as physically active or sedentary). Following these trajectories and their interactions over time gives us the opportunity to produce the standard of evidence needed to inform the design of robust, targeted behaviour change interventions.

In epidemiology, there is a growing appreciation of the need for a temporal perspective for conventional so-called 'adult' risk factors. Age at onset, duration and changes in levels of exposure to conventional risk factors alter their effects on adult disease risk and impact on long-term disease trends. The health behaviours that people adopt will modify their risk of disease across the lifecourse.

Physical *in*activity is associated with an increased risk of NCDs, causing slow, progressive changes such as high blood pressure, elevated blood glucose and cholesterol levels, which will then raise the risk of conditions such as cardiovascular disease and diabetes. This has led to a growing interest in existing and new longitudinal studies that capture certain time windows or other potentially significant features of the lifecourse. The factors which determine how physically active people are include biological, psychological and socioeconomic processes, each acting differently across the stages of life, influencing the development of disease risk.

Physical activity over the lifecourse: whose behaviour changes and why?

Since NCDs such as type II diabetes, cardiovascular diseases and cancer develop gradually over the lifecourse, the most effective way to prevent them is to study the patterned exposures to protective processes such as physical activity and risk processes such as physical *in*activity. However, to develop effective interventions, we need to understand critical periods of change such as in utero conditions, childhood, adolescence, adulthood, middle age and old age.

Childhood and adolescence

The determinants of physical activity in children and adolescents are strongly related to psychological factors. Activity levels in young people are increased by changing individual perceptions and motivations to become active. Other determinants, including intention, previous physical activity and self-efficacy, are positively associated with overall physical activity, with self-efficacy having the strongest evidence. Behavioural determinants of physical activity include active transport and homework, whilst internet usage, reading and sedentary behaviour are associated with low levels of physical activity.

Socioeconomic determinants are reported frequently, and they likely have a strong influence. However, they have been defined so differently across studies that it makes study comparisons difficult. Also, childhood socioeconomic factors such as those defined by the level of parental education and parental income determine how active some young people are. Children experiencing social mobility are ~50% more likely to increase their activity and fitness levels in adulthood compared to children who remain in low socioeconomic status.

Male sex is a positive determinant in children around the ages of 4–9 years. Boys and children are more active than girls and adolescents, which in itself is interesting since the opposite is true in adulthood: low levels of activity are more often seen in men. Behaviours established in childhood regarding diet and physical activity tend to track into adulthood. The transition to adulthood involves drastic biological and social change.

Adults

The transition from adolescence to adulthood is a period of sometimes dramatic change which typically accompanies a reduction in activity levels. To prevent the fall in physical activity, evidence suggests existing levels of activity need to be high, with adults having been physically active in the early years as children. Adults who remain physically active have often walked to and from school, participated independently in active leisure time and carried out more activities without adult supervision (Condello et al. 2017).

In adulthood, lifestyle trajectories vary around key life events which typically involve additional responsibility, leaving less time and motivation to be physically active, such as university, employment, marriage and parenthood, which unsurprisingly lead to lower levels of physical activity. However, the extent to which these transitions lower physical activity is highly dependent on culture, race, gender and age (Puggina et al. 2018), which in turn also influence sedentary behaviour and sleep. For example, a job promotion may result in higher income and socioeconomic circumstances and result in more leisure-time physical activity. However, the higher occupational position, perhaps office-based, may involve long periods of sitting and working well into the evening, sacrificing sleep.

Older adults

In older adults, each passing year results in progressively decreasing physical activity and increased sedentary behaviours. Fewer older people, aged >65 years, are aware of the health benefits of physical activity compared to younger age groups, thus efforts to increase physical activity should focus on promoting its health benefits. Poor health is most common in older individuals, and also the most frequently cited barrier to participation. The remaining determinants mainly relate to individual fears arising from age-related disability and frailty. Fear is a complex factor which can occur in different situations. Barriers include fear of going out alone, fear of falls or injuries, a lack of social support, and constraints related to the physical environment making it less suitable for older adults who have specific needs.

All ages

The sole correlate in children and amongst adults with convincing evidence linking it with physical activity is socioeconomic status. However, socioeconomic status is not a distinct measurement, but rather a theoretical construct involving various measures of income, occupation and education, depending on how it is interpreted. With no agreed definition of socioeconomic status, there is no agreement on what measures should be taken to best assess it. Nonetheless, educational level, income and occupation are most commonly used across studies.

Research into early-life determinants shows that poorer parental socioeconomic status is linked to poor maternal health and low birthweight. However, high birthweight is not linked to low physical activity alone, but results from a combination of low physical activity and overnutrition combined with weight gain, and in some cases, gestational diabetes.

In children and adolescents, socioeconomic position and social mobility show robust associations with physical activity, and this determinant remains throughout the lifecourse. Several studies demonstrate that among adults (≥18 years), socioeconomic status is the sole correlate, with convincing evidence linking it to physical activity, leisuretime physical activity and occupational physical activity (Jaeschke et al. 2017). Among older adults (≥65 years old), leisure-time physical activity is consistently influenced by social mobility, though, compared to younger age groups, the evidence is limited.

Gaps in knowledge

Whether or not individuals choose a healthy lifestyle and are physically active is influenced by a number of inter-dependent and multilevel factors. However, for the majority of determinants, the evidence is inconclusive. This is attributed to three limitations. First, the most common study design used is cross-sectional, which limits the strength of any evidence. In fact, only few determinants achieve a probable level of evidence. Second, the categories of behavioural, psychological and socioeconomic determinants are used to ease interpretation, but these categories feature clusters of factors and are not used uniformly across studies. Third, there is considerable heterogeneity in the methods used to assess physical activity and sedentary behaviour, both across studies and often within the same study from one data sweep to the next.

The DEterminants of DIet and Physical ACtivity-Knowledge Hub (DEDIPAC-KH)

A look at the DEDIPAC European Joint Programming Initiative illustrates this point. Joint programming is a process by which member states engage in defining, developing and implementing a common strategic research agenda. The DEDIPAC-KH project is a multidisciplinary group of scientists from 46 institutions aiming to understand the determinants of dietary, physical activity and sedentary behaviours and to translate this knowledge into more effective promotion of a healthy diet and physical activity (Lakerveld et al. 2014). The work is divided into three key areas: (i) assessment and harmonisation of methods for future research, surveillance and monitoring, and for evaluation of interventions and policies;

(ii) determinants of dietary, physical activity and sedentary behaviours across the lifecourse and in vulnerable groups; and (iii) evaluation and benchmarking of public health and policy interventions aimed at improving dietary, physical activity and sedentary behaviours.

Scientists in the DEDIPAC group conducted a series of umbrella systematic reviews. An umbrella systematic review is a synthesis of existing systematic reviews. The authors aimed to publish the first syntheses of existing systematic reviews on socioeconomic status (O'Donoghue et al. 2018) and behavioural (Condello et al. 2017) and psychological (Cortis et al. 2017) determinants of physical activity across the lifecourse. One umbrella review compared measurements of physical activity including overall physical activity and MVPA from 20 reviews featuring a total 729 primary studies (Carlin et al. 2017). Of the primary studies, 567 studies used self-report/ questionnaire-based measurements, 44 used objective methods, including pedometers, heart rate monitors and accelerometers, seven studies combined subjective and objective measures, and a considerable 111 eligible studies did not report measures of physical activity, but rather estimates based on intentions to carry out physical activity.

Amongst the self-report instruments were the IPAQ, Godin Leisure-Time Exercise Questionnaire (GLTEQ) and Seasonal Pattern Assessment Questionnaire (SPAQ), whilst the remaining studies mainly used study-specific questionnaires or diaries. In the studies using objective measurement instruments, the ActiGraph 7164, GT1M and GT3X accelerometers were predominantly used. Different accelerometer intensity thresholds used to define MVPA resulted in substantial differences in MVPA between studies conducted in the same countries in similar cohorts. Thus, it is unclear from these findings whether large variation across European countries for physical activity in youth is actually due to different measurement protocols.

Recommendations

The evidence regarding behavioural determinants of physical activity is inconclusive. Despite a large number of studies investigating behavioural and psychological determinants in adulthood, the quality of evidence is not strong enough to make robust recommendations (Cortis et al. 2017). The main limitations include non-standardised measurements of physical activity, and the need to incorporate available technologies in activity monitoring to provide objective measurement methods with methodological transparency.

More work is needed to shed light on the full range of determinants which are important at each life stage, let alone whether and at what times those determinants change. Further distillation of the available evidence is needed in children and young adults, to middle age, old age and in those living to be very old. Identifying determinants of change in physical activity in general and around life events is necessary to contribute to our understanding of when and how to intervene, and for whom, most effectively.

The body of literature detailing the correlates and determinants of physical activity across the lifecourse is large, but provides few conclusions. Evidence outlining the determinants and correlates of physical activity across the lifecourse is inconsistent, in terms of both findings and measurement methods. Understanding the determinants governing change in physical activity from one life stage to the next is essential to explain why some people are active and why some are not. This requires the use of vastly improved measurement methods.

Whilst continuous progress has been made through the production of increasingly rigorous study findings, a major discrepancy between studies is the measurement method used to assess physical activity and the outcomes produced by that method. Early studies such as the Harvard Alumni Study only had at their disposal physical activity questionnaires. However, current studies such as NHANES and UK Biobank are using raw accelerometers such as the ActiGraph GT3X+ and GENEActiv. These instruments provide raw acceleration data from which a suite of physical activity measures can be derived.

Summary

This chapter examined the lifecourse theoretical framework, where models of disease progression are used to understand how NCDs and their risk factors can be influenced. Lifecourse adverse exposures gradually accumulate in association with a significant change or event. Useful models involve years of life where exposures have cumulative effects on disease progression and where earlier exposures have no effect on disease risk without the final link in the chain that precipitates disease onset, a so-called 'trigger effect'. Nevertheless, evidence on physical activity exposure–health relationships is voluminous, but still has important knowledge gaps, such as how physical activity changes and why in the presence of increasing age. Tackling this requires the use of accurate yet feasible measurement methods. They are primed for use, and we will take a detailed look at them in Part II.

The key points of Chapter 3 are:

- The lifecourse is segmented into stages. From a lifecourse perspective, these are gestation, childhood, adolescence, young adulthood, middle age, older adults, the very old, and the oldest old. An individual's risk of developing NCDs is accumulated throughout their lifecourse, at different stages and around key life events
- Physical activity demonstrates health benefits throughout the whole lifecourse, from childhood to older age.
- The determinants of physical activity change across the lifecourse, typically revolving around key life events. Where possible, the use of theoretical models improves understanding of correlates and determinants.
- To identify how to make people more active, it is necessary to understand the determinants which act at each life stage, and although evidence is plentiful, it needs to be of better quality.
- Accurate and precise measurements are needed to track secular trends in physical activity. Improved assessments of physical activity will lead to a better understand of determinants at each stage of the lifecourse.

References

Baird, J., C. Jacob, M. Barker, C. H. D. Fall, M. Hanson, N. C. Harvey, H. M. Inskip, K. Kumaran, and C. Cooper. 2017. 'Developmental origins of health and disease: a lifecourse approach to the prevention of non-communicable diseases', *Healthcare (Basel)*, 5: 14.

Carlin, A., C. Perchoux, A. Puggina, K. Aleksovska, C. Buck, C. Burns, G. Cardon, S. Chantal, D. Ciarapica, G. Condello, T. Coppinger, C. Cortis, S. D'Haese, M. De Craemer, A. Di Blasio, S. Hansen, L. Iacoviello, J. Issartel, P. Izzicupo, L. Jaeschke, M. Kanning, A. Kennedy, J. Lakerveld, F. Chun Man Ling, A. Luzak, G. Napolitano, J. A. Nazare, T. Pischon, A. Polito, A. Sannella, H. Schulz, R. Sohun, A. Steinbrecher, W. Schlicht, W. Ricciardi, C. MacDonncha, L. Capranica, and S. Boccia. 2017. 'A life course examination of the physical environmental determinants of physical activity behaviour: a "DEterminants of DIet and Physical ACtivity" (DEDIPAC) umbrella systematic literature review', *PLOS ONE*, 12: e0182083.

Collerton, J., K. Davies, C. Jagger, A. Kingston, J. Bond, M. P. Eccles, L. A. Robinson, C. Martin-Ruiz, T. von Zglinicki, O. F. James, and T. B. Kirkwood. 2009. 'Health and disease in 85 year olds: baseline findings from the Newcastle 85+ cohort study', *BMJ*, 339: b4904.

Condello, G., A. Puggina, K. Aleksovska, C. Buck, C. Burns, G. Cardon, A. Carlin, C. Simon, D. Ciarapica, T. Coppinger, C. Cortis, S. D'Haese, M. De Craemer, A. Di Blasio, S. Hansen, L. Iacoviello, J. Issartel, P. Izzicupo, L. Jaeschke, M. Kanning, A. Kennedy, F. C. M. Ling, A. Luzak, G. Napolitano, J. A. Nazare, C. Perchoux, C. Pesce, T. Pischon, A. Polito, A. Sannella, H. Schulz, R. Sohun, A. Steinbrecher, W. Schlicht, W. Ricciardi, C. MacDonncha, L. Capranica, and S. Boccia. 2017. 'Behavioral determinants of physical activity across the life course: a "DEterminants of DIet and Physical ACtivity" (DEDIPAC) umbrella systematic literature review', *Int J Behav Nutr Phys Act*, 14: 58.

Corder, K., D. Ogilvie, and E. M. F. van Sluijs. 2009. 'Physical activity over the life course: whose behavior changes, when and why?', *Am J Epidemiol*, 170: 1078–83.

Cortis, C., A. Puggina, C. Pesce, K. Aleksovska, C. Buck, C. Burns, G. Cardon, A. Carlin, C. Simon, D. Ciarapica, G. Condello, T. Coppinger, S. D'Haese, M. De Craemer, A. Di Blasio, S. Hansen, L. Iacoviello, J. Issartel, P. Izzicupo, L. Jaeschke, M. Kanning, A. Kennedy, F. C. M. Ling, A. Luzak, G. Napolitano, J. A. Nazare, G. O'Donoghue, C. Perchoux, T. Pischon, A. Polito, A. Sannella, H. Schulz, R. Sohun, A. Steinbrecher, W. Schlicht, W. Ricciardi, L. Castellani, C. MacDonncha, L. Capranica, and S. Boccia. 2017. 'Psychological determinants of physical activity across the life course: a "DEterminants of DIet and Physical ACtivity" (DEDIPAC) umbrella systematic literature review', *PLOS ONE*, 12: e0182709.

Fox, J. 1998. 'A life course approach to chronic disease epidemiology', *BMJ*, 317: 421.

Green, M. J., and F. Popham. 2017. 'Life course models: improving interpretation by consideration of total effects', *Int J Epidemiol*, 46: 1057–62.

Hildebrand, M., E. Kolle, B. H. Hansen, P. J. Collings, K. Wijndaele, K. Kordas, A. R. Cooper, L. B. Sherar, L. B. Andersen, L. B. Sardinha, S. Kriemler, P. Hallal, E. van Sluijs, and U. Ekelund. 2015. 'Association between birth weight and objectively measured sedentary time is mediated by central adiposity: data in 10,793 youth from the International Children's Accelerometry Database', *Am J Clin Nutr*, 101: 983–90.

Jaeschke, L., A. Steinbrecher, A. Luzak, A. Puggina, K. Aleksovska, C. Buck, C. Burns, G. Cardon, A. Carlin, S. Chantal, D. Ciarapica, G. Condello, T. Coppinger, C. Cortis, M. De Craemer, S. D'Haese, A. Di Blasio, S. Hansen, L. Iacoviello, J. Issartel, P. Izzicupo, M. Kanning, A. Kennedy, F. C. M. Ling, G. Napolitano, J. A. Nazare, C. Perchoux, A. Polito, W. Ricciardi, A. Sannella, W. Schlicht, R. Sohun, C. MacDonncha, S.

Boccia, L. Capranica, H. Schulz, and T. Pischon. 2017. 'Socio-cultural determinants of physical activity across the life course: a "DEterminants of DIet and Physical ACtivity" (DEDIPAC) umbrella systematic literature review', *Int J Behav Nutr Phys Act*, 14: 173.

Kouvonen, A., R. De Vogli, M. Stafford, M. J. Shipley, M. G. Marmot, T. Cox, J. Vahtera, A. Väänänen, T. Heponiemi, A. Singh-Manoux, and M. Kivimäki. 2012. 'Social support and the likelihood of maintaining and improving levels of physical activity: the Whitehall II Study', *Eur J Public Health*, 22: 514–18.

Kuh, D. 2013. 'A life course approach to physical capability: findings from the HALCyon research programme', *BMC Proc*, 7 Suppl 4: S4.

Lakerveld, J., H. P. van der Ploeg, W. Kroeze, W. Ahrens, O. Allais, L. F. Andersen, G. Cardon, L. Capranica, S. Chastin, A. Donnelly, U. Ekelund, P. Finglas, M. Flechtner-Mors, A. Hebestreit, I. Hendriksen, T. Kubiak, M. Lanza, A. Loyen, C. MacDonncha, M. Mazzocchi, P. Monsivais, M. Murphy, U. Nothlings, D. J. O'Gorman, B. Renner, G. Roos, A. J. Schuit, M. Schulze, J. Steinacker, K. Stronks, D. Volkert, P. Van't Veer, N. Lien, I. De Bourdeaudhuij, and J. Brug. 2014. 'Towards the integration and development of a cross-European research network and infrastructure: the DEterminants of DIet and Physical ACtivity (DEDIPAC) Knowledge Hub', *Int J Behav Nutr Phys Act*, 11: 143.

O'Donoghue, G., A. Kennedy, A. Puggina, K. Aleksovska, C. Buck, C. Burns, G. Cardon, A. Carlin, D. Ciarapica, M. Colotto, G. Condello, T. Coppinger, C. Cortis, S. D'Haese, M. De Craemer, A. Di Blasio, S. Hansen, L. Iacoviello, J. Issartel, P. Izzicupo, L. Jaeschke, M. Kanning, F. Ling, A. Luzak, G. Napolitano, J. A. Nazare, C. Perchoux, C. Pesce, T. Pischon, A. Polito, A. Sannella, H. Schulz, C. Simon, R. Sohun, A. Steinbrecher, W. Schlicht, C. MacDonncha, L. Capranica, and S. Boccia. 2018. 'Socio-economic determinants of physical activity across the life course: a "DEterminants of DIet and Physical ACtivity" (DEDIPAC) umbrella literature review', *PLOS ONE*, 13: e0190737.

Puggina, A., K. Aleksovska, C. Buck, C. Burns, G. Cardon, A. Carlin, S. Chantal, D. Ciarapica, G. Condello, T. Coppinger, C. Cortis, S. D'Haese, M. De Craemer, A. Di Blasio, S. Hansen, L. Iacoviello, J. Issartel, P. Izzicupo, L. Jaeschke, M. Kanning, A. Kennedy, F. Chun Man Ling, A. Luzak, G. Napolitano, J. A. Nazare, C. Perchoux, T. Pischon, A. Polito, A. Sannella, H. Schulz, R. Sohun, A. Steinbrecher, W. Schlicht, W. Ricciardi, C. MacDonncha, L. Capranica, and S. Boccia. 2018. 'Policy determinants of physical activity across the life course: a "DEDIPAC" umbrella systematic literature review', *Eur J Public Health*, 28: 105–18.

Salinas-Miranda, A. A., L. M. King, H. M. Salihu, E. Berry, D. Austin, S. Nash, K. Scarborough, E. Best, L. Cox, G. King, C. Hepburn, C. Burpee, E. Richardson, M. Ducket, R. Briscoe, and J. Baldwin. 2017. 'Exploring the life course perspective in maternal and child health through community-based participatory focus groups: social risks assessment', *J Health Dispar Res Pract*, 10: 143–66.

Sayer, A. A., and C. Cooper. 2005. 'Fetal programming of body composition and musculoskeletal development', *Early Hum Dev*, 81: 735–44.

PART II

Current measurement methods used across the lifecourse

4

INTERPRETING METHOD COMPARISON STUDIES

To decide on a measurement method, we need to know those available to choose from, compare them against one another and select the best one. This sounds simple: it is not. Choosing the correct measurement method for a study is a challenging task. The first step is to look for method comparison studies.

The design of the method comparison study is aimed at determining if two methods for measuring the same thing do so in an equivalent manner. Often, makers of a new measurement method claim that it has advantages over existing methods, such as lower cost, yet at the same time offers higher validity and repeatability. Method comparison in medical technology often involves small, portable units which quickly measure biological signals such as blood pressure, heart rate and blood glucose. Studies typically report agreement between two methods and/or diagnostic accuracy, sensitivity and specificity. However, the measurement of blood pressure is far simpler than obtaining measures of physical activity.

Measurement methods used in physical activity epidemiology, most often seen in method comparison studies, involve accelerometer-based physical activity monitors. These measurement tools are wearable, sensor-based technologies which involve several computational steps to obtain meaningful measurements of physical activity, namely (i) data collection, (ii) data processing and (iii) data analysis.

First, it is necessary to understand that 'validity of X device' is erroneous language. Since modern activity monitors no longer carry out on-board processing, it is often up to the user to decide how best to process and analyse the data. The release of a new activity monitor typically involves a validation study during which the device itself is tested and open-source analytics are described. Once the device has proven accurate and reliable in recording movement data, more analytical methods are typically validated and published. For example, in the case of modern raw accelerometers, the first analytics provided uncomplicated measures of sedentary, light and moderate to vigorous physical activity. After this, more advanced techniques have been developed such as those used to detect activity type. Method developers typically report the development process and performance during various laboratory tests and/or field tests involving physical activity. These studies should, and typically do, feature a criterion reference to demonstrate criterion validity of the new method.

When carrying out measurement, researchers should know how their chosen measurement method works, why they have chosen it, factors which affect validity and reliability of measurements, and how to interpret the data.

This chapter will:

- Summarise the origins of measurement, from antiquity to the present day and the importance of standardised measurement in the scientific process.
- Describe the study design, terminology and statistics involved in method comparison, calibration and validation studies.
- Establish the study design, protocol and statistics needed so you can be certain your chosen method is the right one.

At the core of science is good measurement. We will start by looking at the origins of measurement, then look at the design and interpretation of method comparison, calibration and validation. Our journey into measurement begins in antiquity.

Origins of measurement

Prior to the birth of modern science, scholars of ancient times interested in the pursuit of knowledge were restricted to their own observations, rational discussion, reason and argument. Observations of the natural world were carried out by ancient Greek and Roman philosophers: the scientists of their day.

However, the earliest measurements were those of the Egyptians, who used standardised units of length, weight and time. The Romans used units of mass to weigh stone and precious metals. The collapse of the empires took with them much of the knowledge and standardisation of measurement. The collapse of the Western Roman Empire in 400 resulted in the stagnation in scientific progress, and it took some considerable time to recover. The loss of centralised power in the West and weakened power in the East was followed by military conflict and political ineffectiveness.

Any advances in technology were aimed military developments. The period from the 5th to the 15th century, the Middle Ages, was marked by scarcity of literary and cultural output. Thereafter, when history transitions into the Renaissance, literally meaning 'rebirth', we see an increase in print media, where classic scientific texts were translated into Greek, Arabic and Latin. Combined, these factors led to an intellectual revitalisation, promoting scientific discussion across Western Europe.

Only after the growing acceptance in the 17th century of the scientific method, in which measurement is central, did an understanding of the importance of measurement in science arise. The organised empirical acquisition of knowledge characterises the 17th century. During this period there was a gradual move away from an implicit trust in man's mind to a more objective approach involving external observations derived from measurement methods. Through scientific experimentation, major contributions to knowledge were swiftly made by applying quantitative measurement, due mostly to measurements expressed in numerical values being less open to interpretation. Thus, scientists were confident in changing their views based on new measurements obtained from experiments. With measurement came great advances in understanding of health and the major factors influencing it.

The term 'scientist' was not coined until the 19th century, by science historian William Whewell (1794–1866), around the time instruments were developed solely for use for measurement (Whewell 1967). In fact, measurement instruments used today rely on clearly recognisable concepts from the famous scholars of history.

Isaac Newton (1642–1726) completed his theory of gravitation, taking the Latin word *gravitas* (weight) to define the effect we know as gravity (Kuhn 2012), which we now see in accelerometer data expressed in gravitational acceleration, or g. Also recognisable in today's accelerometers are Pythagoras's (c.570—c.495 BC) mathematical and scientific discoveries, including the Pythagorean theorem, which calculates angles and distances (Guthrie 2010). Euclid of Alexandria was a Greek mathematician, often referred to as the 'founder of geometry' (Evett and Pirenne 1974). His mathematical treatise *Elements* is said to be one of the most influential works in the history of mathematics in the 19th century. The work of Euclid, which includes Euclid's algorithm, reducing algorithms to their most concise form, one of the oldest in common use, still features in scientific research today: look no further than Vincent van Hees' autocalibrating accelerometer metric, Euclidean norm minus one (van Hees et al. 2013).

The importance of measurement

Typically, measurement involves the assignment of a numerical value to an event, object or characteristic so that it can be compared with other events, objects or characteristics.

Metrology is the science of measurement, and it is crucial in understanding human activities. We carry out measurement of a behaviour by assigning a unit of measurement to it. This unit of measurement must be clearly defined. Quantity is considered separate from measurement as this only depends on the assignment of a value, which in modern measurement is typically a numerical value.

Measuring the human body in motion is notoriously challenging. Accurate measurements are important for assessing within- or between-person change. Poor reproducibility and repeatability may occur because the human body is so complex. Physical activity cannot be directly 'measured'. Instead, we obtain measurements from which we can assess the extent of any change, or simply the amount of physical activity performed. The terms 'measurement' and 'assessment' should not be used interchangeably, though the reader will find this is done frequently throughout the literature; these terms are inherently different.

Assessment of physical activity is a process which allows understanding of the existing state or any changes over time, assessed by gathering and interpreting measurements. Assessment is necessary to understand and evaluate physical activity in the context of a particular research scenario, such as how physical activity changes across the lifecourse and what factors influence change.

Wearable sensors have evolved from rather obtrusive mechanical instruments (LaPorte, Montoye and Caspersen 1985) to a suite of technologies which now feature mainly in accelerometer-based physical activity assessment, computing power and data storage, which advance at a near exponential rate. It is essential that advances in technology, though remarkable, are not used outside the rules of measurement. Rapid advances in the technology available to carry out measurement must only be applied in a way that remains within the boundaries of robust scientific methodology.

The concept of scientific measurement places emphasis on quantification and production of evidence that is meaningful, usable and, most importantly, necessary. The essentials of this form of measurement system require answers to the following questions:

1. What knowledge is required?
2. What measurement method should be used?
3. What is an acceptable level of performance of the measurement method?
4. How are the resulting data to be used?

The weakest step in the process of assessment is the decision about what to measure. This decision – what data to collect – needs to be well informed in order to facilitate the task of translating data into usable knowledge. This process, which forms the backbone of research, involves measurement tightly allied to design and analysis.

The rules of measurement

When we are interested in a characteristic, event or behaviour, we assign a unit of measurement to it. The units that are used to measure an event or behaviour must be standardised and easily interpreted by other researchers. Careful measurement, recording and handling of data are crucial to the research process.

Measurements of physical activity generally require some form of analysis. This typically involves analysis of the output of a measurement instrument such as questionnaire or activity monitor. It is important to remember that the output of measurement is the input of analysis. Unless you can be certain your measurement outputs are valid and reliable, you risk rendering your analysed results meaningless. Measurement and analysis should be carried out under a robust, well-defined research design using appropriate analytical method.

The analytical methods used with certain measurements and the statistical analysis of data depend on what kind of measurements/data you have. Scientific measurements are carried out using one of four different scales: nominal, ordinal, interval and ratio. This classification system was developed by psychologist Stanley Smith Stevens, who considered the properties of the resulting measurements and the statistical tests that could be applied to them (Stevens 1946). Data are expressed either as numerical values or as categories.

Scale

Ratio data involves numerical values with a minimum of zero, such as kcals, which in the context of PAEE could be 200 kcals.

Nominal (named) data exist in groups such as low energy expenditure, moderate energy expenditure and high energy expenditure. Ratio data can be grouped this way.

Interval data involve numerical values representing intervals or numerical groups, such as age groups: 18–30 years, 30–45 years and 45–60 years.

Ordinal (ordered categories) data can be binary (yes/no, male/female, healthy/unhealthy) or non-binary (strongly agree, agree, neither agree nor disagree, disagree, strongly disagree), or rank order (1st, 2nd, 3rd, etc.).

Data in units need to be expressed in a meaningful way. This is achieved by establishing the magnitude, uncertainty and unit.

Magnitude

Magnitude is a number assigned to something indicating its size or quantity so that it can be compared to other things numerically. The magnitude of any number is usually called its 'absolute value', which represents its distance from zero. A man's height could be 182 cm. However, a vector is a quantity that has both magnitude and direction. For example, acceleration is a vector because it describes both how fast something is moving and in what direction it is moving – far more informative. Acceleration is expressed in gravitational units (g), where $1\ g = 9.8\ \text{m/s}^{-2}$.

Uncertainty

All measurements are subject to uncertainty. No measurement is exact. Measurement uncertainty is also referred to as measurement error. It is often expressed statistically via a measure of dispersion such as standard deviation. Uncertainty represents the random and systemic errors of the measurement procedure, and can be used to determine how confident you are in the measurements. Random errors are caused by unknown and unpredictable changes. Systematic errors are introduced by an inaccuracy inherent to the system, involving either the observation or measurement process, and usually of the same magnitude or direction.

Unit

The International System of Units (SI, abbreviated from the French Système International) derived from the metric system is the most widely used measurement system (Bureau and Gosselin 1987). It features measurement units built on seven base units (ampere, kelvin, second, metre, kilogram, candela, mole) and a set of 20 decimal prefixes to the unit names, such as ms (millisecond). The system also specifies names for 22 derived units for other common physical quantities such as lumen or watt.

They are adopted to facilitate measurement in diverse fields of investigation whilst preserving the comparability of data. Good practice dictates that measurements should always be expressed using SI units. SI-derived units often need to be expressed as a combination of one or more of the base units. For example, the SI-derived unit of area is the square meter (m^2). Table 4.1 shows this.

Understanding the type, magnitude, unit and uncertainty of measurements is essential in obtaining good-quality measurements. The quality of measurements obtained is very important since complex behaviours such as physical activity must be assessed using one or more measurements in large numbers of people, often repeated over time.

TABLE 4.1 The seven base SI units and their related constants.

Name	Symbol	Measure	SI constant	Symbol
metre	m	length	speed of light in vacuum, c	L
kilogram	kg	mass	Mass of International Prototype Kilogram	m
second	s	Time	Duration of hyperfine splitting in caesium-133	T
ampere	A	Electric current	Permeability of free space, the value of magnetic permeability	I
kelvin	K	Thermo-dynamic temperature	Absolute zero temperature of the triple point of water.	
mole	mol	Amount of substance	molar mass of carbon-12	N
candela	cd	Luminous intensity	luminous efficacy of a 540 THz source	J

Measurements are combined and assessments made relative to a research question or research perspective; the result of this process is evidence. Vast quantities of evidence have resulted from the assessment of physical activity: for example, public recommended guidelines suggest that 150 minutes of moderate to vigorous physical activity per week are needed to maintain good health; more recently, physical inactivity has been identified as the fourth leading risk factor for serious NCD. Hence, the importance of obtaining good measurements cannot be overstated.

The assessment of physical activity comes with its own rules of best practice. These do not stop at simply obtaining good measurements. Researchers must interpret their measurements, report their data correctly and draw valid conclusions to create new evidence. Researchers aiming to assess physical activity must understand what physical activity is and how it is quantified in order to draw valid conclusions from their data and make worthy contributions to knowledge. Therefore, we must address how physical activity can be quantified, the measurements involved, the instruments used to obtain those measurements, and how to choose the right instrument.

Choosing a measurement method

Measurement allows us to do two things: first, to establish the quantity of a particular characteristic of interest, and second, to establish a correlation or relationship with particular phenomenon. For example, we can measure daily MVPA in a population. Then we can test for any relationship between those activity levels and a particular health outcome in that population, such as the development of depression. If the relationship is strong and negative, we have evidence that physical activity reduces the prevalence of depression.

In medicine, clinicians want to obtain quick and easy, accurate and precise measurements to inform patient care, such as blood pressure, heart rate and blood glucose. Advances in medical technology have increased the popularity of small, portable digital sensors such as continuous glucose monitors. Clinicians often need to know if a new measurement instrument is equivalent to an established one already in clinical use, so newer devices are normally these small, portable digital sensors, which are easier to use and cost less.

Rapid technological innovation means that new measurement methods are continuously being adopted into physical activity research. Prior to using the new measurement method, the prospective user needs to know if the newer technique is equivalent to that already in use (Derosa et al. 2009). You might want to know if a new activity monitor performs as well as the most popular one currently used in your field.

The aim of traditional method comparison studies which generally appear in the medical literature is to determine the agreement between scores from two measurement methods, such as the comparison of a new blood glucose meter with one already in use. However, the assessment of physical activity in epidemiology involves a more complex measurement procedure relying on measurement instruments such as questionnaires and activity monitors. An instrument-based approach requires that you determine the performance of the instrument and stages of data collection, data processing and then data analysis.

Prior to using a new activity monitor, the user should consult method comparison studies that not only compare new and existing monitors, but test the validity and reliability of measurements derived from the activity monitor. However, it is important to bear in mind that widely used accelerometer-based activity monitors are classed as measurement systems, and involve data collection, data processing and data analysis. Differences in each of these steps and the consequences these differences have for the resulting measurements should be understood.

The choice of measurement instrument should be supported by a robust body of evidence demonstrating its validity and reliability in your chosen population of interest. This can be found in validation studies. However, this may require an extensive review of the literature. Researchers should attempt to stay well informed about new devices/device specifications, new data processing techniques and new analytical techniques. However, this is not always possible since the ability to understand and evaluate each stage of measurement often requires knowledge of human physiology, epidemiology, ageing, digital signal processing and statistics. Fear not, as this book aims to provide enough knowledge in one place to help you make the right choice.

We will first define key terms involved in method comparison and validation, then address the design, statistical analysis and interpretation.

Terminology

In a method comparison study, the investigator is comparing a less well-established method with an established method already in use. Typically, the new method is cheaper, easier to use or has higher feasibility in some way. The comparison of two assessment methods involves the use of complex terminology. Statistical reporting terms are often used incorrectly. For example, the terms 'accuracy' and 'precision' are sometimes used interchangeably with 'validity' and 'reliability'. The correct definitions are provided here and presented in Table 4.2.

Accuracy refers to how close measurements are to the 'true' value, while precision refers to how close measurements are to each other (Tosteson et al. 1994). Accuracy is the degree to which an instrument measures the 'true' real value of a variable, and can only be assessed by comparing the measurement method with a gold standard that has been calibrated to be highly accurate.

Precision refers to the extent to which a measuring technique provides the same results if the measurement is repeated (Habibzadeh and Habibzadeh 2015). Precision can be further subdivided into two components: repeatability and reproducibility. Repeatability refers to the how well the method gives the same results when the operator carries out repeated measurements with the same device – that is, the degree to which the method produces similar results on repeated measurements, and the extent to which values cluster around the mean value.

TABLE 4.2 Key terms used in method comparison studies.

Term	Definition
Accuracy	How close the measured values are to the true values of measurements of a quantity to that quantity's true value.
Precision	The extent to which a measuring technique consistently provides the same results if the measurement is repeated.
Bias	difference (variance) between repeated measurements from the estimator's expected value and the true value of the parameter being estimated.
Reliability	The extent to which similar values are produced under consistent conditions.
Reproducibility	The extent to which similar values are obtained by a new operator carrying out measurement procedures as closely matched to the original.
Random error	Errors in experimental measurements are caused by unknown and unpredictable changes.
Systematic error	Error caused by an inaccuracy inherent to the measurement process. Typically, consistent, repeatable error associated with faulty equipment or a flawed instrumentation.
Validity	Does the method measure exactly what it is supposed to measure?
Criterion validity	The extent to which measurements are related to those derived from a definitive technique or 'gold standard'.
Construct validity	The extent to which a test measures what it claims, or purports, to measure.
Concurrent validity	The extent to which the results of a particular test, or measurement, correspond to those of a previously established measurement for the same construct.

Reproducibility refers to the variation observed when different operators carry out the same measurements using the same instrument.

Measurement errors can be divided into two components: random error and systematic error. The first is simply the error that is random from one measurement to the next. Systematic error is not a 'mistake', but rather a difference between a computed, estimated or predicted value and the criterion or true known value (Bland and Altman 1996a, 1996b).

The difference in values obtained when comparing the two methods represents the 'bias' of the newer method relative to the more established one. In statistics, bias is an objective property of a measurement instrument which estimates or predicts a particular value (Magari 2004).

The validity (accuracy of the mean or trueness) of a measurement method is high if it measures exactly what it is supposed to measure. Thus, the validity determines the presence, or lack thereof, of systematic error. Reliability and validity are subsumed in the term 'accuracy'. Accuracy is only high when both precision and validity are high.

Construct validity, concurrent validity and convergent validity are typically assessed when a criterion measure is not available. For example, the comparison of a new accelerometer with an existing one determines concurrent validity (Byun et al. 2016).

The most robust approach to method comparison is comparison with a criterion method. Criterion methods or 'gold standard' techniques are used, for example, when measuring predicted energy expenditure from a new accelerometer against that derived from a metabolic cart or indirect calorimetry. The agreement between the two methods is then measured statistically to determine criterion validity. Where a gold standard is not available to determine criterion validity, the new method is compared to the next best thing to determine concurrent validity or convergent validity.

Calibration of activity monitors focuses on two stages of device function (Welk 2005). 'Unit calibration' ensures the individual activity monitor is correctly measuring the intended signal, such as acceleration. 'Value calibration' is the process of converting the measured signal into established measurement units. Initially, activity monitors converted the signal into accelerometer counts, which are not standardised units of measurement. However, raw accelerometers express the signal in g, which is one of the SI measurement units.

Method comparison: study design

The introduction of a new accelerometer or, more commonly, a new analytical method to derive meaningful measures from the acceleration data typically follows one of two study designs: one involves a laboratory-based design and the other involves testing in free-living conditions. The chosen protocol depends on the estimated variable.

Protocol

The aim of this type of study is normally to determine the validity and reliability of the accelerometer-based method. The laboratory setting involves participants carrying out selected activities of daily living while wearing the activity monitor.

Energy expenditure-related measures can be validated against indirect calorimetry and activity-type measures validated against direct observation. Two main criticisms of this approach are that (i) certain activities such as walking tend to produce high levels of agreement and (ii) study conditions may not generalise well to free-living conditions. The field setting generally involves the comparison of energy expenditure-related measures with those derived from doubly labelled water (DLW; see Chapter 5). However, this remains prohibitively expensive in larger sample sizes.

Timing of measurements

The question being asked in a method comparison study is whether either of two different available methods can be used to measure equivalently. It follows that in order to answer this question, measurements must be recorded at the same time with the two methods. Thus, simultaneous sampling of the variable of interest is a requirement. Stored physiological data, such as VO_2 from indirect calorimetry and movement data from accelerometers, when visualised using computer software, have values which are timestamped. Researchers should be diligent so that data from each measurement method are aligned correctly prior to further analysis.

Criterion measure

Close attention should be paid to the selected criterion method. Indirect calorimetry and DLW require specialist technicians and facilities. Some studies use an activity monitor which has been compared to a criterion in a previous study and use this as justification for its adoption as the criterion in their study. It is common to find studies in the literature which claim that a new physical activity questionnaire demonstrates good validity and therefore can be used imminently, when in fact the reference method used is an activity monitor which, in many cases, has itself performed inconsistently across different populations when detecting different activity intensities.

Where activity classifiers are validated, the comparator method is simply direct observation. For this purpose, a laboratory-based protocol is desirable in order to create a training data set for the classification algorithm. Direct observation in free-living conditions is intrusive and susceptible to the Hawthorne effect (where individuals alter their behaviour due to being observed).

Conditions of measurement

To obtain comparable and objective measurements, the measurement conditions must be standardised. For example, clinical study measurements such as blood pressure must be performed at the same time, in the same room and in the same position. A method comparison study should include parallel measurements taken over a range of physiological conditions (Bland and Altman 2012). For example, in laboratory studies where participants carry out a series of physical activities, the selected activities should reflect all of those typically carried out in daily life, from sedentary to vigorously active.

Study sample

Researchers are often eager to adopt new technologies in their measurement arsenal. Many instances exist where a new activity monitor is made available that has been validated in a large study against the appropriate creation measure, with robust statistical analysis and good reporting of the result. Thereafter, the activity monitor is readily adopted across a range of populations, often in prominent studies. However, it is not uncommon to find such a device used in populations who are unlike those found in the original method comparison, but occasionally authors will justify its use based on that study. For example, if used in population surveillance, some of the study participants will inevitably be overweight and obese, have reduced physical function and suffer from common sleep disorders such as insomnia or sleep apnoea which can cause metabolic dysregulation. Some may have mental health problems, and the effect on activity monitoring is not well understood. Therefore, note that method comparisons should be representative of the sample population you intend to investigate: specifically, they should be validated in children, teenagers, adults and old adults.

When first introduced, all new measurement methods should be placed under close scrutiny and undergo rigorous testing using method comparison to determine validity, reliability and feasibility of the instrument (Bassett, Rowlands and Trost 2012). If method comparison has not already been carried in your population of interest using the measurement method you wish to use, you should conduct it yourself.

Units of measurement

It goes without saying that in a method comparison study, both established and new instruments should measure the same thing. Nevertheless, the type of scale is so important, as both descriptive statistics and statistical test procedures depend on it (Stevens 1946). Transformation from a higher to a lower scale type is in principle possible, although the converse is impossible. For example, the activity intensity may be determined with a metric scale (e.g. kcals) and then be transformed to an ordinal scale (e.g. low activity, moderate activity and high activity level), but not conversely. Similarly, using a clinical example, haemoglobin content may be determined with a metric scale (e.g. as g/dL). It can then be transformed to an ordinal scale (e.g. low, normal and high haemoglobin status), but not conversely.

Method comparison: statistical analysis

Statistical analysis in validation or method comparison studies involving physical activity assessment instruments differs according to the aims of the study. The literature on statistical analysis in method comparison generally refers to clinical scenarios involving clinical measurements. Instruments such as heart rate monitors, pulse oximeters and blood pressure monitors provide simple measurements which must show high levels of agreement to provide trustworthy measurements for the clinician. However, physical activity is a complex behaviour with several dimensions and domains. Therefore, statistical techniques differ, mainly depending to the measurement of interest.

Tests of normality

Visually inspecting the data using frequency distributions and scatterplots, as with any study, is important to see the distribution of the data, and to note outliers and any missing data. Statistical tests should also be used to determine if the distribution is normal, since in some cases normality cannot be determined simply by observing the histogram plot (McKinlay 1951). Appropriate statistical tests to check the distribution of data include the Shapiro-Wilk test, D'Agostino-Pearson test (Demler, Pencina and D'Agostino 2011) and Kolmogorov-Smirnov test. If the data is normally distributed, then parametric testing can proceed, specifically making use of the Bland-Altman plot (Bland and Altman 1986b).

Agreement

Determining the agreement between two measurement methods determines the mean bias (difference in values obtained when comparing the two methods) and measurement error. The Bland-Altman plot is recommended for the analysis of agreement. It features bias and precision statistics, to determine agreement between two methods.

The standard deviation (SD) of all the individual differences is calculated as a measure of variability (repeatability) from which the limits of agreement are determined. The 95% confidence limits of the normal distribution are used (mean difference ±1.96 SD). The limits of agreement represent the range of values in which agreement between methods will lie for approximately 95% of the sample. Figure 4.1 shows a Bland-Altman plot. Although this is a statistical test, I recommend you first visually inspect the data. Are values spread evenly, or are they clustered together? Are they spread evenly across low to higher measurements, or clustered more tightly at lower or higher readings? In Figure 4.1 (which omits units of measurement for simplicity), our data are clustered at readings below 200 (x-axis) and we see mostly negative values over 200. It could be that the new instrument measures differently at lower versus higher values – an important finding.

The plot shows a mean bias of −27.2 (solid horizontal line). Our limits of agreement are 47.1 and −95.4 (dotted lines). Is this acceptable? Many studies decide this after they have performed the Bland-Altman test. You should not do so. The acceptable use of the Bland-Altman test should involve defining acceptable error *a priori*, based on biologically and analytically relevant criteria.

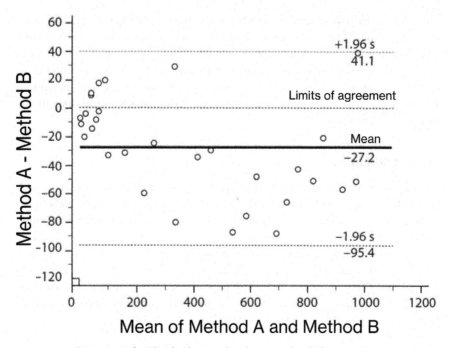

FIGURE 4.1 Structure of a Bland-Altman plot showing the differences between Method A and Method B compared to the mean of both measurements.
Source: Zaki et al. (2012).

Note that bias should be consistent throughout all differences. The values in Figure 4.2 do not appear to show this. Our values appear to cluster closer to a zero bias on the y-axis at values under 200 (y-axis). The bias between two measurement methods is rarely equal for all levels of measurement. For example, many accelerometers tend to underestimate low-intensity activities. Therefore, the difference between measurements is not equal throughout the data. The addition of a regression line is therefore recommended to detect non-consistent systematic bias.

The addition of a regression line (Figure 4.2) shows this more clearly and allows statistical reporting of these findings. If these were data from a new activity monitor plotted against a criterion such as double labelled water (giving PAEE), our activity monitor underestimates (PAEE) more so at higher levels of energy expenditure.

Many studies use correlation coefficients to determine agreement between two measurement methods. However, this is erroneous. Although correlation provides an initial idea of how to measures are related, it is essential that correlation is not used to demonstrate agreement. Where two methods are specifically designed to measure the same thing, it would be surprising to find that they were not related.

Nevertheless, linear regression is used in the development of prediction equations or cut-point values to determine sedentary, light, moderate and vigorous activity. Correlation and regression show the strength of association between

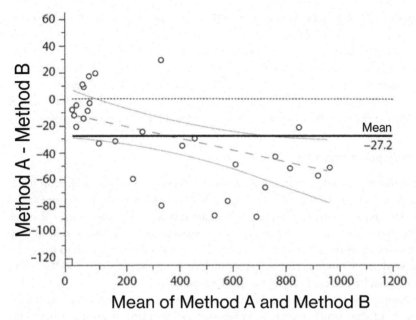

FIGURE 4.2 Structure of a Bland–Altman plot. A regression line added shows a negative trend in differences between the two measurements.

Source: Zaki et al. (2012).

two measurement methods. Correlation shows the strength of linear association between two variables; either Spearman's (r) or Pearson's (ρ) depending on the data (Bland and Altman 1986a). Linear regression is useful as it provides an accompanying P value of statistical significance and the coefficient of determination (r^2) which tells us the proportion of variance explained by the predictor variable, for example the new measurement method.

Cross-validation

The predictive capabilities of accelerometer models and how they will generalise to real-world settings can be assessed using cross-validation. Take, for example, a study developing activity intensity cut-points from raw accelerometer data (g) for moderate-intensity (3–6 METs) and vigorous-intensity (>6 METs) activity. If a regression model shows 100 mg = 3 METs and 420 mg = 6 METs, cross-validation should be used to see how the results will generalise to a new data set. This statistical method involves dividing the data into two subsets. First, analysis is performed on the metabolic subset (the training set), then the model is tested on the other subset (the validation or testing set).

Leave-one-out cross-validation involves leaving out a single observation to use as the validation data, and using the remaining observations for metabolic calibration. The process is repeated until every observation in the sample has served as the validation data.

Cross-validation shows the percentage of individuals who were correctly classified using the regression model. Perhaps the regression model above shows that 92% of prediction values were correct for moderate-intensity activity (3–6 METs), but 32% were correct for vigorous intensity activity. We would conclude that the model performs well for moderate-intensity activity but not for vigorous-intensity activity.

Classification accuracy

Accelerometer-based activity monitors giving access to the raw acceleration signal record for 24 hours/day over 7 days/week. These data are ideally suited for the use of activity type classifiers. These algorithms are different from traditional cut-point techniques as they do not depend on the magnitude of acceleration, instead they obtain characteristic features in the acceleration signal and match them to particular activity types. Consequently, activities such as lying down, sitting, walking and running can be detected in the raw acceleration data.

Classification accuracy describes the performance of a classification model on a test set of data which represents either the gold standard or ground truth. This could be the comparison of MVPA obtained using accelerometer cut-points with that derived from VO_2, or sedentary time identified using a classification algorithm compared with ground truth from direct observation.

In statistics, a contingency table (also known as a cross-tabulation or crosstab) is a type of table in a matrix format. A confusion matrix is a table that is often used to describe classification accuracy (Landgrebe and Duin 2008). The confusion matrix itself is simple to understand and easy to produce. Table 4.3 shows a confusion matrix for a hypothetical binary classifier detecting sedentary activity expressed in minutes per day. The table is first set out in basic terms showing numbers, not percentages.

A 24-hour period contains 1440 minutes (Table 4.3). For each minute, there are two possible predicted classes: 'Sedentary' and 'Not sedentary'.

Predicted sedentary time was (1010 + 80) 1090 minutes, leaving (300 + 50) 350 minutes. In reality, (50 + 1010) 1060 minutes were spent sedentary.

True positives (TPs) are minutes which are predicted as sedentary and are actually sedentary.

True negatives (TNs) are minutes which are predicted as not sedentary and are actually not sedentary.

False positives (FPs) are minutes which are predicted as sedentary and are actually not sedentary (also known as a 'Type I error').

False negatives (FNs) are minutes which are predicted as not sedentary but are actually sedentary (also known as a 'Type II error').

In predictive analytics, a table of confusion, often called a confusion matrix, is a table with two rows and two columns that reports the number of false positives, false negatives, true positives and true negatives (Table 4.4). This allows more detailed analysis than the mere proportion of correct classifications (accuracy).

TABLE 4.3 Confusion matrix showing the performance of an activity type classifier expressed as predicted and true sedentary time or non-sedentary time in minutes per day.

n = 1440	Predicted not sedentary	Predicted sedentary	
Actual not sedentary	TN = 300	FP = 80	380
Actual sedentary	FN = 50	TP = 1010	1060
	350	1090	

TABLE 4.4 Confusion matrix showing the performance of an activity type classifier and true positives, false positives, true negatives and false negatives.

n = 1440 (60 mins x 24 hours)	Predicted not sedentary	Predicted sedentary
Actual not sedentary	300	80
Actual sedentary	50	1010

Accuracy: Overall, how often is the classifier correct?

(TP + TN)/total = (1010 + 300)/1440 = 0.90

Misclassification Rate: Overall, how often is it wrong?

(FP + FN)/total = (80 + 50)/1440 = 0.09 equivalent to 1 minus Accuracy, also known as 'Error Rate'

True Positive Rate: When it's actually yes, how often does it predict yes?

TP/actual yes = 1010/1060 = 0.95, also known as 'Sensitivity' or 'Recall'

False Positive Rate: When it's actually no, how often does it predict yes?

FP/actual no = 80/380 = 0.21

Specificity: When it's actually no, how often does it predict no?

TN/actual no = 300/380 = 0.79, equivalent to 1 minus False Positive Rate

Precision: When it predicts yes, how often is it correct?

TP/predicted yes = 1010/1090 = 0.93

Prevalence: How often does the yes condition actually occur in our sample?

actual yes/total = 1060/1440 = 0.74

Often epoch-by-epoch comparisons are carried out (in this example minute-by-minute) to assess the sensitivity, specificity and accuracy (Table 4.5). Epoch-by-epoch agreement is then calculated from the number of epochs in each category:

Accuracy = [(TP) + TN)/(TP + FN + TN + FP)]*100 = percentage of epochs correctly detected

Sensitivity = [TP/(TP + FN)]*100 = percentage of sedentary epochs correctly detected

Specificity = [TN/(TN + FP)]*100 = percentage of non-sedentary epochs correctly detected.

In our example, sensitivity (sedentary detection) was 95%, specificity (non-sedentary detection) was 79% and accuracy (total agreement for all epochs) was 95%.

Positive Predictive Value (PPV) is very similar to precision, except that it takes prevalence into account. In a case where the classes are perfectly balanced (meaning the prevalence is 50%), the PPV is equivalent to precision.

TABLE 4.5 Confusion matrix showing accuracy, sensitivity and specificity.

Sensitivity (%)	95%
Specificity (%)	79%
Accuracy (%)	90%

Cohen's Kappa is essentially a measure of how well the classifier performed compared to how well it would have performed simply by chance. In other words, a model will have a high Kappa score if there is a big difference between the accuracy and the null error rate.

F Score is a weighted average of the true positive rate (recall) and precision.

ROC Curve is a commonly used graph that summarises the performance of a classifier over all possible thresholds. It is generated by plotting the True Positive Rate (y-axis) against the False Positive Rate (x-axis) as you vary the threshold for assigning observations to a given class.

An alternative statistical approach to determining classification accuracy or cut-off points to determine activity intensity thresholds in the continuous acceleration signal is the receiver operating characteristic (ROC) curve. The ROC curve was developed in the late 1950s for evaluating radar signal detection, and has long been used in medicine to test the accuracy of diagnostic tests. A ROC curve is obtained by calculating the sensitivity and specificity of every observed data value and plotting sensitivity against 1-specificity. An activity classifier which perfectly classifies an activity of interest would yield a curve close to the left and top sides of the plot. An activity classifier which is of no use whatsoever would give a straight line (Figure 4.3). In practice, the curve lies somewhere between the two.

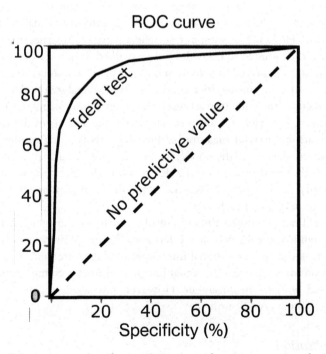

FIGURE 4.3 Receiver operating characteristic curve, showing cut-points determined with optimal sensitivity and specificity.

A strength of ROC curve analyses is that the cut-points are chosen to optimise the balance between sensitivity and specificity (i.e. point nearest 0,1 on the ROC curve), which, in all analyses also coincided with the Youden index, ensuring the optimality of the cut-points (Youden 1950). The intuitive interpretation of the Youden index is that it is the point on the curve farthest from chance. Specifically, the Youden index or Youden's J statistic is a single statistic ranging from 0 to 1 which summarises the performance of a diagnostic test.

J = sensitivity + specificity − 1

A value of zero indicates that the test identifies the given number of epochs with the same number of positive as negatives − in other words, the test is useless. A value of 1 indicates there are no false positives or false negatives − the test is perfect.

Calibration and validation in activity monitoring

Thus far, we have discussed the essentials of comparing two measurement methods. This allows researchers to determine whether measurements from one instrument are acceptably equivalent to an accepted criterion measure. Early physical activity monitors were sold as a complete measurement system with device-specific software packages which the researcher used to download and analyse the activity monitor data. However, as soon as researchers started to use these new pieces of technology, they wanted to know how they worked. It quickly became apparent that testing the validity of an activity monitor was erroneous, as in fact assessing physical activity using an activity monitor involved several steps, namely converting movement of the body into an acceleration signal, processing the acceleration signal to make it suitable for analysis, and finally the analysis of the acceleration data to create meaningful measures of physical activity, such as physical activity intensity (sedentary, light, moderate to vigorous). You may or may not be involved with investigations into the device itself. However, the accelerometer-based activity monitor features several steps. It is a measurement system. It is important to understand each step.

'Unit calibration' ensures the individual activity monitor is correctly measuring the intended signal, such as acceleration. 'Value calibration' is the process of converting the measured signal into established measurement units. Initially, activity monitors converted the signal into accelerometer counts, which are not standardised units of measurement. However, raw accelerometers express the signal in *g*, which is an SI unit.

Unit calibration

An acceleration sensor works on the principle that acceleration is captured mechanically and converted into an electrical signal, for example as voltage (say, in millivolts, mV). How accurately the electrical signal represents acceleration is determined by offset and gain. An offset means that the sensor output is higher or lower than the ideal output. Gain magnifies or diminishes the acceleration value. Therefore, the establishment of the offset and gain factor makes up the sensor calibration procedure (Nez et al. 2016) as part of a process called unit calibration.

Until recently, unit calibration was rarely discussed in the literature. However, as devices allowed access to raw acceleration data, researchers could determine the relationship between acceleration applied to the sensor and the output of the sensor itself.

Unit calibration is necessary in order to minimise the inter-instrument output differences observed under standardised conditions in mechanical setups. However, reducing inter-instrument variability through technical/mechanical calibration would only be important in order to improve field data quality and study power if random variability across units contributed considerably to the total variation in field data. Otherwise, the primary focus can shift to other sources of variation (e.g. variation over time, or position worn on the body, including compliance with the instructions given on how to wear the accelerometer).

Unit calibration for the GENEA accelerometer was carried out using a multi-axis shaker table (Instron Structural Testing Systems, Buckinghamshire, UK). Forty-seven GENEA accelerometers were attached to the shaker table and oscillated at incrementally higher-frequency oscillations. Measured acceleration from the GENEA was expressed as g-seconds (g.s) and compared to true acceleration (g) from the shaker table using Pearson product–moment correlation, which resulted in strong correlations between GENEA and reference acceleration ($r = 0.97$, $P < 0.001$).

Repeated use of the accelerometer over time can increase offset of the sensor signal. Furthermore, this does not account for data collected historically for which the corresponding accelerometer device does not exist any more. Therefore, techniques have been published which check and correct calibration error based on the collected triaxial accelerometer data in the participant's daily life without additional experiments, referred to as autocalibration. First, the acceleration signal is screened for non-movement periods. Next, the moving average over the non-movement periods is taken from each of the three sensor axes. Thus, deviations between acceleration produced by the sensor and 1 g (ideal calibration) can be used to derive correction factors for calibration error specific to each axis.

The GENEActiv accelerometer features both an accelerometer sensor and a temperature sensor. Temperature has been identified as a potential source of calibration error in low-cost acceleration sensors. The GENEActiv contains the ADXL345 sensor chip (Analog Devices, UK). The specification sheet accompanying the ADXL345 states that a change of 1 °C can result in a change in acceleration of up to 1.2 mg change in acceleration value. An autocalibration method for raw accelerometer data is available which has been evaluated and its performance assessed in free-living conditions in the UK (n = 921), Kuwait (n = 120), Cameroon (n = 311) and Brazil (n = 200). The method has been fully described, published (van Hees et al. 2014) and is available for immediate use as part of an open-source analytical package for the processing of raw accelerometer data. It is described in Chapter 8.

Acceleration measured by the accelerometer sensor must be accurate, since the output or metric produced using these processing techniques then becomes the input for value calibration, where useable estimates of physical activity such as energy expenditure and physical activity intensity are derived and used to represent physical activity assessed in that study.

The next stage to evaluate is where the recorded acceleration signal is converted into values which can be used to derive measures of physical activity. For example, a device may process the acceleration signal producing accelerometer counts, or more recently, raw acceleration (g). This process, called 'value calibration', often involves the comparison of the accelerometer output with a physiological value such as VO_2 when the device is attached to someone performing a selection of physical activities. If the device output shows a strong relationship with VO_2 values, then the output is suitable to derive meaningful estimates of physical activity-related measures, commonly by using the device outputs to denote the dividing line between sedentary (<1.5 METs) and MVPA (3–6 METs).

Value calibration

Value calibration could also be called metabolic calibration, since it involves assessing the relationship between accelerometer output and a physiological measure of energy expenditure such as VO_2. A widely used approach is to collect energy expenditure and accelerometer output data on multiple individuals during a range of activities of daily living, then determine the relationship between the two using linear regression. Thereafter, the regression equation allows you to identify where in the accelerometer output would divide different activity intensities. For example, a popular approach is to determine cut-points from the accelerometer output marking 3 METs (the dividing point between light- and moderate-intensity activity) and 6 METs (the dividing point between moderate- and vigorous-intensity activity). This has been done using counts per minute (cpm) and milli$g$ (mg), where 3 METs is identified as 1008 cpm (Aadland and Ylvisåker 2015) and 100 mg (Hildebrand et al. 2014) respectively.

Devices such as the GENEActiv, Axivity AX3 and ActiGraph GT3X+ provide access to the acceleration data expressed as a series of gravity values (g). Initially, studies followed similar patterns by carrying out calibration and validation to provide cut-points for use with children, adolescents and adults. However, rigorous methodological work involving collaborations between physical activity researchers in epidemiology and method development have resulted in the publication of systematically refined and standardised data processing techniques with built-in autocalibration (van Hees et al. 2013) that are used in several large-scale studies (Sabia et al. 2014; Doherty et al. 2017).

Validation

The first accelerometer-based activity monitor specifically intended for use in epidemiological research was validated using indirect calorimetry to demonstrate its suitability for use in real-world research (Montoye and Taylor 1984). It has become routine that a new device is compared to criterion method prior to being used in studies. The ActiGraph accelerometer model 7164 was validated against criterion measured energy expenditure. Participants wore the device (then called the CSA) while walking on a treadmill at different speeds. The authors first determined the relationship between device output, in accelerometer counts, and VO_2 ($r = 0.77$–0.89). Then they developed regression models to predict energy expenditure (kcal.min-1) from accelerometer counts. Finally, they used statistical tests to determine the validity of the prediction models (Melanson and Freedson 1995).

However, modern technologies are not validated so easily. Upon release of the GENEA raw accelerometer, large significant correlations between output in g and VO_2 were reported, and high classification accuracy of raw accelerometer cut-points was also established (Esliger et al. 2011). Note that here it is the performance of the data analysis step which is truly being validated. For example, shortly after the release of the GENEA, activity classification algorithms were validated which use very different analytical techniques (Zhang et al. 2012).

Ultimately, the choice of device, processing techniques and analytical methods should rest on the validation of these techniques in the population used in epidemiological studies. The complete transparency provided by raw accelerometer data means each step of the analytical process is reported in full, validated against a criterion and compared with other analytical techniques. We will explore these complex data processing and analysis methods in Chapter 8. Prior to that, a comprehensive overview of current assessment methods, focusing on activity monitors is needed.

Summary

In this chapter, we learned how to choose a measurement method. Accelerometer-based activity monitors need evidence that they will perform well in your population of interest. This comes before implementation in large-scale studies and ensures the data obtained in the real study is of good quality and can be shared amongst other researchers. Becoming proficient at assessing the strengths and weaknesses of a measurement method is highly recommended. Measurement, to intentionally labour the point, is central to the scientific process. Familiarity with the rules of measurement and the strengths and weaknesses of current technologies puts you at the head of the field. Now you are equipped to appraise current measurement methods in Chapter 5.

The key points in Chapter 4 are:

- Measurement is central to the process of scientific enquiry, and therefore must be carried out with diligence and care. The user must understand how the measurement method works, what factors influence its accuracy and how to interpret the resulting values.
- Understanding method comparison and calibration and validation studies is key to interpreting existing studies correctly and drawing valid conclusions from your own measurements.
- A suite of technologies now feature in accelerometer-based physical activity assessment. However, a balance is always needed between scientific rigour and innovation. Advances in technology will always proceed at a rapid pace.

References

Aadland, E., and E. Ylvisåker. 2015. 'Reliability of the ActiGraph GT3X+ accelerometer in adults under free-living conditions', *PLOS ONE*, 10: e0134606.

Bassett, D. R., Jr., A. Rowlands, and S. G. Trost. 2012. 'Calibration and validation of wearable monitors', *Med Sci Sports Exerc*, 44: S32–8.

Bland, J. M., and D. J. Altman. 1986a. 'Regression analysis', *Lancet*, 1: 908–9.

Bland, J. M., and D. G. Altman. 1986b. 'Statistical methods for assessing agreement between two methods of clinical measurement', *Lancet*, 1: 307–10.

Bland, J. M., and D. G. Altman. 1996a. 'Measurement error', *BMJ*, 312: 1654.

Bland, J. M., and D. G. Altman. 1996b. 'Measurement error proportional to the mean', *BMJ*, 313: 106.

Bland, J. M., and D. G. Altman. 2012. 'Agreed statistics: measurement method comparison', *Anesthesiology*, 116: 182–5.

Bureau, C., and P. Gosselin. 1987. '[Everything you should know about the International System of Units]', *Nurs Que*, 7: 51–2.

Byun, S., J. W. Han, T. H. Kim, and K. W. Kim. 2016. 'Test-retest reliability and concurrent validity of a single tri-axial accelerometer-based gait analysis in older adults with normal cognition', *PLOS ONE*, 11: e0158956.

Demler, O. V., M. J. Pencina, and R. B. D'Agostino, Sr. 2011. 'Equivalence of improvement in area under ROC curve and linear discriminant analysis coefficient under assumption of normality', *Stat Med*, 30: 1410–18.

Derosa, G., S. A. Salvadeo, R. Mereu, A. D'Angelo, L. Ciccarelli, M. N. Piccinni, I. Ferrari, A. Gravina, P. Maffioli, and C. Tinelli. 2009. 'Continuous glucose monitoring system in free-living healthy subjects: results from a pilot study', *Diabetes Technol Ther*, 11: 159–69.

Doherty, A., D. Jackson, N. Hammerla, T. Plotz, P. Olivier, M. H. Granat, T. White, V. T. van Hees, M. I. Trenell, C. G. Owen, S. J. Preece, R. Gillions, S. Sheard, T. Peakman, S. Brage, and N. J. Wareham. 2017. 'Large scale population assessment of physical activity using wrist worn accelerometers: the UK Biobank Study', *PLOS ONE*, 12: e0169649.

Esliger, D. W., A. V. Rowlands, T. L Hurst, M Catt, P Murray, and R. G. Eston. 2011. 'Validation of the GENEA accelerometer', *Med Sci Sports Exerc*, 43: 1085–93.

Evett, A. S., and M. H. Pirenne. 1974. 'Proceedings: an experimental demonstration of the validity of scientific perspective, as developed from Euclid to Einstein', *J Physiol*, 241: 69P–71P.

Guthrie, W. 2010. *A History of Greek Philosophy: Earlier Presocratics and the Pythagoreans, Vol. 1*, Cambridge, UK: Cambridge University Press.

Habibzadeh, F., and P. Habibzadeh. 2015. 'How much precision in reporting statistics is enough?', *Croat Med J*, 56: 490–2.

Hildebrand, M., V. T. van Hees, B. H. Hansen, and U. Ekelund. 2014. 'Age group comparability of raw accelerometer output from wrist- and hip-worn monitors', *Med Sci Sports Exerc*, 46: 1816–24.

Kuhn, T. 2012. 'Introduction: a role for history'. In *The Structure of Scientific Revolutions: 50th Anniversary Edition*, Chicago, IL: University of Chicago Press.

Landgrebe, T. C., and R. P. Duin. 2008. 'Efficient multiclass ROC approximation by decomposition via confusion matrix perturbation analysis', *IEEE Trans Pattern Anal Mach Intell*, 30: 810–22.

LaPorte, R. E., H. J. Montoye, and C. J. Caspersen. 1985. 'Assessment of physical activity in epidemiologic research: problems and prospects', *Public Health Rep*, 100: 131–46.

Magari, R. T. 2004. 'Bias estimation in method comparison studies', *J Biopharm Stat*, 14: 881–92.

McKinlay, P. L. 1951. 'The measurement of normality', *Br Med Bull*, 7: 275–7.

Melanson, E. L., Jr., and P. S. Freedson. 1995. 'Validity of the Computer Science and Applications, Inc. (CSA) activity monitor', *Med Sci Sports Exerc*, 27: 934–40.

Montoye, H. J., and H. L. Taylor. 1984. 'Measurement of physical activity in population studies: a review', *Hum Biol*, 56: 195–216.

Nez, A., L. Fradet, P. Laguillaumie, T. Monnet, and P. Lacouture. 2016. 'Comparison of calibration methods for accelerometers used in human motion analysis', *Med Eng Phys*, 38: 1289–99.

Sabia, S., V. T. van Hees, M. J. Shipley, M. I. Trenell, G. Hagger-Johnson, A. Elbaz, M. Kivimaki, and A. Singh-Manoux. 2014. 'Association between questionnaire- and accelerometer-assessed physical activity: the role of sociodemographic factors', *Am J Epidemiol*, 179: 781–90.

Stevens, S. S. 1946. 'On the theory of scales of measurement', *Science*, 103: 677–80.

Tosteson, A. N., M. C. Weinstein, J. Wittenberg, and C. B. Begg. 1994. 'ROC curve regression analysis: the use of ordinal regression models for diagnostic test assessment', *Environ Health Perspect*, 102 Suppl 8: 73–8.

van Hees, V. T., Z. Fang, J. Langford, F. Assah, A. Mohammad, I. C. da Silva, M. I. Trenell, T. White, N. J. Wareham, and S. Brage. 2014. 'Autocalibration of accelerometer data for free-living physical activity assessment using local gravity and temperature: an evaluation on four continents', *J Appl Physiol (1985)*, 117: 738–44.

van Hees, V. T., L. Gorzelniak, E. C. Dean Leon, M. Eder, M. Pias, S. Taherian, U. Ekelund, F. Renstrom, P. W. Franks, A. Horsch, and S. Brage. 2013. 'Separating movement and gravity components in an acceleration signal and implications for the assessment of human daily physical activity', *PLOS ONE*, 8: e61691.

Welk, G. J. 2005. 'Principles of design and analyses for the calibration of accelerometry-based activity monitors', *Med Sci Sports Exerc*, 37: S501–11.

Whewell, W. 1967. *History of the Inductive Sciences*, London: Cass.

Youden, W. J. 1950. 'Index for rating diagnostic tests', *Cancer*, 3: 32–5.

Zaki, R., A. Bulgiba, R. Ismail, and N. A. Ismail. 2012. 'Statistical methods used to test for agreement of medical instruments measuring continuous variables in method comparison studies: a systematic review', *PLOS ONE*, 7: e37908.

Zhang, S., A. V. Rowlands, P. Murray, and T. L. Hurst. 2012. 'Physical activity classification using the GENEA wrist-worn accelerometer', *Med Sci Sports Exerc*, 44: 742–8.

5

POPULAR ASSESSMENT METHODS

Lifecourse epidemiology requires the long-term tracking of physical activity over several time-points. Therefore, either physical activity questionnaires or physical activity monitors are most suitable. Questionnaires require the individual to record activities as they occur or recall activities retrospectively. Wearable physical activity monitors contain sensors which directly measure one or more variables associated with human movement, such as acceleration, device orientation or heart rate. Assessments of physical activity made across the lifecourse should be both accurate and reliable to test the strength of associations, detect changes in physical activity around key life events and to highlight determinants of behaviour change causing an increase or decrease in physical activity levels.

Much of the evidence identifying physical *in*activity as a major threat to global health comes from research using questionnaire data. Whilst the risk to health due to chronic low levels of physical activity is dramatic, gaining better knowledge of the determinants of physical activity and assessing the effectiveness of any interventions lie beyond the capabilities of questionnaire-based assessments. Instead, sensor-based technologies such as accelerometers are sensitive enough to detect low-movement behaviours such as sedentary activities and-light intensity activity such as standing and walking, both of which questionnaires appear not to capture well. Yet it is around these behaviours that we need increased precision, since the populations at greatest risk are likely to be physically *in*active. Measurement instruments are required which can be used on a large scale, and crucially, are sensitive to the fluctuations in physical activity which occur from childhood to adulthood and into old age.

The introduction of a new measurement method should be accompanied by the publication of several validation studies to demonstrate its strengths and weaknesses in specific populations. This involves the new measurement method being compared with a criterion reference. Assessment methods used in physical activity epidemiology are categorised as those used as (i) criterion reference methods, (ii) inexpensive but subjective questionnaires and (iii) objective accelerometer-based activity monitors. Criterion methods are reserved for testing the criterion validity of instruments used in physical activity epidemiology: questionnaires and accelerometers.

This chapter describes the gold standard methods, then critiques the plethora of questionnaires available to choose from, provides guidelines on how best to improve the measures derived from questionnaire data, and illustrates the move toward the use of accelerometers in large-scale research, ending on the current developments in raw accelerometers that have generated huge leaps in progress.

This chapter will:

- Give an overview of measurement methods involved in physical activity epidemiology, including criterion methods, questionnaires and technologically advanced accelerometer-based activity monitors.
- Compare physical activity questionnaires, in the context of their use across the lifecourse in continuously increasing age-groups.
- Describe the movement of researchers in the field from questionnaires to activity monitors.
- Introduce modern accelerometer-based devices which are defined by their placement at the wrist, output of raw acceleration data and compatibility with open-source algorithms.

As we delve deeper into the evaluation of questionnaire- and accelerometer-based instruments, we need to remain cognisant of the evidence gaps in lifecourse epidemiology, which is well suited to the use of raw accelerometer devices.

Criterion methods

The most valid and reliable measurements are generally obtained by taking direct measurements of the behaviour of interest, such as PAEE, physical activity intensity or activity type. However, this involves the use of expensive instrumentation operated by trained specialists. These methods – indirect calorimetry, doubly labelled water (DLW) and direct observation – are used as criterion methods to determine the validity of a more feasible measurement method such as a questionnaire or physical activity monitor. Criterion validity of a new accelerometer-based activity monitor can be determined by evaluating the agreement between measurements obtained from earlier instruments. In physical activity assessment, criterion methods are often referred to as the 'gold standard'. The gold standard strives to represent the ground truth (the underlying absolute state of information) as closely as possible.

Criterion energy expenditure in free-living conditions can be obtained using double labelled water, and in the exercise laboratory it can be obtained using indirect calorimetry. Criterion measures of activity type can be obtained by direct observation, which is typically carried out in the exercise laboratory.

Indirect calorimetry

Calorimetry is the science or act of measuring changes in state variables of a body for the purpose of deriving the heat transfer associated with changes of its state due, for example, to chemical reactions. Indirect calorimetry calculates heat that living organisms produce by measuring either their production of carbon dioxide and nitrogen waste (frequently ammonia in aquatic organisms, or urea in terrestrial ones) or their consumption of oxygen (Raurich, Ibanez and Marse 1989). Heat production can be predicted from oxygen consumption in this way, using multiple regression. Heat generated by living organisms may also be measured by direct calorimetry, in which the entire organism is placed inside the calorimeter for the measurement.

Direct calorimetry measures heat lost from the body. All chemical processes give off heat. For example, in glycolysis, 62% of the energy required to carry out the breakdown of glucose to form adenosine triphosphate (ATP) is lost as heat (Hill 1949). Heat is lost from the skin surface (radiation) due to increased blood flow through the dermis (convection), via transference to another surface (conduction) and via the production of sweat (evaporation). Direct calorimetry involves placing the participant in a thermally insulated chamber and measuring heat loss using a heat-absorbent medium pumped through the room via piping. Therefore, the difference in temperature between the medium entering and leaving the chamber directly reflects the participant's heat production. Direct calorimetry is highly accurate (1%) and precise (2–3%) (Benzinger and Kitzinger 1949). However, since the participant is sealed inside a metabolic chamber, direct calorimetry places a high level of burden them. For these reasons, calorimetry is mainly used to validate other methods of assessing physical activity or to determine the energy costs of specific activities. However, the principles of calorimetry have been applied to a more feasible method called indirect calorimetry

Indirect calorimetry involves the measurement of the respiratory gases oxygen (VO_2) and expired carbon dioxide (VCO_2). The ratio of inspired oxygen and expired carbon dioxide is used to calculate energy expenditure using specific formulae. During physical activity, carbon-based nutrients (carbohydrate, fats and protein) are converted into CO_2, water (H^2O), and heat in the presence of O_2. Indirect calorimetry assesses the amount of heat generated indirectly according to the amount and pattern of substrate use and by-product production (Epstein 2000). Specifically, energy expenditure can be calculated by measuring the amount of oxygen used and carbon dioxide released by the body:

Substrate O_2 oxidation $3CO_2$ H_2O Heat

Indirect calorimeters, also called metabolic carts, such as the Metalyzer 32B, are becoming more portable, accurate, sensitive and affordable, and require shorter calibration times. Metabolic carts feature masks and mouthpieces/nose clips to allow the measurement of energy expenditure during various physical activities (Figure 5.1).

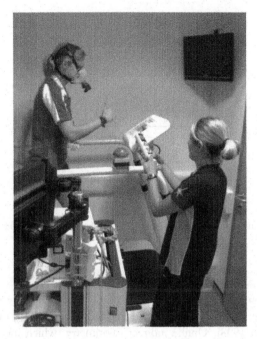

FIGURE 5.1   Cardiopulmonary exercise testing, featuring indirect calorimetry. Metabolic carts measure VO_2 and VCO_2 to determine the intensity of physical activity.

Portable metabolic carts or gas analysis systems such as the Cosmed K4b2 can be used in a field setting, but still feature equipment that is strapped to the body and a mouthpiece into which the individual breathes (da Rocha, Alves and da Fonseca 2006).

Physical activity monitors are routinely validated against indirect calorimetry in a laboratory setting using a protocol featuring several semi-structured activities. However, in free-living conditions, even portable systems are not suitable for long-term measurement of energy expenditure, so the gold standard in free-living conditions is doubly labelled water.

Doubly labelled water

Doubly labelled water is water in which the hydrogen and the oxygen have been replaced with the stable radioisotopes oxygen-18 (^{18}O) and deuterium (^{2}H). These isotopes render these elements 'traceable' and provide the most accurate measures total energy expenditure in free-living conditions over a period of days or weeks. When DLW is consumed, the elimination rate of each isotope is measured by obtaining urine samples. ^{2}H is eliminated as water, and ^{18}O is eliminated as both water and carbon dioxide in air (Figure 5.2). The difference in elimination rate between the two can be used to measure total energy expenditure and physical activity related energy expenditure (Speakman 1998). However, the major limitation of DLW is that it remains prohibitively expensive for use in all but modestly sized studies.

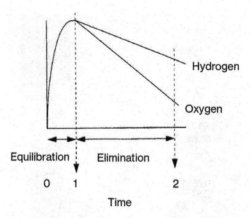

FIGURE 5.2 Elimination rates of oxygen-18 (^{18}O) and deuterium (^{2}H) in doubly labelled water.

Where economically viable, the validation of physical activity monitors aiming to estimate energy expenditure during normal daily life should be carried out against DLW (Speakman 1998). Unlike indirect calorimetry, which involves continuous measurement of respiratory gases, DLW requires only the collection of urine samples. Nevertheless, accelerometer-based activity monitors are increasingly being used to identify specific activity types. Activity type classification should be validated against direct observation.

Direct observation

Direct observation involves a trained observer watching the study participant while they carry out selected activities of daily living. The strength of direct observation is that it provides data close to the ground truth. However, direct observation is suitable only for the laboratory environment. Sending a researcher into a field setting to observe a study participant's physical activity habits is largely impractical. Such close-proximity observation is likely to induce the Hawthorne effect (whereby awareness of being observed causes the individual to alter their behaviour, in this case most likely carrying out more physical activity than normal). Some studies have employed small, body-worn cameras to record free-living activity. However, the advantages of this approach over validation in a laboratory setting have not been demonstrated.

Subjective and objective measurement methods both have their own unique strengths and limitations. However, the decision of which method to use is made even more difficult by the fact that there are so many questionnaires and physical activity monitors to choose from. In order to make the correct choice, it is essential to understand how these popular measurement methods work.

Self-report questionnaires

Subjective instruments, namely physical activity questionnaires, have provided considerable contributions to knowledge of the relationship between physical activity and many serious health complications. Questionnaire-based instruments have been used to establish initial relationships between physical activity and most NCDs. Similarly, they featured in landmark studies such as the Framingham Heart Study (Dorgan et al. 1994), EPIC-Norfolk (Boekholdt et al. 2006), and prior to the incorporation of activity monitors, the NHANES (Hughes, McDowell and Brody 2008) and Whitehall II Study (Singh-Manoux et al. 2005). Put simply, physical activity questionnaires are cheap, easy to use and have played a fundamental role in the evolution of physical activity assessment.

Similarly, the first public health guidelines for physical activity (Pate et al. 1995) aiming at '30 minutes or more of moderate-intensity physical activity on most, preferably all, days of the week', which received much attention at the time, were based on evidence obtained in large numbers of people on a cost-effective basis. However, disparate physical activity recommendations were published soon after which highlighted that important health benefits could be derived at far lighter activity intensities and also that additional benefits could be accrued by carrying out more activity of higher intensity (US Department of Health and Human Services 1996). This was partly due to the absence of evidence showing health benefits at lower activity intensities and by reducing sedentary time, not because they do not exist, but because physical activity questionnaires poorly detect lower-intensity activities. Subsequent recommendations highlight the health hazards of too much sedentary time and advocate regular daily physical activity (US Department of Health and Human Services 2008).

Data published in 2012, obtained using the standardised IPAQ and GPAQ across 122 countries, showed a third of adults and four-fifths of adolescents do not reach public health guidelines for recommended physical activity levels (Lee et al. 2012). Further analysis provided clear evidence that physical *in*activity is the fourth biggest risk factor for NCD.

The major strength of the IPAQ is its standardised design aimed for use across studies and to allow the comparison of data from different countries (Craig et al. 2003). It underwent validity and reliability testing across 12 countries in adults aged 18–65 years. However, substantial overreporting has been seen in people completing the IPAQ (Bauman et al. 2009), and when respondents were further probed on how they answered questions, nearly half reported some physical activity where they should have reported none, and 5% reported physical activity levels so high they were not deemed possible.

A closer look at the IPAQ validity and reliability study reveals that it was deemed to have good criterion validity. However, it was validated against the CSA model 7164 accelerometer (Computer Science and Applications Inc., Shalimar, FL). This highlights two methodological flaws: first, the CSA model 7164 accelerometer is not a criterion measure (Bauman et al. 2009). In fact, studies reveal that the CSA has overestimated light activity and underestimated vigorous activity, and raise concerns regarding the transferability of activity intensity cut-points (METs) from laboratory to free-living conditions (Kozey et al. 2010). Secondly, the agreement between physical activity derived from questionnaires and from accelerometers is significantly influenced by age and socioeconomic status, which is worth consideration if the study age range was 18–65 years.

On balance, when the IPAQ was introduced, it was the only feasible way of collecting such large amounts of physical activity data. Therefore, methodological limitations would not, at the time anyway, represent a strong enough argument to prevent its use. Nevertheless, the limitations of subjective measurement methods and availability of cost-effective yet technologically advanced wearable activity monitors mean that questionnaires are no longer the instrument of choice in the large-scale assessment of physical activity.

Limitations of questionnaires result from their inherent subjectivity. The IPAQ long form is, as its name suggests, relatively lengthy, featuring 27 questions. Thus, the quality of data may be influenced by recall bias (bias due to difficulty recalling past events) and respondent fatigue (tendency for respondents to get tired of the survey), causing some to engage in 'straight line responding'. Respondents may be influenced by social desirability factors, and as a result, over-report physical activity (Sheikh, Abelsen and Olsen 2016). The IPAQ short form is only seven questions long, and undoubtedly less burdensome to complete. I encourage you to try the IPAQ for yourself: it is freely available at www.ipaq.ki.se.

Using self-report methods across the lifecourse

Whether questionnaires are suitable to track long-term trends in physical activity over the lifecourse remains questionable. The IPAQ has shown poor validity and a low response rate in children (Bhargava 2017). Adults aged over 65 years have struggled to accurately complete the questionnaire. They have difficulty recalling activity in the previous 7 days, particularly activity lasting <10 minutes (Heesch 2010). Older adults experience difficulties deciding which of their past activities are moderate-intensity and which are vigorous-intensity.

Although standardised questionnaires like the IPAQ facilitate the comparison of data from different studies, they are not suitable for use across age-groups spanning the lifecourse. To optimise the quality of data from physical activity questionnaires, age group-specific questionnaires should be used where the questionnaire design is informed by the population characteristics and needs.

Children (>6 years)

Several questionnaires aimed at children exist, but they are poorly validated. Validation and reliability studies in children rarely feature a criterion method, and most use one of several accelerometers as the comparison measure. Even then, studies still report unsatisfactory validity and reliability and encourage the use of activity monitors (Bielemann et al. 2011). A number of questionnaires have been used in pre-schoolers (mean age <6 years), children (mean age 6–12 years) and older children, youth and adolescents (mean age >12 years), such as the Children's Physical Activity Questionnaire (CPAQ) (Nor Aini, Poh and Chee 2013) and International Physical Activity Questionnaire modified for Adolescents (IPAQ-A; Ottevaere et al. 2011).

At best, modest relationships are reported between the results from accelerometers and questionnaires in children. Questionnaires for adolescents generally correlate better. This may be due to difficulties of very young individuals in recalling previous activities or in comprehending the questions. Since the use of physical activity questionnaires requires the child to sit and spend time completing the questionnaire to the best of their ability, it is highly likely that wearing a small, unobtrusive activity monitor would prove more feasible and acceptable.

Adults (>18 years)

Standardised questionnaires such as the IPAQ and GPAQ are designed and tested in adults. Some studies classify adults as aged 18–65 years. However, marked reductions in cognitive capacity and physical function occur with increasing age, and this varies between individuals. Therefore, adults are best categorised as young, middle-aged and older (>65 years).

Several studies have compared subjective and objective measurements from questionnaires and activity monitors. These studies report modest correlations, rarely higher than $r = 0.3$ or $\rho = 0.3$, between subjective and objective instruments, regardless of the instrument used. This includes the IPAQ (Boon et al. 2010) and EPIC questionnaire (Cust et al. 2008). Higher socioeconomic status increases correlation between objective and self-reported measures (Sabia et al. 2014), but these individuals are also typically more active and thus have more to recall.

Similarly, higher-intensity activity produces larger correlations, which suggests that older adults, who are generally less active and have lower aerobic fitness and reduced functional capacity, would benefit least from questionnaires. Functional reductions of the ageing process alter the perceived difficulty/intensity of an activity. Similarly, reduced cognitive ability affects the person's ability to recall previous physical activity or complete lengthy questionnaires. As a result, age-specific questionnaires are mostly used with older adults.

Older (>65 years)

Older adults represent a large age demographic who are expanding rapidly, but in whom physical activity shows the largest variation. Many questionnaires designed specifically for older adults are simplified and include lower-intensity activities, in which older adults are more likely to engage. They are also shorter in length owing to the increased susceptibility to responding fatigue in older adults. Specific questionnaires are available, such as the Physical Activity Scale for the Elderly

(PASE) (Schuit et al. 1997) and Community Healthy Activities Model Program for Seniors (CHAMPS) (Stewart et al. 2001). However, they still fail to capture the lower end of the physical activity intensity spectrum. Whatever the design of the questionnaire, older adults asked to complete a paper-based report instrument will provide responses that are influenced by health status, medications, fatigue, pain, concentration and distractibility, changes in mood, depression, anxiety, and problems with memory and cognition.

Very old (>85 years)

Although the very old represent the fastest-growing age group in the world, they are an age group in which robust evidence is only recently emerging. They are also an age demographic in whom physical activity assessment was late in development. The first study to develop an age group-specific study questionnaire was the Newcastle 85+ Study. However, despite participants being highly sedentary with very low levels of physical activity, the questionnaire showed similar correlation coefficients to those seen in studies carried out in younger age groups. However, the accelerometer used in this study was a wrist-worn raw accelerometer, which demonstrates increased capabilities to capture light-intensity activities.

Recommendations to improve physical activity assessed using self-reporting

All instruments feature some level of measurement error. The aim of measurement is to reduce that error as much as possible. Measurement error that is too large can lead to the effects of a behaviour being attenuated or overestimated, and can lead to uncertain conclusions. Therefore, depending on what is being measured, prior to using a measurement instrument, the user should understand the sources of potential error. Self-report instruments and questionnaires feature varying sources of measurement error. However, there are ways to tackle this. Two types of error are common in questionnaires: random error and systematic error.

Random error is caused by unreliable reporting and natural variation in behaviours over time. It is, by nature, random from one measurement to the next. Random error should be normally distributed, in keeping with the central limit theorem. Although it does not generally affect the mean score, it remains unpredictable in how it affects the variation in scores. Increasing sample size is a common way of reducing random error.

Systematic error is typically constant and predictable. Systematic error in questionnaires may be caused by reporting biases in a particular population. For example, where a particular questionnaire systematically underestimates low-intensity activity in older adults, efforts can be made to reduce this error by rephrasing certain questions. A questionnaire should undergo validity and reliability testing prior to being used. If it has not, investigators should first carry this out and publish the results.

Steps can be taken to reduce measurement error. These include (i) careful design of the questionnaire for the population of interest, (ii) using an appropriate comparison method, (iii) standardised delivery by trained researchers and (iv) piloting the instrument prior to implementation in the main study.

First, the design of the questionnaire should be informed by the population of interest, the study in which it will be used and the study aim. The study design and study aim also influence the type of questionnaire used. Large-scale population surveillance aims to identify the percentage of a population who meet a certain criterion. This includes categorising people as active or inactive, grouping people as low-activity, moderate-activity and high-activity, or identifying the number of people meeting national physical activity guidelines.

A clear understanding of the specific physical activity habits of the study cohort is recommended. For example, adults aged ≥85 years typically have some cognitive impairment and reduced memory capacity. Therefore, a questionnaire for this age group should be concise and easy to understand.

Second, the testing the validity and reliability of a questionnaire is critically important. Prior to implementing a questionnaire, users should check whether the questionnaire has been validated in the population of interest for their study. For example, the original IPAQ has not been validated in young children aged 5–12 years and therefore should not be used in this age group unless it has been tested and the results published in peer-reviewed journals. Some authors report conducting testing of the questionnaire used in their study, but do so claiming it is 'unpublished data': this is poor practice.

In addition to this, the correct comparison method should be used. Where possible, a true criterion test, such as indirect calorimetry or doubly labelled water, should be employed. Understandably, this is not feasible for questionnaires used in large-scale epidemiology. As an alternative, accelerometers are commonly used as an objective comparator. The accelerometer should have demonstrated acceptable validity and reliability in the population of interest (preferably tested against a criterion method).

Third, the delivery of the questionnaire should be carried out by qualified individuals. On large-scale longitudinal studies, this might require the recruitment of research nurses, research assistants and other trained personnel to carry out data collection. The aim is to maximise fidelity during data collection. In the case of interviews, those conducting the interviews might need specialist training or, in the case of psychiatric interview assessments, years of medical training. Nevertheless, the ability to standardise the delivery of the questionnaire depends on the use of fully trained personnel. These elements have the potential to increase inter- and intra-participant error that result in wide variability of summary scores within the group, and inconsistency of responses within an individual over repeated measures.

Finally, all questionnaires – particularly those used for the first time – should be piloted in a sub-sample of participants from the main study. This informs the decision of whether the selected instrument is indeed suitable for use in a particular study. Pilot testing may reveal that study participants find the questionnaire lengthy and burdensome, and if respondent fatigue reaches significant levels, possibly even engage in straight line responding.

In summary, recommendations to improve the validity and reliability of data from physical activity questionnaires serves the needs of epidemiologists looking to identify relationships between physical activity and health in previously unexplored populations, or to conduct population surveillance and categorise groups of individuals, for example, as active or inactive. They include (i) carrying out careful design of the questionnaire for the needs of the population of interest, (ii) using an appropriate comparison measurement method for the study aims, (iii) standardised delivery by trained researchers, and (iv) piloting the instrument prior to implementation in the main study. Although it lies outside the scope of this chapter, a working group headed by Barbara Ainsworth has provided a comprehensive conceptual framework for all self-report methods.

Questionnaires are recommended for establishing disease associations in populations whose physical activity habits have not yet been assessed. However, where the aim is to gain further insights into established relationships, increase knowledge about dose–response relationships or accurately track secular trends in physical activity intensity and type, the use of body-worn activity monitors to objectively quantify physical activity is recommended.

Limits to the use of questionnaires in lifecourse epidemiology

The strength of physical activity questionnaires is that they are easy to use: they are feasible. Their limitation is their subjectivity. Until recently, objective alternatives, namely wearable activity monitors, were considered more accurate, but not feasible for use in large-scale physical activity assessment. However, the methodological gap between accuracy and feasibility has closed substantially, and accelerometer-based activity monitors are now being used in a number of studies on a cost-effective basis. This suggests we have reached the peak in design and implementation of physical activity questionnaires. Regardless of the standard of questionnaire design, the subjective nature of questionnaires introduces a catalogue of potential biases listed in Table 5.1.

Questionnaires often express the intensity of physical activity semantically, using a Likert-type scale. Unfortunately, perceptions of the intensity of any stimulus depend on the life experiences and in many cases the personality type of the individual concerned, particularly on characteristics like neuroticism versus stoicism. Some people are particularly prone to report symptoms, and since physical activity is a socially desirable behaviour to report, the over-reporting of some activities and under-reporting of others will never be circumvented.

Over a 10–30-minute bout of physical activity at moderate intensity, the relative difficulty increases with time. Therefore, attempts to contextualise questions with statements such as 'sufficient to cause moderate sweating' or 'causing mild breathlessness' cause the respondent to recall the most difficult part of the activity,

TABLE 5.1 Types of bias in physical activity questionnaires and limitations for use across the lifecourse.

Bias	Description	Example	Limitations for use across the lifecourse
		Question design	
Ambiguous question	Respondents understand the question differently than was intended and therefore answer a different question than was intended	During pregnancy I have been less active than before becoming pregnant.	The response could refer to current and previous pregnancies or the current pregnancy only
Technical jargon	May not be understood by the respondent	How many hours per week do you carry out moderate to vigorous physical activity (MVPA)?	Moderate to vigorous physical activity (MVPA) is interpreted by measurement specialists as 3–6 METs, but responses are influenced largely by physical fitness, which declines in older adults
Vague language	Difficult to quantify	How often do you exercise? [ ] Never [ ] Regularly [ ] Occasionally [ ] All the time	No definition of each, use instead [ ] less than once a week [ ] 1–3 times a week [ ] more than three times a week
Insensitive measure	Questions not detecting meaningful differences	How important do you perceive physical activity to be for good health, on a scale of 1 to 3? 1 – Unimportant 2 – Mildly important 3 – Very Important	Response differences may have statistical significance but too few categories to support strong conclusions
Forced choice	Questions an affirmative or negative response	My mood is better after I have exercised. [ ] Yes [ ] No	Respondents who do not feel better or worse after exercise are forced to select an inaccurate answer.
Horizontal response format	Tends to cause more confusion than vertical responses	Your health is: Excellent ... [ ] Good ... [ ] Fair ... [ ] Poor ... [ ]	Can be unclear where to mark the correct box compared to, [ ] Excellent [ ] Good [ ] Fair [ ] Poor
		Long questionnaires	
Response fatigue	Long questions and questionnaires can induce fatigue among respondents	List up to 3 main activities that you did on the job in the past 12 months e.g. sit, stand, walk, carry loads	The well-known IPAQ features 27 questions making it unsuitable for older adults (>65 years)
Straight-line responding	Long questionnaires can encourage respondents to mark vertically down the page, often close to the end	Please move on to question 71 out of 121 and continue	Questionnaires and surveys should extract maximal data in a concise format. Respondent fatigue and straight-line responding increase in prevalence for; interviews lasting over 50 mins, telephone interviews lasting over 30 mins, self-administered questionnaires typically taking over 20 mins to complete
		Respondent bias	
Faking bad (hello-goodbye effect)	Respondents may downplay their health status, particularly if it fits their personal view of their health	Which of the following symptoms do you have?	Respondents check more of symptoms than they have Older adults with multiple comorbidities, depression or loneliness can have a longing for sympathy
Social desirability bias	Respondents over-report socially desirable behaviours and under-report less desirable behaviours	How many times per week do you exercise got over 30 mins?	Good examples include under-reporting in food intake diaries (socially undesirable) and over-reporting in physical activity questionnaires (socially desirable) Susceptible respondents include children and teenagers, and those who are very sedentary

typically occurring toward the end, and therefore overestimate the intensity of the whole bout of activity. This is compounded by factors such as poor sleep, drowsiness in the post-prandial state and fitness levels.

Conversely, short-duration and light-intensity activity are poorly recalled. Unfortunately, many questionnaires suffer from floor effects, where short-duration activities, common to very old adults and contributing to their health, may be difficult to capture. Some questionnaires do not account for activities lasting under 10 minutes. This is particularly relevant since the populations of interest in many studies are those who are inactive or sedentary.

In general, physical activity questionnaires struggle to detect and assess low levels of physical activity: Considering that two-thirds of the global population are thought to have low levels of physical activity, attention now focuses on the development and implementation of low-cost, easy-to-use accelerometer-based activity monitors.

A large body of evidence has been amassed using questionnaires. Global surveillance carried out with the IPAQ and GPAQ resulted in data from 122 countries, which showed that a third of adults do not reach public health guidelines for recommended physical activity levels (Lee et al. 2012). Nevertheless, there is a shift in the field of physical activity measurement where the strengths of questionnaires are well recognised. However, the advances in accelerometry have resulted in a change in practice and consensus amongst experts for the first time ever: that raw data should be obtained where possible, the data collection protocol should be reported, and never-before-seen measurements are being derived from a single acceleration signal.

Moving from questionnaire to activity monitor

Physical activity epidemiology relied almost exclusively on questionnaires until the early 2000s. However, reductions in the cost of objective activity monitoring mean they are no longer reserved for smaller empirical studies striving for accuracy and reliability. Questionnaires are by no means redundant. They still offer the only means to capture supplementary or contextual data that cannot yet be obtained from a wearable device.

Since activity monitors are objective, they nullify concerns about reporting errors created by misinterpretation, recall bias and social desirability. However, this it not to say that the use of activity monitors is free of any potential issues. After making the decision to use a wearable activity monitor in your study, you must also make several choices. These include:

Which device do I choose?

How do I work the device?

Where is it worn, and for how long?

What data does it produce?

How do I convert the data into meaningful measures of physical activity?

These questions are often hard to answer, and the answers often hard to find.

To assist us, first recall the rules of measurement featured in Chapter 4. Let us remind ourselves that users should understand (i) how their measurement instrument works, (ii) the validity and reliability of the instrument and (iii) the factors affecting validity and reliability.

'Activity monitor' is a term which describes many devices. Some studies report the 'validity of an activity monitor'. In fact, there is no such thing. An activity monitor is part of an instrument-based measurement system.

Figure 5.3 presents a generalised model of a simple instrument. The physical process to be measured, the measurand, is to the left of the image. It is digitally sampled via a sensor and represented as a voltage signal proportional to the original input.

For example, you likely have on or near your person a mobile phone. The probability that it is a smartphone is quite high. Most smartphones orientate the screen depending on whether the phone is placed on its side or placed upright. Inside the phone is a small sensor called an accelerometer. The accelerometer is continuously sensing the force of gravity acting upon it. Thus, when the phone is oriented at any particular angle, the screen display maintains an orientation so that you can view and use it. It is because of this sensitivity, not only to movement, but also fine changes in orientation, that we find accelerometer sensors in so many devices today.

Many activity monitors feature accelerometers. Modern accelerometers are only millimetres in size, to reduce the costs associated with manufacture and improve battery life. These sensors detect gravity. Therefore, they can detect the orientation of the device and movement. However, there are many types of sensor. They all convert a physical phenomenon into an electrical signal. These include microphones (sound), oxygen sensors (in physiology equipment – and your car), gyroscopes (detecting rotation, in smartphones, cars and aircraft), thermometers (detecting temperature, used in medical devices, thermostats, fridges) and many more.

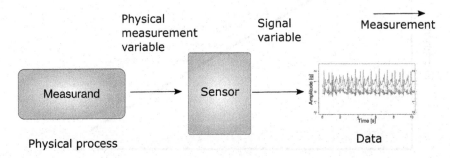

FIGURE 5.3 A generalised model of a simple activity monitor. The process to be measured is the measurand. The sensor converts the physical variable input into a variable output signal. Accelerometers continuously measure gravitational acceleration (g).

The accelerometer inside an activity monitor stores gravity readings, specifically a type of acceleration called g. If the device is set to record at 30 Hz, then it will take a measurement of g 30 times a second. Thus, some activity monitors can record a lot of data. After recording, the device is typically connected to a PC and the data can be uploaded and saved. Some accelerometer-based activity monitors, such as the ActiGraph, come with manufacturer software which contains algorithms which convert the stored data into meaningful measurements such as PAEE or MVPA. This might seem convenient, but remember our rules of measurement. The user should understand how the algorithms work, but some software packages feature proprietary algorithms which are private to the manufacturer.

In response to this, algorithm developers have developed and published algorithms of their own. Some are freely available to access using open-source software such as R. Many have been validated and are being used in large-scale assessments of physical activity. However, a limitation of these algorithms is that the user needs some understanding of the programming language used in R.

Many researchers new to physical activity assessment, obviously eager to use the recommended assessment method, opt to use an accelerometer-based device, but then face a challenge of choosing using more expensive commercial software or finding a way of using open-source algorithms, either through skills upgrade or collaboration. Furthermore, when accelerometer novices review the past literature on objective activity monitoring, they are confronted by a complex, sometimes confusing history involving accelerometer counts, multi-sensor devices such as the ActHeart or SenseWear, and raw accelerometers, now taking the lead in physical activity assessment.

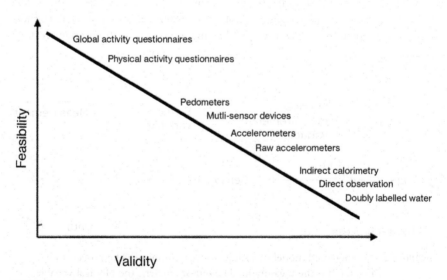

FIGURE 5.4 Physical activity assessment tools and their relative positions on a feasibility validity continuum.

The reader should note that as much of this history as is essential to know is reported within these pages. Of far greater importance is the understanding that continued progress in accelerometer technology has increased the feasibility of these devices for use on a large scale. Where early accelerometers were objective and more reliable than questionnaires, current devices have moved their position on the feasibility/validity continuum, a common method for comparing measures by determining their validity in relation to their feasibility. Figure 5.4 shows criterion methods occupying one end of the scale, questionnaires the other, and in the centre, accelerometers.

Summary

This chapter has covered the necessary ground on criterion methods, physical activity questionnaires and activity monitors. In lifecourse epidemiology, criterion methods are well suited to the purpose of validating novel measurement methods which are developed for use in large-scale monitoring. Physical activity questionnaires have strengths and limitations, such as cost-effectiveness and subjectivity. However, the rapid advances seen in sensor-based wearable technologies have rendered questionnaires useful only for adding context to physical activity measurements which cannot be captured by a device. Questionnaires are not considered redundant. Rather, they are a useful adjunct to objective measurements, providing contextualisation or additional data not currently available from the activity monitor. The technology of accelerometery has come a long way, researchers have worked around the technical limitations of early devices, and in the process the use of accelerometry in epidemiology is growing.

The key points of Chapter 5 are:

- Criterion methods such as DLW, indirect calorimetry and direct observation are commonly used in laboratory- or field-based calibration and validation studies of new sensor-based measurement systems.
- Measurement instruments suitable for use in epidemiological research must be low-cost and easy to implement. For some time, questionnaires filled these requirements best. However, questionnaires are subjective, and their data feature consistent measurement error.
- Advances in accelerometer technology resulting in reduced unit cost and free, open-source analytics mean that accelerometers are now cost-effective enough for use in large-scale studies.
- These innovations represent method developers' efforts to overcome the limitations of early accelerometers. These devices were worn on the waist and were more expensive, and this precluded them from use in all but the best-funded epidemiological studies.
- Measurement using accelerometers can be daunting to the non-specialist. The potential user should understand how the device works and what factors affect measurements from it.

References

Bauman, A., B. E. Ainsworth, F. Bull, C. L. Craig, M. Hagstromer, J. F. Sallis, M. Pratt, and M. Sjostrom. 2009. 'Progress and pitfalls in the use of the International Physical Activity Questionnaire (IPAQ) for adult physical activity surveillance', *J Phys Act Health*, 6 Suppl 1: S5–8.

Benzinger, T. H., and C. Kitzinger. 1949. 'Direct calorimetry by means of the gradient principle', *Rev Sci Instrum*, 20: 849–60.

Bhargava, M. 2017. 'Use of International Physical Activity Questionnaire-short form for assessment of physical activity of children', *J Family Community Med*, 24: 131.

Bielemann, R. M., F. F. Reichert, V. M. Paniz, and D. P. Gigante. 2011. 'Validation of the Netherlands physical activity questionnaire in Brazilian children', *Int J Behav Nutr Phys Act*, 8: 45.

Boekholdt, S. M., M. S. Sandhu, N. E. Day, R. Luben, S. A. Bingham, R. J. Peters, N. J. Wareham, and K. T. Khaw. 2006. 'Physical activity, C-reactive protein levels and the risk of future coronary artery disease in apparently healthy men and women: the EPIC-Norfolk prospective population study', *Eur J Cardiovasc Prev Rehabil*, 13: 970–6.

Boon, R. M., M. J. Hamlin, G. D. Steel, and J. J. Ross. 2010. 'Validation of the New Zealand Physical Activity Questionnaire (NZPAQ-LF) and the International Physical Activity Questionnaire (IPAQ-LF) with accelerometry', *Br J Sports Med*, 44: 741–6.

Craig, C. L., A. L. Marshall, M. Sjostrom, A. E. Bauman, M. L. Booth, B. E. Ainsworth, M. Pratt, U. Ekelund, A. Yngve, J. F. Sallis, and P. Oja. 2003. 'International physical activity questionnaire: 12-country reliability and validity', *Med Sci Sports Exerc*, 35: 1381–95.

Cust, A. E., B. J. Smith, J. Chau, H. P. van der Ploeg, C. M. Friedenreich, B. K. Armstrong, and A. Bauman. 2008. 'Validity and repeatability of the EPIC physical activity questionnaire: a validation study using accelerometers as an objective measure', *Int J Behav Nutr Phys Act*, 5: 33.

da Rocha, E. E., V. G. Alves, and R. B. da Fonseca. 2006. 'Indirect calorimetry: methodology, instruments and clinical application', *Curr Opin Clin Nutr Metab Care*, 9: 247–56.

Dorgan, J. F., C. Brown, M. Barrett, G. L. Splansky, B. E. Kreger, R. B. D'Agostino, D. Albanes, and A. Schatzkin. 1994. 'Physical activity and risk of breast cancer in the Framingham Heart Study', *Am J Epidemiol*, 139: 662–9.

Epstein, C. D. 2000. 'Applications of indirect calorimetry', *Crit Care Nurs Clin North Am*, 12: 187–98.

Heesch, K. C. 2010. 'What do IPAQ questions mean to older adults? Lessons from cognitive interviews', *Int J Behav Nutr Phys Act*, 7: 35.

Hill, A. V. 1949. 'Adenosine triphosphate and muscular contraction', *Nature*, 163: 320.

Hughes, J. P., M. A. McDowell, and D. J. Brody. 2008. 'Leisure-time physical activity among US adults 60 or more years of age: results from NHANES 1999–2004', *J Phys Act Health*, 5: 347–58.

Kozey, S. L., J. W. Staudenmayer, R. P. Troiano, and P. S. Freedson. 2010. 'Comparison of the ActiGraph 7164 and the ActiGraph GT1M during self-paced locomotion', *Med Sci Sports Exerc*, 42: 971–6.

Lee, I. M., E. J. Shiroma, F. Lobelo, P. Puska, S. N. Blair, and P. T. Katzmarzyk. 2012. 'Effect of physical inactivity on major non-communicable diseases worldwide: an analysis of burden of disease and life expectancy', *Lancet*, 380: 219–29.

Nor Aini, J., B. K. Poh, and W. S. Chee. 2013. 'Validity of a children's physical activity questionnaire (cPAQ) for the study of bone health', *Pediatr Int*, 55: 223–8.

Ottevaere, C., I. Huybrechts, I. De Bourdeaudhuij, M. Sjostrom, J. R. Ruiz, F. B. Ortega, M. Hagstromer, K. Widhalm, D. Molnar, L. A. Moreno, L. Beghin, A. Kafatos,

A. Polito, Y. Manios, D. Martinez-Gomez, and S. De Henauw. 2011. 'Comparison of the IPAQ-A and ActiGraph in relation to VO(2)max among European adolescents: The HELENA Study', *J Sci Med Sport*, 14: 317–24.

Pate, R. R., M. Pratt, S. N. Blair, W. L. Haskell, C. A. Macera, C. Bouchard, D. Buchner, W. Ettinger, G. W. Heath, A. C. King, A. Kriska, A. S. Leon, B. H. Marcus, J. Morris, R. S. Paffenbarger, K. Patrick, M. L. Pollock, J. M. Rippe, J. F. Sallis, and J. H. Wilmore. 1995. 'Physical activity and public health: a recommendation from the Centers for Disease Control and Prevention and the American College of Sports Medicine', *JAMA*, 273: 402–7.

Raurich, J. M., J. Ibanez, and P. Marse. 1989. 'Validation of a new closed circuit indirect calorimetry method compared with the open Douglas bag method', *Intensive Care Med*, 15: 274–8.

Sabia, S., V. T. van Hees, M. J. Shipley, M. I. Trenell, G. Hagger-Johnson, A. Elbaz, M. Kivimaki, and A. Singh-Manoux. 2014. 'Association between questionnaire- and accelerometer-assessed physical activity: the role of sociodemographic factors', *Am J Epidemiol*, 179: 781–90.

Schuit, A. J., E. G. Schouten, K. R. Westerterp, and W. H. Saris. 1997. 'Validity of the Physical Activity Scale for the Elderly (PASE): according to energy expenditure assessed by the doubly labeled water method', *J Clin Epidemiol*, 50: 541–6.

Sheikh, M. A., B. Abelsen, and J. A. Olsen. 2016. 'Differential recall bias, intermediate confounding, and mediation analysis in life course epidemiology: an analytic framework with empirical example', *Front Psychol*, 7.

Singh-Manoux, A., M. Hillsdon, E. Brunner, and M. Marmot. 2005. 'Effects of physical activity on cognitive functioning in middle age: evidence from the Whitehall II Prospective Cohort Study', *Am J Public Health*, 95: 2252–8.

Speakman, J. R. 1998. 'The history and theory of the doubly labeled water technique', *Am J Clin Nutr*, 68: 932S–38S.

Stewart, A. L., K. M. Mills, A. C. King, W. L. Haskell, D. Gillis, and P. L. Ritter. 2001. 'CHAMPS physical activity questionnaire for older adults: outcomes for interventions', *Med Sci Sports Exerc*, 33: 1126–41.

US Department of Health and Human Services. 1996. *Physical Activity and Health: A Report of the Surgeon General*, Atlanta, GA: US Department of Health and Human Services, Centers for Disease Control and Prevention, National Center for Chronic Disease Prevention and Health Promotion.

US Department of Health and Human Services. 2008. 'Physical activity'. Accessed 10 April 2019. www.health.gov/PAGuidelines.

6

PHYSICAL ACTIVITY MONITORS IN EPIDEMIOLOGY

Recent advances in accelerometer technology have resulted in their use in large-scale research such as NHANES and UK Biobank. The devices used now are inexpensive and analysed using freely available analytics. Prior to this, accelerometers were more expensive and used proprietary software. Consequently, consensus opinions were near absent from the literature. However, users are now guided to use raw accelerometer data, collect sociodemographic and anthropometric information, and to fully describe data collection protocols in the study.

Physical activity monitors used in epidemiological research have evolved dramatically. Since they first appeared in 2003, a growing number of highly varied monitors were developed and validated, and in some cases live on today, and in other cases have been discontinued. The first devices used in epidemiology were the ActiGraph family, which have featured in the NHANES from 2003 to the present day. Attempts to improve the data from early devices involved the upgrade of ActiGraph technology, such as the battery life, sensor specification and size of the device. Elsewhere, the development of multi-sensor devices combining movement sensor data with biosensors never became cost-effective enough to be used in high-level epidemiological research.

Meanwhile, the technology of activity monitors has advanced in numerous aspects, including device specification, the use of raw data and advanced analytical methods. This describes an evolution of sorts, resulting in wrist-worn, accelerometers producing detailed triaxial acceleration data in a raw, unprocessed format recorded at the sub-second level.

This chapter will:

- Take a short journey through the history of physical activity monitors, from the first device aimed at epidemiological research introduced in 1979 to the first study to feature accelerometers, the NHANES data sweeps from 2003 onward.
- Examine consumer activity monitors such as the Fitbit and Apple iWatch which are also gaining in popularity and may well be part of a network of

sensor-based patient care in the near future. We will see how these devices are intended for public consumption, and therefore differ from research-grade devices.

- Examine the considerable number of wearable activity monitors, including uniaxial, biaxial and triaxial devices and those which feature multiple sensors tracking motion and biological changes.
- Identify the key strengths of wrist-mounted raw accelerometers used in the UK Biobank (Axivity), the NHANES 2011–2012 and 2013–2014 cycles (ActiGraph GT3X+) and the Whitehall II Study (GENEActiv), and investigate the technology underpinning these devices.

The evolution of physical activity monitoring in epidemiology has seen many changes. Single-site activity monitors have moved from the waist to the wrist, removed the proprietary 'black box' processing methods, and allowed method developers to produce open-source analytics to monitor the entire 24-hour movement cycle.

History of physical activity monitors

Mechanical devices have been worn on the body to assess physical activity since antiquity. Leonardo da Vinci (1452–1519) is thought to have designed a pedometer-style instrument with military applications. Fifteenth-century paintings by da Vinci show a device that was used by the ancient Romans for military purposes to calculate the approximate daily distance the troops had travelled on foot (MacCurdy 1938). The device features a pendulum arm that would swing back and forth with every leg motion while walking, much like the modern pedometer. Devices produced during the 1950s also followed the general design of a pedometer. However, digital wrist-worn pedometers such as those first produced by Seiko feature error that is too large for lifecourse epidemiology (Tudor-Locke et al. 2006).

Cavagna and colleagues developed a strain gauge accelerometer-based device in 1961 to quantify human body movement (Cavagna, Saibene and Margaria 1961). However, the first activity monitor aimed at epidemiological research was developed in 1979 (LaPorte et al. 1979). The device, called the Large-scale Integrated Motor Activity Monitor (LSI), featured an internal a cylinder containing a ball of mercury and at one end of the cylinder, a mercury switch. Rotation of the device caused the ball to make contact with the switch, and every 16 contacts was registered by an internal counter as one unit.

The device, which could be described more accurately as a pedometer, was worn on the waist and on the ankle for two days by graduate students (n = 20). Mean hourly counts were correlated with energy expenditure derived from equations. Accelerometer output at the waist was better correlated with estimated energy expenditure than output from the ankle.

In the 1980s, Montoye and colleagues validated the LSI and a device which measured acceleration and deceleration in a vertical direction (Montoye et al. 1983).

The device, 400 g in weight and 14 × 8 × 4 cm in size, housed a sensor containing piezoelectric material. These are materials such as crystals and some ceramics which produce an electrical charge in response to mechanical stress applied during acceleration. LSI and acceleration readings were compared with VO_2 from a metabolic cart. Both devices were worn at the waist and wrist during treadmill walking at 2 mph at 0, 6 and 12% gradient, treadmill walking at 4 mph at 0, 6 and 12% gradient, treadmill walking at 6 mph at 0, 6 and 12% gradient, half knee bends and floor touches). The activities were intentionally chosen to determine whether the devices detected the increased energy cost of incline walking and whether the waist-worn device detected static physical activity. Both devices failed to detect incline walking, but it still remains questionable today how important this is considering the rich suite of data available from body-worn monitors. Devices worn at the waist failed to reflect the energy expenditure of static activities such as knee bends and floor touches. Higher correlations with VO_2 were shown for the LSI worn at the wrist across all activities.

Throughout the 1990s there was a proliferation of new accelerometer-based devices generally introduced via the publication of a laboratory-based validation study which linked accelerometer output to energy expenditure estimated from VO_2. Numerous devices with varying technical specifications were made available for researchers, including the uniaxial Computer Science and Applications, Inc. (CSA) accelerometer, later renamed the ActiGraph 7164, the Tracmor$_D$ (Philips Research Laboratories, Eindhoven, the Netherlands) and triaxial Tritrac-R3D accelerometer.

However, Ronald LaPorte, Carl Caspersen and colleagues developed a mechanical body-worn device for use in epidemiology which gave basic estimates of energy expenditure (LaPorte et al. 1979). The Large-scale Integrated Motor Activity Monitor (LIS) was worn at the hip, and though much more obtrusive, resembled the accelerometer-based devices that would follow over 20 years later. Henry Montoye refined this design with his colleagues and introduced a device which was tested at the waist and the wrist, correlating well with estimated VO_2 in both instances (Montoye et al. 1983).

Only two years later, in 1985, LaPorte and colleagues reported that over 30 different instruments were already being used in physical activity epidemiology, including survey questionnaires, physiological markers such as heart rate, and mechanical and electronic monitors (LaPorte, Montoye and Caspersen 1985). In fact, over the next 10 years, no single instrument would fulfil the criteria of being valid, reliable and practical: those that were precise tended to be impractical on a population basis, and vice versa. The potential to use wearable devices to carry out the objective monitoring of physical activity was evident, but the technology of the time was not yet good enough.

As a result, data from pedometers were used in several studies in the 1990s to provide early public health guidelines. These encouraged adults to achieve 10,000 steps/day. Thereafter, pedometer indices were used to produce a classification system of activity level based on steps/day: sedentary (<5000 steps/day), low active (<5000–7499 steps/day), somewhat active (<7500–9999 steps/day), active (<10,000–12,499 steps/day) and highly active (<12,500 steps/day) (Tudor-Locke and Bassett 2004).

Over time, the internal mechanical counting systems were replaced by piezoelectric sensors. Piezoelectric materials generate an electrical charge when deformed; lead zirconate titanate crystals generate measurable electricity when they are deformed by only 0.1% of their original shape. Piezoelectric accelerometer sensors were quickly incorporated into body-worn instruments, and studies were published in which the accelerometer output was used to develop prediction equations from VO_2 where participants performed a series of semi-structured activities during a laboratory experiment to derive estimates of energy expenditure.

During the 1990s, several accelerometers were developed, such as the Caltrac (Miller, Freedson and Kline 1994; Richardson et al. 1995) TriTrac (Sherman et al. 1998) and Computer Science and Applications, Inc. accelerometer (Melanson and Freedson 1995; Freedson, Melanson and Sirard 1998). From 2000 onwards, accelerometer-based activity monitors were developed and validated that were intended for use in epidemiology. A large number of studies were published comparing new and existing accelerometer monitors with each other and with the criterion methods indirect calorimetry, in lab-based studies, and DLW, in free-living studies.

Accelerometers were used in epidemiological research from 2003, when the NHANES introduced an accelerometer worn at the hip to their 2003–2005 data sweep. Technological advances resulted gradual reductions in production costs. However, only in 2008 was physical activity data from accelerometers gathered in sufficient quantities to be compared to existing questionnaire data, when the most striking observation was that questionnaire data indicated that >26% of the US population met physical activity guidelines (Macera et al. 2005), whereas only 5% did so according to accelerometer-based data (Troiano et al. 2008).

A few other epidemiological studies adopted accelerometers to provide objective measures of physical activity, whilst smaller studies, methodological, validation studies and experiments saw a rapid increase in accelerometer use. As accelerometers gained popularity in physical activity research, manufacturers responded by producing an astonishing number of devices.

As accelerometer sensors and batteries became smaller, more was packed into the device itself. Devices appeared which incorporated several sensors into a single device. Typically, movement-related sensors combined with biosensors were used to feed more complex algorithms in an effort to derive more accurate and reliable measurements. Monitors such as the Actiheart combined accelerometer data with heart rate, whilst the SenseWear armband utilised sensors to detect movement, thermal flow, galvanic skin response, skin temperature and air temperature.

Until roughly 2009, researchers aiming to measure physical activity using activity monitors faced considerable barriers to doing so. First, the objective assessment of physical activity using activity monitors was prohibitively expensive. The NHANES remained one of the few studies to use activity monitors for some time. Costs included that of the device itself, typically >£100, a single software license at ~£1000, plus adequate storage space. Second, the question of which activity monitor to use was near impossible to answer. This was due to a lack of methodological standardisation across studies.

Available devices lacked transparency about the specifications of the hardware inside them, and they differed greatly regarding their internal hardware and technical specification, data sampling techniques, device output and manufacturer-supplied analytical methods used to give the user meaningful measures of physical activity. Although new devices were typically tested in laboratory- or field-based validation studies, evaluation of the performance of the devices themselves was inadequate. For example one study (Farooqi et al. 2013) claiming to carry out 'validation of SenseWear Armband and Actiheart monitors for assessments of daily energy expenditure' reported that they 'can reliably assess TEE in women. However, the SenseWear Armband and Actiheart monitors underestimate TEE'.

Keeping analytical methods private to the manufacturer led to the use of activity monitors by researchers with little understanding of how their measurements were derived, and based solely on the findings of validation studies. The current popularity of accelerometers in epidemiological studies such as Whitehall II and UK Biobank, was only possible due to the development of accelerometers with transparency at each stage of measurement: device specification, data collection, data processing and analysis.

The wrist-worn raw accelerometer was developed by a number of co-workers in the UK and US. The release of devices such as the GENEA (Esliger et al. 2011) led the way for researchers to conduct cost-effective measurement using continuous movement data recorded over 24 hours to derive daytime measurements such as physical activity and nighttime measurements during sleep. The measurements obtained show greater validity and reliability than costly multi-sensor devices. Thus, movement data from raw accelerometers is routinely used to track a range of variables in large studies such as UK Biobank and NHANES.

Surrounded by sensor technology, we are now seeing the integration of health data with healthcare and research, making use of both research devices and sensors housed in devises such as smartphones and consumer-grade activity monitors.

Consumer- versus research-grade monitors

Consumer activity monitors are used mostly outside the field of research by people who are simply interested in quantifying their own activities. The use of body-worn sensors has seen an expansive growth in personal use as well as applications in industries including medicine and healthcare. I have not mentioned them so far as their target market is the lay public, whilst research-grade activity monitors are accurate, feasible and therefore ideally suited for physical activity surveillance. Nonetheless, within the area of health and fitness, wearable technology topped the worldwide fitness trends in 2016 and 2017.

The popularity of consumer-wearable devices, activity sleep trackers or fitness trackers is undoubtedly increasing, and approximately 3.3 million were sold between

April 2013 and March 2014, with the leading examples being sold by Fitbit (67%), Jawbone (18%) and Nike (11%) (Lee, Kim and Welk 2014). The motivations for their development was part of the Quantified Self movement, where interested members of the public have taken advantage of the ubiquitous technologies at their disposal (smartphones, smartphone applications, tablets and PCs). Combined, these technologies are becoming more pervasive in modern life, and more affordable.

Arguably, any vehicle leading the public to become more interested in their physical activity and sleep behaviours is good for health (Turner-McGrievy et al. 2019). These devices are user-friendly. Many have attractive displays for immediate behaviour feedback and come with freely available mobile and internet-based applications, providing users with feedback on a variety of metrics including step-count, calories burned, stairs climbed, distance travelled, active time and sleep. Many of these measures can be shown publicly, allowing the user to share and interact with other users via online sites and social networks, which in itself shows positive health behaviour changes.

The main advantage of step-count is that it can be so easily interpreted. Step count is a ubiquitous measurement found across consumer activity monitors and in various smartphone applications. However, the measurement of step-count is not accurate, greatly depending on the population of interest. Step-count error occurs during both slow walking speeds and fast walking speeds. At slow walking speeds (<4.5 km/h), step-count error has been reported as 50–90%; many devices struggle to detect the steps of individuals who walk at a slower pace. Steps are also underestimated at fast walking speeds due to a proposed ceiling effect. Therefore, pedometers are not suitable for use in populations with altered gait. This includes older adults, who often have some degree of orthopaedic degeneration, obese individuals, who tend to walk at slower speeds, people with Parkinson's disease, whose gait is characterised by small shuffling steps and a general slowness of movement (hypokinesia), and conversely, individuals who regularly walk swiftly, jog or run.

A survey based in the US (Coughlin and Stewart 2016) indicated that ~70% of adults tracked ≥1 of their own lifestyle behaviours or those of a family member or friend, 21% of those also monitored health data, whilst 46% indicated that tracking changed their approach to maintaining their health or the health of the person they cared for. Of the total survey respondents, 40% indicated that it led them to communicate more with their doctor during consultations, ask new questions or obtain a second opinion, and 34% stated that the data influenced their decision making about their own medical treatment.

Several manufacturers claim their devices accurately capture activity levels while worn on various body sites. Considering these features and flexibility, consumer-level activity monitors, coupled with smartphone technology, have potential to enhance user experience and utility. A complete review of consumer devices is outside the scope of this book, and would include the Fitbit(s), Jawbone Up, Jawbone 24, Garmin Vivosmart, Garmin Forerunner, Polar Loop, Samsung Gear S, and Apple iWatch. Note this list is not exhaustive, but a summary is featured below.

Validity

Available devices provide estimates of steps, distance covered, physical activity, energy expenditure and sleep. Criterion methods used in these studies are restricted to indirect calorimetry and the ActiGraph GT3X+. Studies show that validity varies across devices. Steps tend to be underestimated, but not by much. However, compared to research-grade accelerometers, consumer monitors tend to overestimate MVPA, with large differences of up to 1.5 hours/day reported (Imboden et al. 2018). Perhaps unsurprisingly, consumer monitors tend to overestimate sleep time and sleep efficiency, although this is widespread across accelerometer-based monitors using movement to classify sleep and awake.

Reliability

Contrastingly, both inter-device reliability and intra-device reliability were very high for energy expenditure, and equally so for steps. Similarly, reliability for sleep, even at the minute-by-minute sleep/wake classification, was high (Ferguson et al. 2015). However, all the studies used participants with healthy, non-disordered sleep. Findings in sleep-disordered individuals with highly variable sleep may yield different results.

Recommendations

Consumer activity monitors are designed for public use and are hugely popular, allowing self-monitoring of important wake/sleep activities. This consumer popularity presents promise to researchers and clinicians working to help people increase their physical activity and modify their sleep behaviours. Nevertheless, these devices are commercial, consumer-targeted technologies, so there is limited scientific evidence regarding their reliability and validity.

A challenge in evaluating consumer activity monitors is the rate at which new models are introduced, old models become redundant and the technological changes which occur between models during this process. For example, The Fitbit company (San Francisco, CA; www.fitbit.com) has offered at least nine activity trackers since 2008. The first Fitbit, released in 2008, was superseded by the Fitbit Ultra in 2011 and the Fitbit One in 2012, all now discontinued, as are the Fitbit Flex (2013) and the Fitbit Force (2013). Fitbits in production at the time of writing include the Fitbit Zip, released in 2012, the wrist-worn devices Fitbit Alta, Charge and Ionic, released in 2016–2018 and designed to compete with the Apple iWatch. The Jawbone company (San Francisco, CA; https://jawbone.com) has offered at least six activity trackers since 2011. As a consequence, it is common for researchers assessing the validity and reliability of these products to find that by the time their study is published, the device used has been replaced by a totally different model or is no longer in production.

If they hope to gain greater involvement in research and healthcare, I give three bits of advice to the manufacturers. First, whilst the user is rarely interested in how the measures are created, researchers need to know. Many devices feature an analytical 'black box' hiding proprietary analytical methods. Second, researchers need to know if the device has been removed. At present, consumer monitors do not provide this information, which is perhaps expected, since it is of little use to the person wearing it. However, missing data is a big problem in activity monitoring, especially in large-scale studies. Third, it is necessary to have the facility to access device specifications, data processing techniques and analytical methods used to provide activity/sleep measures. Any changes in these areas due to technical improvements need to be declared.

Consumer activity monitors allow people to collect data about themselves. These devices are part of an array of sensor-based technologies at our disposal which can be used to quantify many aspects of daily life. The practice of tracking personal behaviours such as physical activity and sleep is typically used as a way of monitoring personal behaviour and improving individual well-being. Knowledge about oneself easily translates as a tool for self-improvement to enhance daily functioning and optimise various aspects of life through the practice of self-tracking, auto-analytics, body hacking, self-quantifying, self-surveillance and personal informatics

All too often, by the time devices can be scientifically evaluated and results published in peer-reviewed process, the consumer market may have moved on, with new models, new devices and software updates being released continually. Future research examining other aspects of the consumer-level devices, such as their reliability, acceptability, usability and durability, are warranted. A challenge for research in this field will be keeping pace with the rapidly evolving consumer market. Devices are being developed at an extraordinary rate, generally without any published data on validity. The general public are using these devices to make decisions about physical activity and sleep.

Research-grade activity monitors are developed in a systematic and transparent way. The history of research-grade physical activity monitors, in contrast to consumer activity monitors, features more robust testing of new technologies. It also shows that researchers have generally been aware of measurement limitations, but the limitations of technology available at the time have often prevented a solution being implemented. The first accelerometer-based activity monitors differ markedly from those available now. Physical activity monitors used in lifecourse research include accelerometers.

Accelerometers

Accelerometers are the most popular instruments used to objectively assess physical activity. The internal accelerometer sensor continuously records movement of the body. Modern devices feature triaxial micromachined microelectromechanical systems (MEMS) accelerometer sensors which store high-resolution acceleration data in units of gravitational acceleration (g) at frequencies up to ~100 Hz, often recorded for 7 days. These sensors are sensitive to gravitational acceleration in both static ($\pm 1g$) and dynamic forces along vertical, anteroposterior and mediolateral axes.

This sensitivity provides information about inclination of the device and the posture of the person wearing it. This acceleration data can be analysed using a number of different techniques which provide estimates of energy expenditure, physical activity intensity (sedentary, light, moderate-to-vigorous), activity type (sitting, walking, running) and sedentary behaviour.

Large-scale assessments of physical activity using accelerometers reported in the literature typically feature one of the following popular devices: the ActiGraph accelerometer, the GENEActiv (Activinsights Ltd, UK) and its predecessor, the GENEA, the Axivity accelerometer (Axivity Ltd, UK), Actical (Philips Respironics, USA), and activPAL (PAL Technologies Ltd, UK), all shown in Figure 6.1. It is essential that the user understands how accelerometers work, how monitors differ and how those differences affect the measurement process.

The GENEActiv, Axivity and ActiGraph GT3X+ are the most popular tri-axial accelerometers used in epidemiological research. They are quite similar: they feature comparable sensors and internal hardware, and are worn on the wrist. However, a number of instruments are available with different specifications that are sometimes difficult for users to ascertain. Selecting an accelerometer-based activity monitor for a particular project depends on the objectives of the study, and the resources available to purchase and use the instruments. Determining the suitability of an accelerometer for use in a particular study can be challenging.

Depending on the particular model, accelerometers can differ markedly, in terms of sensor specification, data analysis techniques and recommended wear location. The first devices used in epidemiological research featured different sensors,

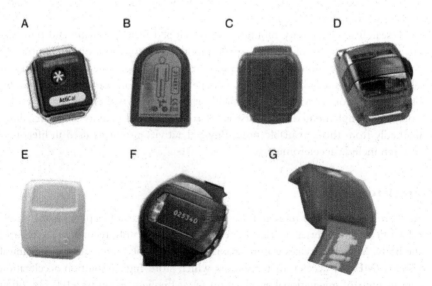

FIGURE 6.1 Accelerometer-based activity monitors used in large-scale epidemiological research. Devices include the Actical (A), activPAL (B), ActiGraph GT1M (C), ActiGraph GT3X (D), GENEA (E), GENEActiv (F) and Axivity (G).

data processing methods and device outputs, and used device-specific algorithms accessed via manufacturer software. They were also worn on the hip or waist.

In order to evaluate and compare evidence from past studies, the user needs to be well-informed about the different specifications of accelerometers and how this affects measurements derived from them. Differences in sensor specification, data analysis techniques and wear location of available accelerometers are best described in the context of the rapid technological evolution that has occurred since accelerometers were first used in 2003 until the present day.

Evolution of accelerometer-based activity monitoring

By the time accelerometers were implemented in epidemiological research, a multitude of accelerometers were available, but only a minority were suitable for use on a large scale. The ActiGraph had established itself as the *de facto* standard accelerometer-based activity monitoring. The increasing prominence of the ActiGraph accelerometers in the early 2000s coincided with the addition of the ActiGraph 7164 to the NHANES 2003–2004 data sweep. The ActiGraph 7164 was replaced by the uniaxial GT1M model. This was the largest accelerometer deployment carried out at the time. Participants wore the accelerometer on a waist belt, over the right hip, for seven consecutive days, removing the device for showering, bathing and before bed.

Other studies added accelerometers such as the ActiGraph GT1M to their measurement protocols, including the EPIC-Norfolk (Cust et al. 2008) and Health Survey for England (Basterfield et al. 2008). Devices such as the ActiGraph GT1M and Actical had limited storage space compared to modern technologies. Therefore, manufacturers incorporated onboard processors which converted the acceleration signal into summary measures for easier storage on the device and less battery drain. To derive summary measures, the acceleration signal was first converted from analogue to digital, filtered, rectified and summarised into condensed units called activity counts (Chen and Bassett 2005).

Activity counts were typically summed to give counts/minute. To estimate physical activity intensity, the output in counts/minute was uploaded to a PC using the manufacturer software and categorised as sedentary, light-, moderate- and vigorous-intensity activity, depending on the number of counts/minute. Cut-points were applied to the data to classify average time spent in certain activity intensities. For example, a popular cut-point for MVPA was ≥1952 counts/minute, and for sedentary behaviour is <100 counts/minute.

The cut-points used to estimate activity intensity are typically developed in a laboratory setting by aligning accelerometer counts with a measured physiological variable, such as VO_2, energy expenditure or METs. Linear regression models are used to establish cut-points that correspond to light, moderate and vigorous intensity (<3 METs, 3–6 METs and >6 METs, respectively) which can be applied to the data in activity counts.

A sizeable proportion of this methodological work, mostly involving the ActiGraph models used in the NHANES, is owed to Patty Freedson and colleagues (Freedson, Melanson and Sirard 1998; Freedson 1991; Freedson et al. 2008) and marks a significant contribution to the use of accelerometry in physical activity epidemiology.

Alternative methods to the cut-point approach exist. Pattern recognition or 'machine learning' approaches were first employed to estimate PAEE and activity type. Some early pattern recognition algorithms, whilst promising, were too complex for use on a large scale (Pober et al. 2006). Conversely, simplified algorithms have shown some success in classifying activity type. However, the authors used the proprietary filtered activity counts from uniaxial ActiGraph 7164, thus somewhat negating the methodological transparency associated with pattern recognition (Staudenmayer et al. 2009).

Accelerometer-based activity monitors such as the Tracmor$_D$ (Philips New Wellness Solutions, Lifestyle Incubator, the Netherlands) performed well when predicting energy expenditure in free-living conditions using DLW (Bonomi et al. 2009, 2010; Plasqui et al. 2005; Plasqui and Westerterp 2005). However, the use of proprietary activity counts as device output and the incomplete reporting of prediction models meant these methods were never adopted in epidemiological studies.

Interest in sedentary behaviours resulted in the validation of devices such as the activPAL, aiming to distinguish different body postures. This is specifically aimed at quantifying time spent sitting/lying, standing and ambulatory activities. However, the device features some limitations. The use of proprietary algorithms means users cannot be sure how their data is calculated. Unlike other devices, the algorithms have not been made public. Stepping accuracy is compromised at very slow (i.e., <0.5 m/s) walking speeds (Harrington, Welk and Donnelly 2011). In addition, placement of the device on the front of the thigh makes it impossible to differentiate sitting from lying down. Around 2008, the activPAL increased in popularity. However, dramatic technological advances in single-sensor accelerometers such as the ActiGraph devices dramatically and permanently changed the field of accelerometer-based activity assessment.

Limitations

The ActiGraph accelerometers have been the most popular for use in epidemiological research, most notably the NHANES, featuring in the 2008–2009 data sweep. However, these devices had well recognised limitations which modern devices circumvent:

- Worn at the waist – Despite the success of using an accelerometer device in NHANES and the widely used data, participant compliance was recognised as a major issue. Only about 25% of participants provided the requested 7 days of data, which was mostly attributed to the discomfort or inconvenience of wearing a device on the hip over time, and forgetting to put the monitor back on after taking it off at night.

- Counts as output – Proprietary accelerometer output 'activity counts' differ from one device to the next and across different models of the same device. Thus, varying acceleration output could be obtained from different monitors for the

same physical activity. Counts are created using brand-specific computational methods considered proprietary to the device manufacturer. This hinders the comparison of data across different studies and presents problems when different accelerometers are used at follow-up.
- Lack of methodological transparency and consistency – The packaging of accelerometer-specific prediction equations in commercial manufacturer software results in a methodological 'black box' hidden from the user.

In response to these long-standing limitations, coordinated efforts to produce a next-generation accelerometer gathered momentum amongst method developers. First, they are worn on the wrist and feature a waterproof casing. Therefore, devices can be worn continuously, 24 hours per day, and support collection of 7 days of continuous accelerometer data. The device would feature a MEMs triaxial accelerometer, detecting acceleration on vertical, anteroposterior and mediolateral axes. The output of these devices is a three-dimensional time series of accelerations, and they are able to collect and store high-throughput, sub-second-level acceleration data at 10–200 observations per second, providing continuous accelerometry. Triaxial sensors detect orientation of the device and therefore posture of the wearer (lying, sitting, standing). Crucially, device output is expressed as the unprocessed raw acceleration signal in units of g instead of proprietary accelerometer counts. Raw acceleration data can be analysed using open-source analytical methods instead of proprietary manufacturer software.

The arrival of this wrist-mounted, triaxial, raw accelerometer was marked by the introduction and validation of the GENEA accelerometer, which started in 2008 (Esliger et al. 2011) and marked the beginning of a move toward the use of raw, unprocessed accelerometer data from devices worn continuously at the wrist, using transparent, open-source data analysis techniques to derive measurements of physical activity.

Meanwhile, method developers were also focusing their efforts on the combination of several sensors instead of a single movement-sensitive accelerometer, which carry out synchronous measurements of acceleration, heart rate, body temperature and other physiological responses.

Multi-sensor arrays

Multi-sensor arrays typically combine accelerometry with other physiological indicators such as heart rate and skin temperature. Initially, it was hoped that these devices would overcome the limitations of early accelerometers. However single-site accelerometers became smaller and more affordable, and as technology advanced, more robust measures of physical activity were available without the burden of considering additional sensors. Nevertheless, the most popular multi-sensor arrays are the Actiheart (CamNtech Ltd, Cambridge, UK) and SenseWear Armband (Bodymedia Inc., Pittsburgh, PA).

The Actiheart uses accelerometry and heart rate monitoring to provide an estimate of physical activity. The rationale behind the combined use of acceleration and heart rate is that acceleration data verifies that elevations in heart rate are due to physical activity. Unsurprisingly, a major criticism of heart rate as an additional input variable is that it is influenced by a range of factors other than body movement. Heart rate is influenced by age, gender, fitness level, environmental temperature and health status, and is increased by lack of sleep, anxiety and the consumption of stimulatory substances such as caffeine, but decreased by pharmacological therapies such as opioid analgesics or hypnotics (Brage et al. 2006; Brage et al. 2005).

The SenseWear Armband combines several sensors to measure acceleration, steps, galvanic skin response, skin temperature and heat flux from the skin. Users are able to extract a wide range of variables using the manufacturer software (METs, AEE, TEE and sleep). Validation studies of the SenseWear report non-significant differences in energy expenditure during treadmill walking compared to indirect calorimetry and during free-living conditions when compared with DLW, but not to levels surpassing less costly accelerometers (Papazoglou et al. 2006; Arvidsson et al. 2007; Mackey et al. 2011; Feehan et al. 2016). Furthermore, the SenseWear has been shown to underestimate the energy cost of low-intensity activities, which often make up a large proportion of physical activity in inactive people who are commonly the population of interest.

In future, technological advances may well make multi-sensor arrays cost-effective and suitable for use in epidemiological research. However, it is uncertain how far future technology will evolve to incorporate several biosensors into devices as small and cost-effective as current wrist-worn accelerometers.

Continuous wave 'raw' accelerometers

Modern accelerometers, including the ActiGraph GT3X+, GENEActiv, GENEA and Axivity, are sometimes called 'raw accelerometers' as they give output in raw, unprocessed acceleration. The combination of waterproof casing and placement on the wrist eliminates the need to remove the device and reduces participant burden. Therefore, devices are worn continuously, and this facilitates the continuous recording and storage of high-throughput, triaxial, sub-second-level acceleration data, ranging between 10 and 100 Hz.

Raw accelerometers differ from the first accelerometers used in physical activity epidemiology. Studies such as the NHANES and Health Survey for England featured devices that, due to battery and memory limitations, returned only aggregated minute-level data in the form of proprietary activity counts. The combined limitations of (i) arbitrary activity counts used as device output, (ii) missing data resulting from wearing the device at the waist and (iii) inconsistent use of accelerometer cut-points across studies were increasingly recognised by measurement experts (Figure 6.2). Collectively, these limitations were overcome by the introduction of raw accelerometers giving access to the unprocessed, raw acceleration data expressed in g or m/s^2 that are worn at the wrist.

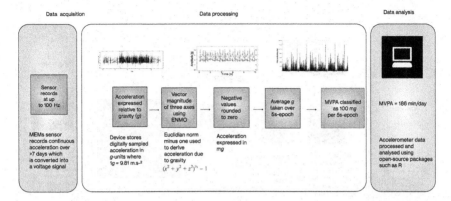

FIGURE 6.2 The stages of accelerometer data processing. The filtering, rectification and integration of raw acceleration data is carried out using proprietary techniques, creating a 'black box' effect highlighted here by black boxes.

The beginnings of these methodological developments appeared from around 2008, when a group of researchers first focused on the development of a suitable device. The introduction of the GENEA, developed by Unilever Discover (Colworth, UK), was possible due to continuous innovations in sensor technology. Two validation papers suggested that the strengths of using the raw acceleration signal were numerous and significant (Esliger et al. 2011; Zhang et al. 2012). The successor to the GENEA, the GENEActiv, was manufactured and distributed by ActivInsights Ltd (Kimbolton, Cambridgeshire, UK).

The 2011–2014 NHANES data collection features the ActiGraph GT3X+, which is waterproof and supports collection of 7 days of continuous triaxial accelerometer raw signal data. Rather than repeating the waist location used in 2003–2006, wrist wear on the non-dominant wrist was chosen. Wrist wear of a waterproof device allows the device to be worn around the clock for 7 days. This body location and protocol were chosen to improve wear compliance and had the additional benefit of allowing the measurement of movement during sleep.

A growing number of longitudinal studies, particularly those with larger cohorts, use wrist-worn raw accelerometers. These include the NHANES in the 2011–2012 and 2013–2014 cycles (ActiGraph GT3X+), Whitehall II Study (GENEActiv), Pelotas Birth Cohort (GENEA), Fenland Study (GENEActiv), INTERVAL Study (Axivity) and UK Biobank (Axivity). However, many studies employ other devices, such as the Women's Health Study (ActiGraph GT3X+), Maastricht Study (activPAL) and Framingham Heart Study (FHS) 3rd Generation cohort (Actical), to maintain a standardised assessment approach or facilitate the comparability of accelerometer data with previous time-points.

The collection of raw accelerometry data opens up a spectrum of new opportunities. First, the use of data expressed in SI units such as g facilitates the pooling

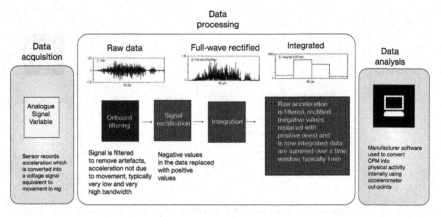

FIGURE 6.3 The stages of raw accelerometer data processing. The acceleration signal is processed using published methods, thus creating transparency at each stage.

of data between studies. Researchers do not need to rely on proprietary output such as activity counts. The raw acceleration signal offers a rich amount of data and detects a wider range of activities when a device is worn on the wrist. Figure 6.3 shows the stages of data processing using raw accelerometer data.

Raw data is well suited for use with machine learning algorithms which classify activity type. Researchers are free to use well-described, open-source metrics to summarise the data. The Newcastle 85+ Study was the first to publish several measures of physical activity intensity (light, moderate, vigorous) and activity type (sitting, walking, running, activities of daily life) using open-source analytics derived from a single acceleration signal (Innerd et al. 2015) and derive objective measures of sleep (Anderson et al. 2014).

The increased granularity of the sub-second-level data may contain important additional information, but it also creates new challenges. Raw data allows a welcome move away from activity counts which are produced via proprietary algorithms developed and patented by the manufacturers of these monitors (entailing different amplifiers, filters, frequencies etc.) and therefore lead to a 'black box' effect preventing any researcher from understanding count values. However, processing the raw acceleration signal involves procedures which many researchers in physical activity epidemiology may not well understand. Hence, there is a necessity for development and implementation of rigorously designed and tested methods to process the data, and to explain them well.

Summary

This chapter took a brief look at the history of activity monitoring using wearable devices. In epidemiological research, the main developments in physical activity monitoring include improved device specification, the popularity of raw accelerometers, a shift amongst experts from placement of the monitor at the waist to the wrist, and to fully exploit this placement, the availability of raw unprocessed data not expressed in activity counts, but in standardised units of g.

The key points of Chapter 6 are:

- Use of accelerometer-based activity monitors in epidemiology gained popularity after the inclusion of the ActiGraph GT1M in the 2003–2006 NHANES studies.
- Limitations included the use of activity counts, poor adherence due to hip placement, and the use of analytical methods that required the manufacturer software.
- Efforts by selected groups of method developers to improve accelerometer performance included upgrading sensor hardware, the introduction of multi-sensor arrays, and the development of cost-effective raw accelerometers worn at the wrist with free analytical methods.

References

Anderson, K. N., M. Catt, J. Collerton, K. Davies, T. von Zglinicki, T. B. Kirkwood, and C. Jagger. 2014. 'Assessment of sleep and circadian rhythm disorders in the very old: the Newcastle 85+ Cohort Study', *Age Ageing*, 43: 57–63.

Arvidsson, D., F. Slinde, S. Larsson, and L. Hulthen. 2007. 'Energy cost of physical activities in children: validation of SenseWear Armband', *Med Sci Sports Exerc*, 39: 2076–84.

Basterfield, L., A. J. Adamson, K. N. Parkinson, U. Maute, P. X. Li, and J. J. Reilly. 2008. 'Surveillance of physical activity in the UK is flawed: validation of the Health Survey for England Physical Activity Questionnaire', *Arch Dis Child*, 93: 1054–8.

Bonomi, A. G., G. Plasqui, A. H. Goris, and K. R. Westerterp. 2009. 'Improving assessment of daily energy expenditure by identifying types of physical activity with a single accelerometer', *J Appl Physiol*, 107: 655–61.

Bonomi, A. G., G. Plasqui, A. H. Goris, and K. R. Westerterp. 2010. 'Estimation of free-living energy expenditure using a novel activity monitor designed to minimize obtrusiveness', *Obesity (Silver Spring)*, 18: 1845–51.

Brage, S., N. Brage, U. Ekelund, J. Luan, P. W. Franks, K. Froberg, and N. J. Wareham. 2006. 'Effect of combined movement and heart rate monitor placement on physical activity estimates during treadmill locomotion and free-living', *Eur J Appl Physiol*, 96: 517–24.

Brage, S., N. Brage, P. W. Franks, U. Ekelund, and N. J. Wareham. 2005. 'Reliability and validity of the combined heart rate and movement sensor Actiheart', *Eur J Clin Nutr*, 59: 561–70.

Cavagna, G., F. Saibene, and R. Margaria. 1961. 'A three-directional accelerometer for analyzing body movements', *J Appl Physiol*, 16: 191.

Chen, K. Y., and D. R. Bassett, Jr. 2005. 'The technology of accelerometry-based activity monitors: current and future', *Med Sci Sports Exerc*, 37: S490–500.

Coughlin, S. S., and J. Stewart. 2016. 'Use of consumer wearable devices to promote physical activity: a review of health intervention studies', *J Environ Health Sci*, 2.

Cust, A. E., B. J. Smith, J. Chau, H. P. van der Ploeg, C. M. Friedenreich, B. K. Armstrong, and A. Bauman. 2008. 'Validity and repeatability of the EPIC physical activity questionnaire: a validation study using accelerometers as an objective measure', *Int J Behav Nutr Phys Act*, 5: 33.

Esliger, D. W., A. V. Rowlands, T. L Hurst, M. Catt, P. Murray, and R. G. Eston. 2011. 'Validation of the GENEA accelerometer', *Med Sci Sports Exerc*, 43: 1085–93.

Farooqi, N., F. Slinde, L. Haglin, and T. Sandstrom. 2013. 'Validation of SenseWear Armband and Actiheart monitors for assessments of daily energy expenditure in free-living women with chronic obstructive pulmonary disease', *Physiol Rep*, 1: e00150.

Feehan, L. M., C. H. Goldsmith, A. Y. F. Leung, and L. C. Li. 2016. 'SenseWearMini and ActiGraph GT3X accelerometer classification of observed sedentary and light-intensity physical activities in a laboratory setting', *Physiother Can*, 68: 116–23.

Ferguson, T., A. V. Rowlands, T. Olds, and C. Maher. 2015. 'The validity of consumer-level, activity monitors in healthy adults worn in free-living conditions: a cross-sectional study', *Int J Behav Nutr Phys Act*, 12: 42.

Freedson, P. S. 1991. 'Electronic motion sensors and heart rate as measures of physical activity in children', *J Sch Health*, 61: 220–3.

Freedson, P. S., K. Brendley, B. E. Ainsworth, H. W. Kohl, 3rd, E. Leslie, and N. Owen. 2008. 'New techniques and issues in assessing walking behavior and its contexts', *Med Sci Sports Exerc*, 40: S574–83.

Freedson, P. S., E. Melanson, and J. Sirard. 1998. 'Calibration of the Computer Science and Applications, Inc. accelerometer', *Med Sci Sports Exerc*, 30: 777–81.

Harrington, D. M., G. J. Welk, and A. E. Donnelly. 2011. 'Validation of MET estimates and step measurement using the activPAL physical activity logger', *J Sports Sci*, 29: 627–33.

Imboden, M. T., M. B. Nelson, L. A. Kaminsky, and A. H. Montoye. 2018. 'Comparison of four Fitbit and Jawbone activity monitors with a research-grade ActiGraph accelerometer for estimating physical activity and energy expenditure', *Br J Sports Med*, 52: 844–50.

Innerd, P., M. Catt, J. Collerton, K. Davies, M. Trenell, T. B. Kirkwood, and C. Jagger. 2015. 'A comparison of subjective and objective measures of physical activity from the Newcastle 85+ Study', *Age Ageing*, 44: 691–4.

LaPorte, R. E., L. H. Kuller, D. J. Kupfer, R. J. McPartland, G. Matthews, and C. Caspersen. 1979. 'An objective measure of physical activity for epidemiologic research', *Am J Epidemiol*, 109: 158–68.

LaPorte, R. E., H. J. Montoye, and C. J. Caspersen. 1985. 'Assessment of physical activity in epidemiologic research: problems and prospects', *Public Health Rep*, 100: 131–46.

Lee, J. M., Y. Kim, and G. J. Welk. 2014. 'Validity of consumer-based physical activity monitors', *Med Sci Sports Exerc*, 46: 1840–8.

MacCurdy, E. 1938. *The Notebooks of Leonardo Da Vinci*, New York: Reynal & Hitchcock.

Macera, C. A., S. A. Ham, M. M. Yore, D. A. Jones, B. E. Ainsworth, C. D. Kimsey, and H. W. Kohl, 3rd. 2005. 'Prevalence of physical activity in the United States: Behavioral Risk Factor Surveillance System, 2001', *Prev Chronic Dis*, 2: A17.

Mackey, D. C., T. M. Manini, D. A. Schoeller, A. Koster, N. W. Glynn, B. H. Goodpaster, S. Satterfield, A. B. Newman, T. B. Harris, and S. R. Cummings. 2011. 'Validation of an armband to measure daily energy expenditure in older adults', *J Gerontol A Biol Sci Med Sci*, 66: 1108–13.

Melanson, E. L., Jr., and P. S. Freedson. 1995. 'Validity of the Computer Science and Applications, Inc. (CSA) activity monitor', *Med Sci Sports Exerc*, 27: 934–40.

Miller, D. J., P. S. Freedson, and G. M. Kline. 1994. 'Comparison of activity levels using the Caltrac accelerometer and five questionnaires', *Med Sci Sports Exerc*, 26: 376–82.

Montoye, H. J., R. Washburn, S. Servais, A. Ertl, J. G. Webster, and F. J. Nagle. 1983. 'Estimation of energy expenditure by a portable accelerometer', *Med Sci Sports Exerc*, 15: 403–7.

Papazoglou, D., G. Augello, M. Tagliaferri, G. Savia, P. Marzullo, E. Maltezos, and A. Liuzzi. 2006. 'Evaluation of a multisensor armband in estimating energy expenditure in obese individuals', *Obesity (Silver Spring)*, 14: 2217–23.

Plasqui, G., and K. R. Westerterp. 2005. 'Accelerometry and heart rate as a measure of physical fitness: proof of concept', *Med Sci Sports Exerc*, 37: 872–6.

Plasqui, G., A. M. Joosen, A. D. Kester, A. H. Goris, and K. R. Westerterp. 2005. 'Measuring free-living energy expenditure and physical activity with triaxial accelerometry', *Obes Res*, 13: 1363–9.

Pober, D. M., J. Staudenmayer, C. Raphael, and P. S. Freedson. 2006. 'Development of novel techniques to classify physical activity mode using accelerometers', *Med Sci Sports Exerc*, 38: 1626–34.

Richardson, M. T., A. S. Leon, D. R. Jacobs, Jr., B. E. Ainsworth, and R. Serfass. 1995. 'Ability of the Caltrac accelerometer to assess daily physical activity levels', *J Cardiopulm Rehabil*, 15: 107–13.

Sherman, W. M., D. M. Morris, T. E. Kirby, R. A. Petosa, B. A. Smith, D. J. Frid, and N. Leenders. 1998. 'Evaluation of a commercial accelerometer (Tritrac-R3 D) to measure energy expenditure during ambulation', *Int J Sports Med*, 19: 43–7.

Staudenmayer, J., D. Pober, S. Crouter, D. Bassett, and P. Freedson. 2009. 'An artificial neural network to estimate physical activity energy expenditure and identify physical activity type from an accelerometer', *J Appl Physiol*, 107: 1300–7.

Troiano, R. P., D. Berrigan, K. W. Dodd, L. C. Masse, T. Tilert, and M. McDowell. 2008. 'Physical activity in the United States measured by accelerometer', *Med Sci Sports Exerc*, 40: 181–8.

Tudor-Locke, C., and D. R. Bassett, Jr. 2004. 'How many steps/day are enough? Preliminary pedometer indices for public health', *Sports Med*, 34: 1–8.

Tudor-Locke, C., S. B. Sisson, S. M. Lee, C. L. Craig, R. C. Plotnikoff, and A. Bauman. 2006. 'Evaluation of quality of commercial pedometers', *Can J Public Health*, 97 Suppl 1: S10–15, S10–16.

Turner-McGrievy, G., D. E. Jake-Schoffman, C. Singletary, M. Wright, A. Crimarco, M. D. Wirth, N. Shivappa, T. Mandes, D. S. West, S. Wilcox, C. Drenowatz, A. Hester, and M. J. McGrievy. 2019. 'Using commercial physical activity trackers for health promotion research: four case studies', *Health Promot Pract*, 20: 381–9.

Zhang, S., A. V. Rowlands, P. Murray, and T. L. Hurst. 2012. 'Physical activity classification using the GENEA wrist-worn accelerometer', *Med Sci Sports Exerc*, 44: 742–8.

PART III

Optimal measurement of physical activity across the lifecourse

7

THE TECHNOLOGY OF ACCELEROMETRY

The modern accelerometer used in large-scale assessment of physical activity is a small, light-weight device. The technology used in modern accelerometers has evolved considerably since accelerometers were first used in physical activity epidemiology. It is important to understand this technology, namely the internal hardware, data processing methods and analytical methods. However, this can be challenging, since there is large variation across different devices and the analytical methods compatible with each one.

Devices typically feature a triaxial MEMS accelerometer sensor which produces raw data in g on three axes. This data is rich in information about movement intensity and type, and often complex analysis must be undertaken to extract the desired variables. The first step is to convert the data into a chosen metric. The metric of choice was, at first, the activity count. However, the use of activity count is criticised since it is not a standardised SI unit of measurement. Analytical methods compatible with raw accelerometer data are free of charge and include cut-points (MVPA), machine learning (activity type) and posture change using arm angle elevation (sedentary behaviour and sleep). When using the raw data, care must be taken to process and analyse it using appropriate techniques. The choice of technique is best made with a good understanding of the technology of accelerometry.

This chapter will:

- Examine the internal hardware of the devices and clarify the way in which accelerometer-based sensors work to produce raw signal, offering data greater in size and detail than ever before.
- Provide a clear outline of precisely what activity counts are and how they are calculated, and clarify the concerns created by the use of non-standardised, proprietary units of output.

- Outline the correct steps for an user looking to summarise the raw data, for example to apply cut-points or signpost the available metrics available for use with raw acceleration data.
- Examine how the measures that feature in studies are best obtained through the use of certain analytical techniques: user-friendly regression equations and cut-points (MVPA), machine learning techniques to exploit the full raw signal to carry out pattern recognition, and arm angle algorithms to obtain measurements of sedentary behaviour and sleep.

Specific measures of physical activity can be obtained using different approaches. Here we explore the internal hardware, data processing techniques and analytical methods involved in accelerometer-based activity monitoring.

Hardware

Strictly speaking, an accelerometer is a sensor which records the magnitude of acceleration. Modern accelerometers are triaxial, measuring acceleration along three axes. Thus, the sensor can detect both acceleration and orientation of the device or instrument. Accelerometers measure gravitational acceleration, expressed in g (1 g = 9.8 m/s^2). Gravitational acceleration, which also goes by the more familiar names of 'g-force' or 'g-units', expresses acceleration due to Earth's gravity. For example, an accelerometer worn whilst standing still (on the Earth's surface) will register a g-force of 1 g.

Sensors

The sensor is housed inside a hermetically sealed (airtight) device casing and attached to a printed circuit board (PCB). The PCB mechanically supports and electrically connects components generally soldered onto the PCB to both electrically connect and mechanically fasten them to it.

The accelerometer sensor converts physical movement (acceleration) of the body into a signal of variable output (voltage). Signal variables are transmitted and manipulated in an electrical circuit, expressed as a digital signal (acceleration). The aim of accelerometer-based measurement is to generate an output which is proportional to acceleration of the body part to which the device itself is attached.

Sensors detect acceleration and orientation of the device and typically convert the input into a readable voltage. Modern accelerometer sensors are typically micromachined microelectromechanical systems (MEMS), whereas earlier accelerometer sensors, such as that housed in the ActiGraph GT1M, feature parts, albeit very small, which do move and affect the measurement over time. To interpret data collected using these devices, you need to understand how they work.

'Piezo' comes from the Greek word *piezein*, which means 'squeeze' or 'apply some pressure'. Piezoelectric components convert mechanical energy to electrical energy. Whether they take the form of a transducer or sensor, piezo components all operate as the result of some degree of physical pressure placed upon them. Most piezo devices are piezoelectric or piezoresistive, and each has its appropriate applications.

Piezoelectric sensors rely on the piezoelectric effect to measure acceleration (Figure 7.1). Piezoelectric sensors are electromechanical components exhibiting near zero deflection and are responsive to high frequencies. Piezoresistive sensors are slightly more complex in their design, featuring thin resistors and single-crystal silicon.

Transducers

Transducers convert energy from one form to another. Piezoelectric transducers convert mechanical energy such as pressure and vibration to electrical energy like voltage or current.

When pressure is applied to a piezoresistor, depending on the material, its resistance increases.

The ActiGraph AM7164, which features a piezoelectric sensor, was used in the NHANES 2002–2003 data sweep. Shortly, afterward ActiGraph replaced the ActiGraph AM7164 with the ActiGraph GT1M. Inside the GT1M is an ADXL320 capacitative accelerometer (Analog Devices, Norwood, MA) which detects change in capacitance of the sensing element, causing specific voltage changes to the existing electric flow. The capacitative sensor detects both static and dynamic acceleration, whereas the piezoelectric sensor found in the AM7164 detects only dynamic acceleration (John and Freedson 2012). An analogue-to-digital converter and phase-demodulation techniques amplify, digitise (at a sampling rate of 30 Hz) and full-wave rectify the signal (Rothney et al. 2008). This determines the directions (vertical, anteroposterior and mediolateral axes) of acceleration. Finally, the signal is filtered at a bandwidth of 0.25–2.5 Hz, trimming unwanted frequencies in the signal before it is converted into activity counts for storage on the device.

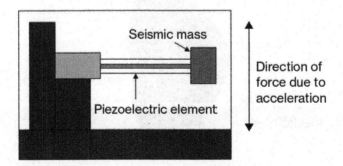

FIGURE 7.1 Schematic of the piezoelectric accelerometer sensor. Accelerational forces bend the seismic mass, and a voltage output is generated.

Micromachined microelectromechanical systems

By 2008, accelerometer-based activity monitors were fitted with micromachined accelerometer sensors featuring MEMS technology. MEMS are made of nanotechnology (near microscopic-sized elements) components between 1 and 100 micrometres in size. They are 'solid state', featuring no mechanical parts, so there is little the researcher needs to understand about how they work. These sensors consist of a polysilicon surface-micromachined structure built on top of a silicon wafer. Wrist-worn raw accelerometers such as the GENEA, GENEActiv and ActiGraph GT3X feature MEMS accelerometers: specifically, the ADXL335 accelerometer, a triaxial capacitive MEMS with a full-scale range of ±3 *g* is housed in the ActiGraph GT3X and ADXL345 with ±8 *g* housed in the GENEActiv (Figure 7.2). The ActiGraph GT3X provides access to the raw, unprocessed acceleration data. To accommodate the storage needs resulting from the collection of high-resolution raw acceleration data, the ActiGraph GT3X+ features greater storage capacity and a wider sampling rate (10–100 Hz) (Troiano et al. 2014).

Modern acceleration sensors generally consist of the sensor (centre black square) mounted on a circuit board with power supply (battery), as seen in Figure 7.3.

MEMS accelerometers can measure acceleration ranging from −8 *g* to 8 *g* at a user-defined frequency, typically of 10–100 Hz. These accelerometers can record continuously for days, weeks and even months due to the low power draw of the sensor. Acceleration data recorded and stored on the device, when downloaded, consists of a stream of discrete, digital values of acceleration across three axes.

A measured acceleration signal consists of three parts: a gravitational component, a movement component and noise (Veltink et al. 1996). Once uploaded and stored, data processing is carried out to eliminate the gravity component from the signal.

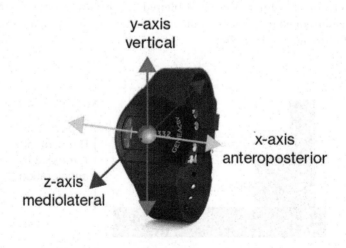

FIGURE 7.2 Axes of acceleration of MEMs triaxial sensors.

FIGURE 7.3   The internal hardware of a wrist-worn triaxial accelerometer.

Raw accelerometers which simply store the acceleration signal are smaller and less obtrusive as they do not contain the onboard processors needed to condense the signal into activity counts.

Understanding how the internal hardware of an accelerometer works is essential when using accelerometers to measure physical activity. Accelerometers feature specific sensor type and technical capabilities, compatible with specific analytical methods, as shown in Table 7.1.

Since accelerometers first featured in epidemiology, the internal hardware has improved significantly. The ActiGraph AM7164 featured in the NHANES from 2003 featured a uniaxial sensor which recorded at a maximum of 10 Hz over a range of up to 2 g. Only 5 years later, researchers were using much smaller, cheaper triaxial sensors capable of recording up to 8 g on a much larger scale. These devices, such as the ActiGraph GT3X+ and GENEActiv, feature in the NHANES and UK Biobank studies.

TABLE 7.1   Technical specification of accelerometers suitable for lifecourse epidemiology.

Device name	Manufacturer	Sensor type	Possible sampling frequencies	Dynamic range	Memory	Output	Released	Studies featured
ActiGraph AM7164	ActiGraph LLC, Pensacola, FL US	Piezoelectric uniaxial	10 Hz	0.05–2g	-	Accelerometer counts	1998	NHANES 2003–2004 2005–2006 cycles
ActiGraph GT1M	ActiGraph LLC, Pensacola, FL US	MEMs biaxial	30 Hz	±5g	1 MB	Accelerometer counts	2005	
ActiGraph GT3X+	ActiGraph, Fort Walton Beach, FL, US	MEMs triaxial	30–100 Hz	±8g	4 GB	Accelerometer counts Raw acceleration (g)	2010	NHANES 2011–2012 and 2013–2014 cycles
GENEA (not commercially available)	Unilever Discover, Colworth, UK	MEMs triaxial	10–80 Hz	±6g	0.5 GB	Raw acceleration (g)	2011	Newcastle 85+ study
GENEActiv	Activinsights Ltd., Kimbolton, Cambridgeshire UK	MEMs triaxial	10–100 Hz	±8g	0.5 GB	Raw acceleration (g)	2011	Whitehall II Pelotas Birth Cohort UK Biobank
Axivity AX3	Newcastle University, Open Lab, Newcastle upon Tyne UK	MEMs triaxial	12.5–3200 Hz	±8g	512 Mb flash	Raw acceleration (g)	2012	UK Biobank

Accelerometer data

The purpose of accelerometry is to convert acceleration of the body into a quantifiable, digital signal. The process of converting a real-world signal into a digital signal is called digital signal processing, and is shown in Figure 7.4. Real-world acceleration is, by definition, an analogue signal or continuous time signal, as it occurs continuously in time. Acceleration is sampled at a user-defined frequency (commonly 10–100 Hz) and converted into a digitised signal using an analogue-to-digital converter (ADC). The resulting digital signal, consisting of a stream of discrete digital values of acceleration, can be visualised or further processing carried out using computer software packages such as MATLAB or R.

Modern raw accelerometers giving access to the unprocessed signal in g provide the opportunity to carry out signal processing under full control of the user. The three axes could be combined to give one omnidirectional acceleration signal, then summarised into signal magnitude vector (SMV) minus the value of gravity (g) averaged over 1-second epochs. The resulting data would probably be a series of values roughly between 2 and 200 g, much like standardised transparent versions of activity counts. Raw accelerometer cut-points could easily be applied to these measurements, for example using 100 mg as the cut-off for MVPA (Hildebrand et al. 2014). The use of more complex analyses such as statistical machine learning, and angle of the device for sedentary activities and sleep would involve different processing steps.

However, the first accelerometers used in epidemiology required onboard processors to condense the raw acceleration signal into activity counts – an aggregate

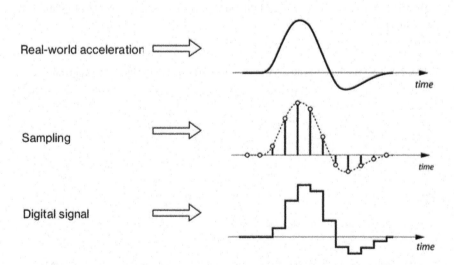

FIGURE 7.4 A digitally sampled signal. Real-world acceleration is sampled by the accelerometer at a user-defined frequency (10–100 Hz). The discrete points in time are used to create a representation of the original signal.

measure of the intensity and magnitude of accelerations over a given time epoch. Note that two commonly used devices, the ActiGraph GT1M and Actical, use proprietary algorithms to calculate activity counts. Count-based accelerometers still feature heavily in the literature. Therefore, it is essential that the user understands what counts are, and anyone attempting to interpret data derived from activity counts needs an understanding of how counts are created.

What are accelerometer counts?

Activity counts or accelerometer counts were ubiquitous and widely accepted in the physical activity literature from the time accelerometers first gained popularity in the late 1990s until around 2009. Where possible, users are advised to avoid the use of counts as accelerometer output. Nevertheless, they feature in hundreds of published studies. Therefore, it is essential to understand what they are.

The confidentiality regarding how accelerometer counts are derived initially led some researchers to assume that counts were identical across devices. However, counts are non-standardised units of measurement. The computational methods used to calculate counts differ across brands of device and different models of the same brand. Therefore, performing a single activity can result in a different number of counts, depending on the device used.

The acceleration signal is summarised into counts using one of three computational methods illustrated in Figure 7.5: the zero-crossing approach, time above threshold or digital integration.

The zero-crossing approach involves the use of a threshold value, often 0 *g* (bearing in mind *g* can be positive or negative) or a significant threshold that represents movement. A digital counter measures the number of times the signal crosses that threshold in a given epoch, and from that value creates an activity count value. Zero-crossing methods have been criticised as they favour high-frequency components of the signal, whereas most normal human movement is restricted to lower frequencies, especially during low-intensity activity, sedentary behaviour and sleep.

The time above threshold approach involves the use of a threshold value (often 0.1–0.2 *g*) and the duration of time that the acceleration signal exceeds that value within that epoch is then logged by the device and the count reset to zero for the next epoch. The main limitation of this approach is that it does not accurately reflect the magnitude of acceleration, and the muscle force required to carry that out.

Digital integration involves sampling the acceleration signal using analogue-to-digital conversion, then calculating the area under the curve for each epoch. Comparisons of all three methods show that the integration approach is more accurate in identifying movement, therefore this method is more commonly used.

Before the integration algorithm, the steps of the digital signal processing normally include converting the negative values into positive ones (full-wave rectification) or taking only the positive side (half-wave rectification). This is to ensure that the integration does not include both positive and negative counts. The digital integration

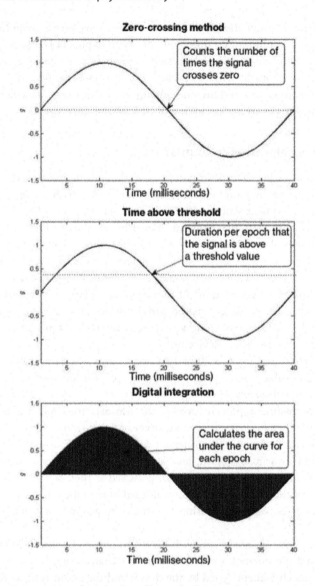

FIGURE 7.5 Computational methods used to calculate accelerometer counts. The methods used to derive counts are typically a zero-crossing approach, time above threshold or digital integration. The precise computational methods employed by accelerometer processors are proprietary, therefore researchers cannot be sure which method is used.

algorithm then sums the rectified values within a given time window or epoch (normally 1 minute). This provides the counts, typically expressed as counts/minute.

The advantages of using the integrated signals include simplicity for general understanding, and ease of processing for both hardware and software needs.

However, this comes at a cost. First, the integration process diminishes the details of the signals within each time window. Second, although the common duration for a time window is 1 minute, this varies across devices, which can affect the interpretation of data.

Choosing a short epoch yields higher resolution of bout durations, which is useful if physical activity is accumulated in multiple short bouts, such as in children. Conversely, a disadvantage of short epochs is that the PAEE associated with 10–30-second epochs has little physiological value. Choosing a longer epoch has the normal data-smoothing advantage of time averaging. However, if the long epoch contains a mixture of two activities of different intensity, then the data will be averaged to reflect an intermediate intensity. If a bout of higher-intensity activity within a particular epoch is markedly shorter than the width of the epoch, the averaged count for the epoch will be lower than the actual activity intensity. This can lead to misclassifying higher-intensity activity (which confers the greatest health benefits) that are more intermittent into moderate or light categories. Thus, there is a trade-off between choosing shorter versus longer epochs. For most applications, the use of 1-minute epochs is suggested as a reasonable compromise.

Raw acceleration data

The output from accelerometers is expressed in units of gravitational acceleration or g, where $1\ g = 9.8\ \mathrm{m.s^{-2}}$. Gravitational units, or g-units, are part of the SI system developed to provide a standardised, universally recognised system of unit measurements. More and more studies opt to use the raw acceleration signal in g, particularly those using modern accelerometer technology which can exploit the high-resolution raw data.

There are practical advantages associated with raw accelerometry in addition to technological ones. Firstly, the individual devices are less costly than count-based accelerometers. As devices are discontinued or used less often, component parts become more expensive and harder to find. Also, many of the onboard components needed to convert the raw signal into counts are not needed. Second, raw accelerometers are designed to be worn on the wrist. Placement of the device on the wrist instead of the waist or hip increases compliance and reduces participant burden.

Recall that the process of measurement should involve (i) careful consideration of what is being measured, (ii) an understanding of how the measurement method works and (iii) the use of a standardised unit of measurement. Therefore, researchers are increasingly using devices which give access to the raw accelerometer data. Raw accelerometers are different from count-based accelerometers as the acceleration signal is not converted into counts using on-board processors. Instead, users can access the raw acceleration signal expressed in gravitational units (g).

Raw accelerometers can be initialised to record at high frequencies, well above 10 Hz, for long periods of time, if necessary 1 or 2 months. Since g is relative to gravity, raw acceleration data reflects acceleration during both dynamic and static conditions, and as most accelerometers are now triaxial, the signal can be processed to reflect sensor orientation, from which we can infer static body posture and changes in body posture. Figure 7.6 shows raw accelerometer data plotted during four different circumstances: with the device removed from the wrist, when sitting, when walking and while running.

Device sensors are capable of sampling at very high frequencies. This results in large amounts of data. For example, a device set to record at 80 Hz takes one observation 80 times per second. Therefore, a week of data would consist of roughly $80 \times 60 \times 60 \times 24 \times 7 = 48,384,000$ for each of the three axes. Thus, most studies would feature billions of data points. Thus, the size and complexity of raw accelerometer data generates a number of potential consequences at each step of further investigation. Nonetheless, such size and complexity could provide previously unobtainable information on the physical condition of individuals. It seems counterintuitive to summarise the raw data, as it seems that vital new information is being lost. Yet several open-source metrics have been developed to summarise accelerometer data. Conversely, analysis of the non-summarised data reveals the problems caused by high heterogeneity of data, both within and between subjects: within-subject due to simple factors such as changes in stride length (Urbanek et al.

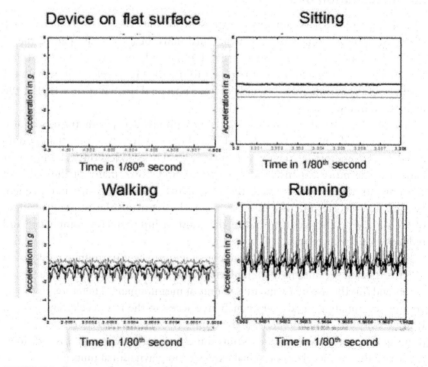

FIGURE 7.6 Raw accelerometer data in mg. Output from a wrist-worn accelerometer during four different activities: device flat on surface (typical during non-wear time), sitting, walking and running.

2015) and between-subject due to differences in body size, physical ability and mental will to perform the task. Analytical methods which do not summarise the data focus on activity type recognition. However, their use requires knowledge of machine learning algorithms.

Accelerometer metrics

The methodological transparency created by the use of raw accelerometry creates an ideal opportunity for the development of metrics: standardised procedures to obtain measurements relating to physical activity. Some of these are relatively simple ways to combine three-axis, sub-second data to generate a single omnidirectional measure of acceleration by taking the vector magnitude from the three axes and then the value of gravity (g) as in $\sqrt{x2 + y2 + z2} - 1$. The generation of summary units of acceleration in g could theoretically be described an improved activity count, since no proprietary steps are involved and instead transparent, standardised steps are performed so that other users can replicate each step.

Method developers consistently strive to extract the most from raw signals. Some of the first metrics to be published include the rigorously developed ENMO (van Hees et al. 2013), Activity Intensity (Bai et al. 2014), the refined version named Activity Index (Bai et al. 2016) and Mean Amplitude Deviation (MAD) (Bakrania et al. 2016). Each metric provides similar output in mg. Slight differences in metric performance claimed by the authors are discussed in Chapter 8. The output from data processing acts as the input for data analysis. Depending on what measures are of interest, a range of different analytical techniques are freely available for use.

A plethora of physical activity related outcomes can be derived from a single acceleration signal. The analytical methods used to obtain these measures are varied. However, the outcomes necessary to provide robust assessments of lifelong physical activity are well defined. Measurements relating to activity intensity are obtainable, namely light-intensity physical activity and MVPA can be obtained using cut-point techniques or more advanced machine learning techniques. The use of signal features and a pattern recognition approach fully exploit the high-resolution, high-volume data obtained from current devices. Consequently, an increasing number of large-scale studies are using machine learning techniques to classify activity types, such as sitting, walking and household activities, as well as the detection of sleep. Finally, activities involving a near total lack of movement, namely sedentary behaviour and sleep, can detected using arm angle elevation from the orientation of the device.

Data analysis

Regression equations

The first analytical methods developed for the early ActiGraph models were typically based on linear regressions to predict energy expenditure from accelerometer counts (Vanhelst et al. 2011). Development of prediction equations is done using a laboratory-based protocol of selected activities carried out with the participant VO_2 under continuous measurement. Early analyses published using raw accelerometers used the same algorithmic approach. Prediction equations were used to estimate PAEE using the raw acceleration signal (van Hees et al. 2011). However, the classification of activity intensity such as MVPA was preferred by method developers using raw accelerometry.

Physical activity intensity: the cut-point approach

By the end of the 2005–2006 NHANES data sweep, over 15 regression equations were available to estimate activity intensity from activity counts from the ActiGraph. The available cut-points for MVPA ranged from 574 to 3250 counts/minute, and cut-points for sedentary time, ranged from 50 to 500 counts/minute. In fact, the inconsistent use of cut-points could well result in MVPA ranging from 4 to 80 minutes/day and sedentary time ranged from 7 hours 55 minutes to 11 hours 5 minutes, or 62–86% of the day spent sedentary (Gorman et al. 2014).

The development of raw accelerometer cut-points was done with more methodological rigour. When the wrist-worn GENEA was introduced, authors published cut-points for use with raw acceleration data (Esliger et al. 2011), identifying sedentary (<1.5 METs) light (<3 METs), moderate (3–6 METs) and vigorous (>6 METs) physical activity in adults. Soon after, activity intensity cut-points were made available for children (Rowlands et al. 2014) and older adults (Innerd and University of Newcastle upon Tyne Institute for Ageing 2015). However, some studies using raw accelerometers have employed MVPA cut-points typically at 100 mg (da Silva et al. 2014), whilst large-scale studies such as the UK Biobank (Doherty et al. 2017) and Whitehall II (Sabia et al. 2015) reported only summary measures of physical activity in mg.

Although raw acceleration data provides necessary transparency, much more than estimates of activity intensity can be derived from the detailed, high-frequency signal. Raw data provides the potential to derive a rich suite of physical activity measures. In the Newcastle 85+ Study, we obtained measures of daily sedentary time, low-intensity physical activity and activity type classified as sedentary, activities of daily living and walking via simple reanalysis of the stored data (Innerd et al. 2015). The classification of sitting and walking was carried out using an activity type classifier (Zhang et al. 2012).

Activity type classification does not involve summary measures applied to the raw data. Therefore, it makes better use of the granularity of sub-second-level data and may contain important additional information. Machine learning techniques use signal features and signature patterns in the data to produce improved estimates of energy expenditure/activity intensity. Activity type classification algorithms have been proposed (Xiao et al. 2016; Bai et al. 2012). This approach to data processing, whilst theoretically valuable, requires specialist knowledge of machine learning algorithms. Nevertheless, the machine learning approach is one of the fastest-growing fields in computer science. As data becomes continuously 'bigger', the potential of machine learning applications for pattern recognition and intelligent systems which adapt to changing environments represents the opportunity to bring about significant advances in physical activity assessment.

Activity type classification

Activity type classifiers represent a more complex type of analysis involving machine learning algorithms designed to perform pattern recognition. Machine learning algorithms were developed to analyse continuous streams of large and complex data. Classification algorithms carry out unsupervised learning, where the algorithms find patterns in the data and group them into categories, in this case to identify activity type.

A pattern recognition machine does not work directly on the raw sensor data, but rather a data representation of it is built from feature variables or 'features' obtained from the raw signal which act as summaries of the data. Feature variables from the raw sensor data are selected from a sliding window, with a finite and constant width, typically called a data frame. A data frame might be 12.8 seconds in length. Frequency domain features represent the number of times an event occurs, and time domain features refer to variation of amplitude of the signal over time. The aim is to achieve the best reconstruction of the data or the most efficient method for making predictions: the optimum combination of features is generated, then performance of the model is assessed using various machine learning algorithms.

Windowing techniques

Most activity classification methods use windowing techniques to divide the sensor signal into smaller time segments (windows). Activity classification algorithms are then applied separately to each window. In real-time applications, windows are defined concurrently with data collection and a continuous real-time activity profile is produced. When the sensor data are processed off-line, the windows are defined first and classification algorithms applied sequentially to each window. This information is then combined to give an activity profile along the entire signal. The sliding window approach does not require pre-processing of the sensor signal, and is therefore ideally suited to real-time applications. Due to its implementational simplicity, most activity classification studies have employed this approach.

Feature generation

Time domain features are derived directly from a window of sensor data and are typically statistical measures. In order to derive frequency domain features, the window of sensor data must first be transformed into the frequency domain, normally using a fast Fourier transform (FFT). The output of a FFT typically gives a set of basis coefficients which represent the amplitudes of the frequency components of the signal and the distribution of the signal energy. Features in the time domain include mean, variance, covariance, minimum, maximum, mean and variance of monitor orientation, and the 10th, 25th, 50th, 75th and 90th percentiles of the acceleration signal are calculated separately for x-, y- and z-axes.

Classification schemes

Once features have been derived to characterise a window of sensor data, they are used as input to a classification algorithm. The degree of complexity of these different classification schemes varies from simple threshold-based schemes to more advanced algorithms, such as artificial neural networks or hidden Markov models. With these advanced classification algorithms, software learns to recognise and associate patterns in the features with each activity type.

In previous studies various machine learning algorithms have been used, including decision tree, neural network, hidden Markov model and support vector machine, all of which have been well described (Mannini and Sabatini 2010). This approach not only recognises the basic parameters of activities of daily living such as sitting, lying or standing, but can also highlight extended periods of ambulatory behaviour such as performing random chores involved during housework. These algorithms fall into the subfield of computer science known as machine learning (whereby correct algorithmic decisions are reinforced and incorrect ones discarded), and have their roots in artificial intelligence. Figure 7.7 shows a hierarchical classification scheme.

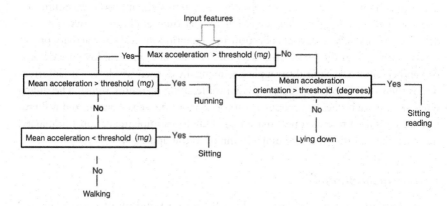

FIGURE 7.7   Hierarchical classification scheme. A binary decision structure is created which consists of a number of consecutive nodes; at each node, a binary decision is made depending on the input features.

Posture detection

Activities featuring low levels of movement produce correspondingly low-magnitude acceleration signals. This is perhaps problematic for analytical methods using accelerometer cut-points or feature extraction. However, classification systems using arm angle elevations are used to detect two behaviours with significant effects on health. Sedentary activities – sitting, lying watching TV – are important to detect. Furthermore, sedentary activity must be differentiated from sleep, since adequate sleep is critical for health.

The classification of posture from raw acceleration data obtained from the wrist involves the simple premise that elevations greater than 15° below horizontal indicate elevation of the wrist. If acceleration is low – below the cut-point for moderate intensity – the activity is coded as sitting or reclining. Arm angle elevations greater than 15° below horizontal indicate the arm is positioned vertically by the side, and the activity is coded as standing. Moderate to vigorous acceleration signals also code as standing active behaviours. Rowland and colleagues describe an analytical method called the Sedentary Sphere, which is similar to this (Rowlands et al. 2016).

Sleep has also been assessed using wrist-worn accelerometer data. Arm angle averaged per 5-second time window has been used as input for a sleep detection algorithm. Since sleep is highly variable and can occur throughout the day, especially later in the lifecourse during old age, algorithm development involves heuristic decisions to avoid overfitting to a particular study sample. Heuristics underlie the whole field of artificial intelligence and the computer simulation of thinking, as they may be used in situations where there are no known algorithms. A comprehensive description of this analytical method is given by van Hees and colleagues (van Hees et al. 2015; van Hees et al. 2018). Arm angle was estimated using the equation:

$$angle = \left(tan^{-1} \frac{a_z}{a_{x^2} + a_{y^2}} \right)$$

where a_x, a_y and a_z are the median values of the three orthogonally positioned raw acceleration sensors in gravitational (g) units derived based on a rolling 5-second time window.

The posture-based accelerometer analyses described above are freely available. An open-source approach to algorithm development increases innovation and facilitates collaboration between researchers.

Summary

This chapter uncovered essential knowledge about accelerometer hardware, data processing techniques and data analysis methods. The only task left for the user is to implement this knowledge to carry out the measurement of physical activity using accelerometry.

The key points of Chapter 7 are:

- Accelerometer hardware includes a sensor which converts analogue acceleration into a digitally sampled signal.
- Where possible, users opt to use the raw acceleration data expressed in g and avoid the use of accelerometer counts. The computational methods used to calculate counts differ across brands of device and different models of the same brand. Acceleration expressed in g is a standardised, universally recognised unit of measurement.
- Several data processing techniques are available, with metrics published specifically for use with raw accelerometers.
- The use of raw accelerometers gives great analytical freedom. Data analysis such as cut-points, machine learning and posture detection can generate measures relating to physical activity, sedentary behaviour and sleep.

References

Bai, J., C. Di, L. Xiao, K. R. Evenson, A. Z. LaCroix, C. M. Crainiceanu, and D. M. Buchner. 2016. 'An activity index for raw accelerometry data and its comparison with other activity metrics', *PLOS ONE*, 11: e0160644.

Bai, J., J. Goldsmith, B. Caffo, T. A. Glass, and C. M. Crainiceanu. 2012. 'Movelets: a dictionary of movement', *Electron J Stat*, 6: 559–78.

Bai, J., B. He, H. Shou, V. Zipunnikov, T. A. Glass, and C. M. Crainiceanu. 2014. 'Normalization and extraction of interpretable metrics from raw accelerometry data', *Biostatistics*, 15: 102–16.

Bakrania, K., T. Yates, A. V. Rowlands, D. W. Esliger, S. Bunnewell, J. Sanders, M. Davies, K. Khunti, and C. L. Edwardson. 2016. 'Intensity thresholds on raw acceleration data: Euclidean Norm Minus One (ENMO) and Mean Amplitude Deviation (MAD) approaches', *PLOS ONE*, 11: e0164045.

da Silva, I. C., V. T. van Hees, V. V. Ramires, A. G. Knuth, R. M. Bielemann, U. Ekelund, S. Brage, and P. C. Hallal. 2014. 'Physical activity levels in three Brazilian birth cohorts as assessed with raw triaxial wrist accelerometry', *Int J Epidemiol*, 43: 1959–68.

Doherty, A., D. Jackson, N. Hammerla, T. Plotz, P. Olivier, M. H. Granat, T. White, V. T. van Hees, M. I. Trenell, C. G. Owen, S. J. Preece, R. Gillions, S. Sheard, T. Peakman, S. Brage, and N. J. Wareham. 2017. 'Large scale population assessment of physical activity using wrist worn accelerometers: the UK Biobank Study', *PLOS ONE*, 12: e0169649.

Esliger, D. W., A. V. Rowlands, T. L. Hurst, M. Catt, P. Murray, and R. G. Eston. 2011. 'Validation of the GENEA Accelerometer', *Med Sci Sports Exerc*, 43: 1085–93.

Gorman, E., H. M. Hanson, P. H. Yang, K. M. Khan, T. Liu-Ambrose, and M. C. Ashe. 2014. 'Accelerometry analysis of physical activity and sedentary behavior in older adults: a systematic review and data analysis', *Eur Rev Aging Phys Act*, 11: 35–49.

Hildebrand, M., V. T. van Hees, B. H. Hansen, and U. Ekelund. 2014. 'Age group comparability of raw accelerometer output from wrist- and hip-worn monitors', *Med Sci Sports Exerc*, 46: 1816–24.

Innerd, P., and University of Newcastle upon Tyne Institute for Ageing. 2015. *Assessment of Physical Activity and Sleep Using Raw Accelerometry*, Newcastle upon Tyne, UK: Newcastle University.

Innerd, P., M. Catt, J. Collerton, K. Davies, M. Trenell, T. B. Kirkwood, and C. Jagger. 2015. 'A comparison of subjective and objective measures of physical activity from the Newcastle 85+ Study', *Age Ageing*, 44: 691–4.

John, D., and P. Freedson. 2012. 'ActiGraph and Actical physical activity monitors: a peek under the hood', *Med Sci Sports Exerc*, 44: S86–9.

Mannini, A., and A. M. Sabatini. 2010. 'Machine learning methods for classifying human physical activity from on-body accelerometers', *Sensors (Basel)*, 10: 1154–75.

Rothney, M. P., G. A. Apker, Y. Song, and K. Y. Chen. 2008. 'Comparing the performance of three generations of ActiGraph accelerometers', *J Appl Physiol*, 105: 1091–7.

Rowlands, A. V., K. Rennie, R. Kozarski, R. M. Stanley, R. G. Eston, G. C. Parfitt, and T. S. Olds. 2014. 'Children's physical activity assessed with wrist- and hip-worn accelerometers', *Med Sci Sports Exerc*, 46: 2308–16.

Rowlands, A. V., T. Yates, T. S. Olds, M. Davies, K. Khunti, and C. L. Edwardson. 2016. 'Sedentary sphere: wrist-worn accelerometer-brand independent posture classification', *Med Sci Sports Exerc*, 48: 748–54.

Sabia, S., P. Cogranne, V. T. van Hees, J. A. Bell, A. Elbaz, M. Kivimaki, and A. Singh-Manoux. 2015. 'Physical activity and adiposity markers at older ages: accelerometer vs questionnaire data', *J Am Med Dir Assoc*, 16: 438.e7–13.

Troiano, R. P., J. J. McClain, R. J. Brychta, and K. Y. Chen. 2014. 'Evolution of accelerometer methods for physical activity research', *Br J Sports Med*, 48: 1019–23.

Urbanek, J. K., V. Zipunnikov, W. Fadel, N. Glynn, A. Koster, P. Caserotti, C. Crainiceanu, and J. Harezlak. 2015. 'Prediction of sustained harmonic walking in the free-living environment using raw accelerometry data'. Accessed 10 April 2019. https://arxiv.org/abs/1505.04066.

van Hees, V. T., L. Gorzelniak, E. C. Dean Leon, M. Eder, M. Pias, S. Taherian, U. Ekelund, F. Renstrom, P. W. Franks, A. Horsch, and S. Brage. 2013. 'Separating movement and gravity components in an acceleration signal and implications for the assessment of human daily physical activity', *PLOS ONE*, 8: e61691.

van Hees, V. T., F. Renstrom, A. Wright, A. Gradmark, M. Catt, K. Y. Chen, M. Lof, L. Bluck, J. Pomeroy, N. J. Wareham, U. Ekelund, S. Brage, and P. W. Franks. 2011. 'Estimation of daily energy expenditure in pregnant and non-pregnant women using a wrist-worn tri-axial accelerometer', *PLOS ONE*, 6: e22922.

van Hees, V. T., S. Sabia, K. N. Anderson, S. J. Denton, J. Oliver, M. Catt, J. G. Abell, M. Kivimäki, M. I. Trenell, and A. Singh-Manoux. 2015. 'A novel, open access method to assess sleep duration using a wrist-worn accelerometer', *PLOS ONE*, 10: e0142533.

van Hees, V. T., S. Sabia, S. E. Jones, A. R. Wood, K. N. Anderson, M. Kivimaki, T. M. Frayling, A. I. Pack, M. Bucan, M. I. Trenell, D. R. Mazzotti, P. R. Gehrman, B. A. Singh-Manoux, and M. N. Weedon. 2018. 'Estimating sleep parameters using an accelerometer without sleep diary', *Sci Rep*, 8: 12,975.

Vanhelst, J., L. Beghin, D. Turck, and F. Gottrand. 2011. 'New validated thresholds for various intensities of physical activity in adolescents using the ActiGraph accelerometer', *Int J Rehabil Res*, 34: 175–7.

Veltink, P. H., H. B. Bussmann, W. de Vries, W. L. Martens, and R. C. van Lummel. 1996. 'Detection of static and dynamic activities using uniaxial accelerometers', *IEEE Trans Rehabil Eng*, 4: 375–85.

Xiao, L., B. He, A. Koster, P. Caserotti, B. Lange-Maia, N. W. Glynn, T. B. Harris, and C. M. Crainiceanu. 2016. 'Movement prediction using accelerometers in a human population', *Biometrics*, 72: 513–24.

Zhang, S., A. V. Rowlands, P. Murray, and T. L. Hurst. 2012. 'Physical activity classification using the GENEA wrist-worn accelerometer', *Med Sci Sports Exerc*, 44: 742–8.

8

ASSESSING PHYSICAL ACTIVITY USING A SINGLE ACCELEROMETER

Raw accelerometry provides greater transparency and methodological freedom. Whilst this is good for innovation, efforts must be made to maintain a standardised approach where necessary. The first choice the user faces is to choose the right device. Then, a location for device placement must be selected. Expert consensus promotes placement at the wrist. While initialising the device, you will be asked to select the sampling frequency. The effect of sampling frequency varies according to what you plan to do with the data when it is stored.

After data collection, the device should be connected to a PC and the data uploaded to a safe and secure approved location. Studies where data exceeds the capacity of traditional hard drive disc storage should make use of cloud servers, discussed later in this chapter. The first stages of signal processing, done on one or more devices, should be carried out carefully to preserve the quality of output.

The choice of metric is somewhat informed by the data analysis, which is directly determined by the desired measurement. Measurements relating to physical intensity can be obtained using uncomplicated methods. However, activities at the lower end of the movement spectrum, such as sedentary activity and sleep, are best dealt with using either machine learning techniques or the angle of the device.

The strengths of raw accelerometry mean that 24-hour movement measurement is increasingly carried out, which requires the utilisation of the complete wake/sleep cycle. Movement guidelines combining physical activity, sedentary behaviour and sleep are set to be published across the globe. Therefore, the final practical guidance this book will give is to assist you in deriving measures of physical activity, sedentary behaviour and sleep from a single acceleration signal.

This chapter will:

- Provide practical guidance on the assessment of physical activity using a single-site accelerometer, starting with device choice, body placement and device initialisation.
- Provide guidance on how to store the data when you receive the device back from data collection, discussing the recommended metrics specifically compatible with raw accelerometer data, and a step-by-step guide to processing and analysing accelerometer data using GGIR, which involves autocalibration of sensor data and is the best way to provide measures of MVPA, sedentary activity and sleep.
- In light of 24-hour movement guidelines appearing across the globe, the combined measurement of physical activity, sedentary behaviour and sleep are essential to create robust activity recommendations throughout a 24-hour cycle.

A wealth of novel measurement opportunities results from current technologies in raw accelerometry. What follows is a guide to data collection, data processing and data analysis. First, we will check the consensus opinions of measurement experts, highlighting best practice.

Best practice

Carrying out the assessment of physical activity using a single-sensor accelerometer requires a number of decisions to be made when designing the study, each of which can affect the quality of evidence eventually produced. The types of questions researchers are faced with focus on which device to use, how long it should be worn, where it should be worn, what to do with the accelerometer data and how to analyse the data to produce meaningful measures of physical activity. The 'best practice' recommendations you will find in the literature gradually change as technology evolves, creating new opportunities.

The recommendations made in recent publications, aimed at maximising the potential of raw accelerometer data, differ markedly from those you will find in earlier papers from around the early 2000s. Guidelines from Dianne Ward and colleagues (Ward et al. 2005) and Charles Matthews (Matthews et al. 2012) help users to make their choice of device, though this is difficult due to the proprietary nature of device specifications at this time, calculating the numbers of devices a study needs and giving tips for improving compliance. However, many of the challenges highlighted in these texts can be avoided through the use of wrist-worn raw accelerometers.

Modern accelerometers offer a great deal of methodological freedom. Thus, a rigid framework for data collection is difficult to provide, and perhaps defeats the object by restricting innovation. It seems a case of striking a healthy balance. Also, the production of a consensus paper should include experts from all necessary disciplines. A 2015 open-access paper (Wijndaele et al. 2015) features consensus points proposed by 16 measurement experts formed using the Delphi method. This process involves all participants remaining anonymous. In this case, participants responded to questions in rounds, refining their responses in the second round. The advantage of the Delphi method is that it prevents influence by authority or personality from others and minimises personal biases such as the 'bandwagon effect' or 'halo effect'. The authors reported that it yielded some useful points.

First, much can be done with the considerable amount of accelerometry data available internationally, collected from >275,000 participants across 36 countries and increasing by the day. The unprocessed accelerometer data can be combined from different studies to make cross-country/cross-population comparisons. The production of raw accelerometer data that is highly comparable between studies relies mainly on the standardisation of monitor calibration, data collection and data processing procedures.

A second recommendation is to ensure optimal wear compliance. The use of wrist-worn devices alone has improved this, with recent studies such as UK Biobank and Whitehall II requiring a minimum wear time of 7 days of valid data, reporting 93% and 96.1% adherence respectively compared to some of the first NHANES studies which reported 68% adherence, which was usually based on ≥10 hours on at least 4 days (Troiano et al. 2008).

Third, accelerometer data does not hold all of the answers. Additional data other than accelerometry data is required. In order of priority, this additional data has been identified as basic sociodemographic data (e.g. age, sex, race/ethnicity, country) and socioeconomic status (i.e. income, education, employment status), anthropometric data (i.e. weight, height, waist circumference) and health status data (i.e. diabetes, cardiovascular disease, cancer). These data are pertinent to a lifecourse approach where we seek to target the determinants of physical activity.

Close scrutiny of the accelerometer literature shows the interesting dynamics of a scientific 'shift' and the reactions from researchers in the field. For example, the GENEA, the first raw accelerometer suitable for use in large-scale studies, was introduced to the scientific community and validated in 2011. Open-source analytical methods were made available for children (Phillips, Parfitt and Rowlands 2013), young and middle-aged adults (Hildebrand et al. 2014) and older adults (Innerd and University of Newcastle upon Tyne Institute for Ageing 2015). Many studies, perhaps inevitably, were already invested in the use of traditional devices, but the investigators in others waited to see evidence that a new measurement method delivered enough advantages to warrant consideration, and some smaller studies opted purely to maintain consistency across timepoints. Alternatively, some studies, such as NHANES, amended their accelerometer protocol around the same time (Troiano et al. 2014).

Methods should not become popular simply as a result of being the first of their kind or because large studies choose, for example, the use of count-based uniaxial waist-worn accelerometers in 15,000 individuals in the early NHANES or the use of raw triaxial wrist-worn accelerometers in >100,000 individuals in the UK Biobank. Consequently, the reader is advised to appraise the accelerometer literature with this in mind and remain sensibly critical when familiar names are linked to device manufacturers, author their validation studies and use those methods in their research.

When designing an accelerometer-based protocol, the researcher will likely interrogate the literature on physical activity measurement. It is pertinent to bear in mind the three key stakeholders in accelerometry: device manufacturers, algorithm developers and measurement method users. Individuals can be part of more than one group. For example, there are device manufacturers who publish algorithms and can also employ them in their research. Although this is not absent from other areas of science, the novice accelerometer user is wise to be aware of this. New trends in accelerometry should evolve naturally through ongoing accumulation of empirical evidence on the feasibility and validity of methods.

The major questions faced when attempting to measure physical activity with an accelerometer-based approach revolve around the following questions: Which device do I use? How long should people wear it for? What is the best placement on the body? How do I set up the device – does sampling frequency make much difference? What do I do with the accelerometer data? How do I get measurements that I can use to assess physical activity?

Choosing a device

Believe it or not, this choice is far simpler than it might once have been. Prior to the introduction of the raw accelerometers, an eyewatering number of activity monitors could be found in the literature, some more popular than others, but all available for purchase. To put this into context, a systematic review from 2011, perhaps unwittingly, highlights the problem. Authors carried out a search of validation studies from 2000 to 2012 featuring adults with or without chronic disease. Forty activity monitors were identified. The devices included 31 accelerometers: 12 uniaxial, 3 biaxial, 16 triaxial and 9 multi-sensor devices (van Remoortel et al. 2012). This ambitious review found that single sensor accelerometers such as the ActiGraph GT3X performed equally well as more complex, expensive devices, many with various biosensors. However, the main observation was the vast range of monitor outputs. Thus, when choosing a device suitable for lifecourse research, economically priced raw accelerometers are recommended.

Several manufacturers produce raw accelerometers: GENEA, Unilever Discover, Ltd, UK, GENEActiv, ActivInsights Ltd, UK, Axivity Ltd, UK, and ActiGraph LLC, USA. Sensor output across all devices is expressed in standardised units of g. Since these sensors are used in large numbers for the purpose of collecting large amounts of data, the main requirement is that the acceleration signal from one device is as accurate as possible and is as identical as possible to that from other devices. Bear in mind that processing applied to the signal after it has been stored from the device can influence any relationship with a given outcome from another device (John et al. 2013). For manufacturers, product development is primarily driven by physical requirements such as small size, long battery life, durability and low manufacturing costs.

Placement

Accelerometer placement in epidemiological research started off at the hip or waist and migrated to the wrist. The wrist is recommended wherever possible as it is more comfortable and encourages the wearing of the device for 24 hours continuously. Epidemiological studies using accelerometers almost exclusively opt to place the monitor at the wrist. However, the wrist and waist are not the only placements of interest. In addition to the wrist and waist, method development studies have compared positioning of the device at the chest, thigh and ankle. Placement makes a difference, as can be seen in Figure 8.1.

Initially, researchers favoured the waist due to its close proximity to the centre of mass. Since the development of the first activity monitor for use in epidemiology (LaPorte et al. 1979), and after the addition of the ActiGraph, worn at the waist, to the NHANES in 2003, other epidemiological studies followed suit. The plethora of prediction equations and cut-points that were published were mostly developed with the monitor worn at the waist (Crouter et al. 2010; Freedson, Pober and Janz 2005; Matthew 2005).

As studies grew larger, the impact of missing data became more prominent. Since traditional accelerometers were not fully waterproof, missing data often

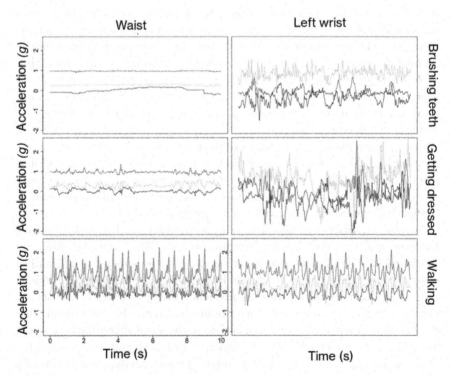

FIGURE 8.1 Acceleration data (*g*) from the waist and left wrist differ during three different activities: brushing teeth, getting dressed and walking.

resulted from the removal of devices for bathing and before bed. Since it was such a major factor, this was noted by investigators of the NHANES. Only about 25% of participants provided the requested 7 days of data, which was mostly attributed to the discomfort or inconvenience of wearing a device on the hip over time, and forgetting to put the monitor back on after taking it off at night.

Positioning at the waist reduces the devices' ability to detect low-intensity movements, particularly in old people whose walking is hard to detect, and sedentary activities. Furthermore, this location misses activities involving the upper torso such as those associated with self-care, which for some populations are important to maintain. Studies showed that the comparability of acceleration signals recorded from different body locations was poor. The waist and hip gave different accelerometer output. Thus, moving placement to the wrist would require the development of a new accelerometry and analytical methods. For example, the correlation between activity counts and PAEE from uniaxial accelerometers was found to be much lower when positioned on the wrist rather than at the hip.

The consensus on monitor placement is to use the wrist. This reduces participant burden and has resulted in the development of analytical methods which extract much more from the data, allowing the move toward 24-hour monitoring.

Sampling frequency

Sampling is a process of converting an analogue signal, in this case movement, into a numeric sequence. Frequency is measured in hertz (Hz), defined as one cycle per second. So an accelerometer recording at 10 Hz samples ten times per second. Early accelerometers were limited in the sampling frequency the user could select, and the maximum was often ~30 Hz. However, modern devices typically sample acceleration at up to 100 Hz. The maximum sampling frequency you can use is often limited by the duration of data collection. Most studies collect data over 7 days, but UK Biobank follows a 9-day protocol to ensure that at least 7 full days have been recorded. Users looking to carry out data collection over 14 days or more may not be able to use higher sampling frequencies such as 80–100 Hz.

Although studies often lack a clearly stated motivation for using a given frequency, researchers often make their choice based on popularity. Sampling frequencies have been used as low as 10 Hz or up to 100 Hz for long-term monitoring.

Firstly, it is worth bearing in mind that the advantage of raw data is that it can be sampled at the sub-second level and give remarkably high levels of detail. If simple analytics will be used, such as applying cut-points to the data, then sampling frequency is less of a concern. But do consider whether your data may be pooled with other data in the future.

A motivation for simply using the highest frequency possible could be to collect as much information as possible. Current machine learning algorithms already benefit from having a rich data signal to which pattern recognition techniques can be applied. Furthermore, the ability of analytical methods to utilise more and more of the signal increases continuously.

The Shannon-Nyquist theorem should be used when selecting sample frequency. This is more relevant for accelerometers which produce activity counts, as the use of different frequencies is reported to affect the outcome measures (Brond and Arvidsson 2016). However, it is less relevant when using raw, unprocessed data. The Shannon-Nyquist theorem states that the sampling frequency should be greater than twice the maximum frequency of the original analogue signal. A full discussion of this theory is outside the scope of this book, but studies which have tested it report it is unlikely to miss any acceleration due to physical activity unless sampling is carried out at <5 Hz (Zhang et al. 2012a)

Storage

After the device has been returned by the participant to the investigator, it should be connected to allow data upload and storage. The larger studies become, the greater the storage needs. Conventionally, researchers have used password-protected networked PCs. Standard procedures for data storage, management and control should be agreed, adhered to and reported in studies. However, this is rarely done.

As storage needs grow, researchers are beginning to move away from traditional physical storage such as a hard disc drive to using cloud-based technology. To support the efforts of studies collecting large data sets, web-based platforms are available for use. Increasingly, these platforms offer enhanced security and control over data governance. The pooling of data is offered by many online platforms.

The International Children's Accelerometry Database (ICAD) (Sherar et al. 2018) combines accelerometer data from several participating studies to give greater insights into exposure–health relationships in children. Other web-based services exist for studies requiring storage space which exceeds the capabilities of an institutional network.

Metrics

Early devices carried out onboard processing, summarising the accelerometer signal and condensing it to produce activity counts. With the wall of secrecy created by proprietary activity counts gone, method developers have produced open-source metrics which process the accelerometer data. For the non-specialist, the technique of data processing can be unfamiliar. Processing techniques are needed to resolve any problems caused by device calibration, missing data and essentially to convert the three axes of data into a format that can be analysed, from which the desired measurement can be derived. Some outcome measures can be obtained using different analytical methods. For example, MVPA can be obtained using a cut-point approach or machine learning techniques. These two approaches, shown in Figure 8.2, represent vastly different approaches to obtaining the same outcome measures. Further, particular analytical methods are only compatible with certain accelerometer outputs.

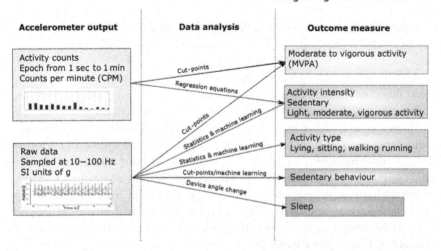

FIGURE 8.2 Common accelerometer output, data analysis and outcome measures.
Accelerometers used in large-scale research produce output in counts or
raw acceleration. Counts are typically analysed using regression equations
and cut-point thresholds. Raw acceleration yields more analytical
possibilities and a wider range of outcome measures.

The raw acceleration signal consists of acceleration not only due to movement,
but also gravity and noise. Method developers have produced metrics which aim
to convert raw signals into something that accurately represents the movement
it recorded. This revolves around several factors: the management of the vast
amount of data generated, the requirement to remove the gravitational and noise
components incorporated within the signals, and the requirement for feasible
mathematical and/or statistical tools to accurately analyse and make valid inter-
pretations from the data.

From the first techniques used to process raw data, successive techniques have
involved gradually evolving methods. However, the transparency of reporting and
justifying each step means it is done in a scientific way, which keeps users informed.

The choice of signal processing technique used to summarise raw accelerometer data can influence the accuracy with which acceleration due to movement is
isolated from the raw acceleration signal. This impacts subsequent analyses when
obtaining measurements such as PAEE or MVPA.

Vincent van Hees's Euclidian norm minus one (ENMO) metric is most easily accessible to researchers unfamiliar with computational analysis. The metric
calculates one set of acceleration data from the three axes then performs an
autocalibration based on environmental gravity recorded by the device, a linear
transformation on the raw data before computing the Euclidean norm, resulting in
ENMO. The metric can be carried out using the open-source program R and is
being used in large-scale studies (Doherty et al. 2017).

Other metrics are available. The Activity Index (Bai et al. 2014) was developed and later refined (Bai et al. 2016), demonstrating improved ability to capture sedentary activity and MVPA. Similarly, the Mean Amplitude Deviation (Bakrania et al. 2016) was used to generate cut-points for hip- and wrist-worn accelerometers, although the authors used the software Stata/IC V13.1 (Stata Corporation, College Station, Texas, USA), which is not accessible free of charge.

However, it is debatable whether attempting to classify activity intensity with ever-increasing accuracy makes the most of raw acceleration data. Modern devices are wrist-worn, to facilitate continuous 24-hour wear, and there is growing recognition of sedentary behaviour and sleep as essential components of the 24-hour movement cycle. Current interest in the combined assessment of physical activity, sedentary activity and sleep has reached high-level proportions (Rosenberger et al. 2019), and guidelines have recently been proposed (Tremblay, Carson and Chaput 2016).

Due to growing concern over the public's 24-hour movement patterns, ENMO, as part of the GGIR package, offers the user the opportunity to derive measurements over the whole 24-hour cycle. It is noteworthy that van Hees's work has been pivotal to the huge progress made in physical activity measurement (van Hees, van Lummel and Westerterp 2009; van Hees et al. 2011), thus these innovations are in line with the original aims of those researchers who envisaged and developed physical activity assessment using raw accelerometry.

Analysis

A range of analytical methods are available, which were reviewed in Chapter 7. The most common measures pertaining to activity intensity, such as MVPA, are obtainable using a cut-point approach. Cut-points for MVPA can be found as part of GGIR and are easily changeable, for example, if working with an older population with reduced physical function. The choice of cut-point should be chosen from well-designed validation studies which use the population of interest. MVPA is typically derived from mg, for example >100 mg used in the Pelotas Birth Cohort (da Silva et al. 2018). Some studies have not opted to apply cut-points, but rather report mean physical activity in mg. For example, a UK Biobank study (n = 103,712) reported this in the 45–54 years age group as 31.17 ±9.10 mg, but it reduced to 22.9 ±6.8 mg in adults aged 75–79 years (p < 0.001) (Doherty et al. 2017).

The first study to report objective measures of physical activity in adults aged over 85 years, the so called 85+, derived several measures of 24-hour movement via reanalysis of the same accelerometer data (Innerd et al. 2015). Using the GENEA accelerometer, the authors used simple algorithms, namely activity intensity cut-points, to measure light, moderate and vigorous activity (Esliger et al. 2011), and an early pattern recognition algorithm to detect lying, sitting and walking (Zhang et al. 2012b) and sleep (Anderson et al. 2014).

For users looking to measure sedentary behaviour, the cut-point approach is unlikely to prove effective. Traditional accelerometers were widely known to detect low-level movement poorly, mainly due to the loss of information from condensing the data into activity counts. However, several large-scale studies have used sedentary cut-points on raw accelerometer data (Gabriel et al. 2018; Jefferis et al. 2015). There is greater difficulty in differentiating between sedentary activities such as lying awake, sitting and TV watching, which are detrimental to health. There are other methods available. Approaches shown to be effective include the use of arm angle change to carry out posture classification from the wrist. Rowland's Sedentary Sphere uses the arm angle of 15° and movement intensity to classify participants as 'reclining/sitting' or 'upright/standing' correctly 74% and 91% of the time, respectively using either the GENEActiv or the ActiGraph GT3X+ (Rowlands et al. 2016b).

Finally, sleep can be accurately measured using raw accelerometer data, though the available analytical methods are diverse. It has long been accepted that sleep measurement using accelerometer methods based on the presence or absence of movement miscodes wakefulness as sleep if the person is not moving, as is common in insomniacs. However, a novel approach using arm angle change was used in the Whitehall II Study and validated against a criterion reference (van Hees et al. 2015). More recently, sleep and activity type were measured using machine learning algorithms in 96,220 UK Biobank participants (Willetts et al. 2018). The arm angle analysis is available as part of GGIR (van Hees 2014), whilst implementing machine learning techniques requires some specialist knowledge of computational analysis.

Perhaps the most comprehensive and user-friendly metric package is that developed by Vincent van Hees and colleagues. This involved the systematic development of raw accelerometer metrics which carried out autocalibration (van Hees et al. 2014; van Hees et al. 2013) of the device and provided easy-to-use output in mg. A cut-point of, for example, 100 mg can then be used to classify MVPA. This approach is the metric most commonly adopted across epidemiological studies.

Data processing and analysis using GGIR

Euclidean norm minus one by van Hees and colleagues was developed for wrist-worn accelerometry-based activity monitors and has been used in the Whitehall II Study and UK Biobank. It is suitable for use with the GENEA and GENEActiv and ActiGraph monitors (Rowlands et al. 2016a).

The open-source package GGIR enables the processing and analysing of raw accelerometer signals in R (http://cran.r-project.org). Signal processing in GGIR includes: (1) autocalibration using gravity as a reference, (2) detection of abnormal values, (3) detection of non-wear and (4) calculation of the vector magnitude of acceleration corrected for gravity (Euclidean norm minus 1g) for 5-second epochs in mg.

Accelerometer data downloaded as .gt3x files should be converted to .csv format for data processing.

A shell function called g.shell allows you to interact with the accelerometer data. GGIR is made of five parts. Part 1 loads the raw data.

Part 1:

Line 33 'windowsizes' allows you to set the epoch length for summarising acceleration values and the non-wear time window.

Line 34 'do.cal' allows you to alter the gravity autocalibration. I would advise you to leave this as it is, separating gravitational from movement-related acceleration.

Part 2:

Here you can ignore parts of the data (line 44). If a participant did not put on the device until 5 hours after it started recording, you can ignore the first 5 hours of data. If the participant returned the device earlier than planned and you need to trim the end of the data by 10 hours, you can do this at line 45.

Part 3:

This stage carries out some pre-processing for Part 4, sleep detection. Parts of the signal not considered as 'sleep' are removed from the data. You can see the angle threshold set at 5° within a time window of 5 minutes, in keeping with published accelerometer methods. Only alter this where improved analyses are published using different arm angle thresholds.

Part 4:

Here you can link the data to a sleep diary, also called a 'sleep log'. If you have used a sleep diary, then enter the file location after 'loglocation'. If you have not used a sleep diary in your study, then simply leave the file location blank. In 'def.noc.sleep', GGIR always uses the latest computational method for sleep detection.

Part 5:

GGIR performs separation of different behaviours in the acceleration signal. On lines 88–90 you can see thresholds set for light (30 mg), moderate (100 mg) and vigorous (400 mg) physical activity. Ensure you alter this according to the latest validation study for your study population, for example MVPA in older adults.

Now you can start to analyse the data by clicking the 'source' button with the left mouse button. This analyses the data, stores the output in a .csv file and allows you to open the file to reveal values for weekdays, valid hours of data per day, light, moderate and vigorous physical activity, and sleep duration.

These open-source packages can derive a multitude of variables from a single acceleration signal, including energy expenditure, METs, MVPA, activity types such as sitting, standing, walking and running, sedentary behaviour, and sleep.

Enthusiasm for accelerometer use in population surveillance is growing. In addition to this, the size of longitudinal studies using accelerometers as their principal method of physical activity assessment is rising, from NHANES in 2003 (n = 2174) to UK Biobank in 2017 (n = 106,053). With the advancement of technology, researchers have at their disposal body-worn activity monitors that are practical and affordable. Figure 8.2 shows the greater flexibility offered by using raw accelerometer data.

However, despite rapid advances in measurement technology, strict adherence to measurement rules must be maintained. Methodological consistency is critical for valid comparisons of physical activity data from different populations, and at different points in time.

It is now more common than ever to see multi-disciplinary teams, including clinicians, physiologists or psychologists, collaborating with method developers and measurement experts to produce impactful research in physical activity epidemiology.

However, researchers are now faced with new, equally challenging decisions. Sensor technology, data storage and data analysis have advanced with such rapid pace that specialist knowledge is needed to understand the technology of modern accelerometers, the data they produce and how to carry out the advanced analytical procedures required to derive measures of physical activity from the acceleration signal. Specialists in the areas of advance analytics must develop methods to analyse accelerometer data that are user-friendly so that they can be implemented outside laboratory-based validation studies, in epidemiological research.

Toward 24-hour movement surveillance and guidelines

Substantial evidence has led to recommendations for adequate physical activity, limited sedentary behaviour and healthy sleep habits to achieve increased longevity, improved health and disease prevention. Health research has focused on these different daily activities, but in order for researchers to better understand activity–health relationships, it is necessary to study the complete 24-hour activity cycle. Combined measurement of physical activity, sedentary behaviour and sleep is essential to create robust activity recommendations throughout a 24-hour cycle. Current activity and sleep guidelines are limited to 30 minutes per day of exercise and 7–8 hours of sleep, leaving roughly 16 hours of time with vague recommendation to avoid too much sitting.

Prior to the development of 24-hour activity monitoring, the collection of objective measures of physical activity, sedentary behaviour and sleep was challenging Technological advances now make these measurements possible, using small wearable devices such as the GENEActiv, Axivity and ActiGraph GT3X+. Researchers have used data from studies such as the UK Biobank to derive objective measures of physical activity, sedentary behaviour and sleep from a single acceleration signal in large numbers of participants (>90,000) (Willetts et al. 2018).

Summary

This chapter has provided a step-by-step guide to data collection, data processing and data analysis. The aim was to show how to use raw accelerometers to obtain measurements of MVPA, sedentary activity and sleep derived from the continuous 24-hour movement data.

Considering the analytical freedom provided by raw data, the most important guidance refers to the running of accelerometer metrics and carrying out data analysis. Nevertheless, as studies get larger, these resources will move online, forming large web-based infrastructures.

The key points of Chapter 8 are:

- The use of raw accelerometers, worn at the wrist, gives users the chance to derive measures of physical activity, sedentary behaviour and sleep from a single acceleration signal.
- Obtaining several measurements from one raw signal requires careful storage of the data and use of a well-validated metric such as ENMO. This carries out autocalibration and detection of non-wear time for you.
- Future studies are likely to shift away from measuring physical activity, instead obtaining measures of physical activity, sedentary behaviour and sleep to promote 24-hour movement guidelines.

References

Anderson, K. N., M. Catt, J. Collerton, K. Davies, T. von Zglinicki, T. B. Kirkwood, and C. Jagger. 2014. 'Assessment of sleep and circadian rhythm disorders in the very old: the Newcastle 85+ Cohort Study', *Age Ageing*, 43: 57–63.

Bai, J., C. Di, L. Xiao, K. R. Evenson, A. Z. LaCroix, C. M. Crainiceanu, and D. M. Buchner. 2016. 'An activity index for raw accelerometry data and its comparison with other activity metrics', *PLOS ONE*, 11: e0160644.

Bai, J., B. He, H. Shou, V. Zipunnikov, T. A. Glass, and C. M. Crainiceanu. 2014. 'Normalization and extraction of interpretable metrics from raw accelerometry data', *Biostatistics*, 15: 102–16.

Bakrania, K., T. Yates, A. V. Rowlands, D. W. Esliger, S. Bunnewell, J. Sanders, M. Davies, K. Khunti, and C. L. Edwardson. 2016. 'Intensity thresholds on raw acceleration data: Euclidean Norm Minus One (ENMO) and Mean Amplitude Deviation (MAD) approaches', *PLOS ONE*, 11: e0164045.

Brond, J. C., and D. Arvidsson. 2016. 'Sampling frequency affects the processing of ActiGraph raw acceleration data to activity counts', *J Appl Physiol (1985)*, 120: 362–9.

Crouter, S. E., E. E. Kuffel, J. D. Haas, E. A. Frongillo, and D. R. Bassett, Jr. 2010. 'A refined 2-regression model for the ActiGraph accelerometer', *Med Sci Sports Exerc*, 42: 1029–37.

da Silva, S. G., K. R. Evenson, I. C. M. da Silva, M. A. Mendes, M. R. Domingues, M. F. da Silveira, F. C. Wehrmeister, U. Ekelund, and P. C. Hallal. 2018. 'Correlates of accelerometer-assessed physical activity in pregnancy: the 2015 Pelotas (Brazil) Birth Cohort Study', *Scand J Med Sci Sports*, 28: 1934–45.

Doherty, A., D. Jackson, N. Hammerla, T. Plotz, P. Olivier, M. H. Granat, T. White, V. T. van Hees, M. I. Trenell, C. G. Owen, S. J. Preece, R. Gillions, S. Sheard, T. Peakman, S. Brage, and N. J. Wareham. 2017. 'Large scale population assessment of physical activity using wrist worn accelerometers: the UK Biobank Study', *PLOS ONE*, 12: e0169649.

Esliger, D. W., A. V. Rowlands, T. L. Hurst, M. Catt, P. Murray, and R. G. Eston. 2011. 'Validation of the GENEA Accelerometer', *Med Sci Sports Exerc*, 43: 1085–93.

Freedson, P., D. Pober, and K. F. Janz. 2005. 'Calibration of accelerometer output for children', *Med Sci Sports Exerc*, 37: S523–30.

Gabriel, K. P., S. Sidney, D. R. Jacobs, Jr., K. M. Whitaker, M. R. Carnethon, C. E. Lewis, P. J. Schreiner, R. I. Malkani, J. M. Shikany, J. P. Reis, and B. Sternfeld. 2018. 'Ten-year changes in accelerometer-based physical activity and sedentary time during midlife: CARDIA Study', *Am J Epidemiol*, 187: 2145–50.

Hildebrand, M., V. T van Hees, B. H. Hansen, and U. Ekelund. 2014. 'Age group comparability of raw accelerometer output from wrist- and hip-worn monitors', *Med Sci Sports Exerc*, 46: 1816–24.

Innerd, P., and University of Newcastle upon Tyne Institute for Ageing. 2015. *Assessment of Physical Activity and Sleep Using Raw Accelerometry*, Newcastle upon Tyne, UK: Newcastle University.

Innerd, P., M. Catt, J. Collerton, K. Davies, M. Trenell, T. B. Kirkwood, and C. Jagger. 2015. 'A comparison of subjective and objective measures of physical activity from the Newcastle 85+ Study', *Age Ageing*, 44: 691–4.

Jefferis, B. J., C. Sartini, E. Shiroma, P. H. Whincup, S. G. Wannamethee, and I. M. Lee. 2015. 'Duration and breaks in sedentary behaviour: accelerometer data from 1566 community-dwelling older men (British Regional Heart Study)', *Br J Sports Med*, 49: 1591–4.

John, D., J. Sasaki, J. Staudenmayer, M. Mavilia, and P. S. Freedson. 2013. 'Comparison of raw acceleration from the GENEA and ActiGraph GT3X+ activity monitors', *Sensors (Basel)*, 13: 14,754–63.

LaPorte, R. E., L. H. Kuller, D. J. Kupfer, R. J. McPartland, G. Matthews, and C. Caspersen. 1979. 'An objective measure of physical activity for epidemiologic research', *Am J Epidemiol*, 109: 158–68.

Matthew, C. E. 2005. 'Calibration of accelerometer output for adults', *Med Sci Sports Exerc*, 37: S512–22.

Matthews, C. E., M. Hagstromer, D. M. Pober, and H. R. Bowles. 2012. 'Best practices for using physical activity monitors in population-based research', *Med Sci Sports Exerc*, 44: S68–76.

Phillips, L. R., G. Parfitt, and A. V. Rowlands. 2013. 'Calibration of the GENEA accelerometer for assessment of physical activity intensity in children', *J Sci Med Sport*, 16: 124–8.

Rosenberger, M. E., J. E. Fulton, M. P. Buman, R. P. Troiano, M. A. Grandner, D. M. Buchner, and W. L. Haskell. 2019. 'The 24-hour activity cycle: a new paradigm for physical activity', *Med Sci Sports Exerc*, 51: 454–64.

Rowlands, A. V., T. Yates, M. Davies, K. Khunti, and C. L. Edwardson. 2016a. 'Raw accelerometer data analysis with GGIR R-package: does accelerometer brand matter?', *Med Sci Sports Exerc*, 48: 1935–41.

Rowlands, A. V., T. Yates, T. S. Olds, M. Davies, K. Khunti, and C. L. Edwardson. 2016b. 'Sedentary sphere: wrist-worn accelerometer-brand independent posture classification', *Med Sci Sports Exerc*, 48: 748–54.

Sherar, L. B., P. Griew, D. W. Esliger, A. R. Cooper, U. Ekelund, K. Judge, and C. Riddoch. 2018. 'International Children's Accelerometry Database (ICAD)'. Accessed 10 April 2019. www.mrc-epid.cam.ac.uk/research/studies/icad/.

Tremblay, M. S., V. Carson, and J. P. Chaput. 2016. 'Introduction to the Canadian 24-Hour Movement Guidelines for Children and Youth: an integration of physical activity, sedentary behaviour, and sleep', *Appl Physiol Nutr Metab*, 41: iii–iv.

Troiano, R. P., D. Berrigan, K. W. Dodd, L. C. Masse, T. Tilert, and M. McDowell. 2008. 'Physical activity in the United States measured by accelerometer', *Med Sci Sports Exerc*, 40: 181–8.

Troiano, R. P., J. J. McClain, R. J. Brychta, and K. Y. Chen. 2014. 'Evolution of accelerometer methods for physical activity research', *Br J Sports Med*, 48: 1019–23.

van Hees, V. T. 2014. 'GGIR: raw accelerometer data analysis'. Accessed 10 April 2019. https://cran.r-project.org/web/packages/GGIR/.

van Hees, V. T., Z. Fang, J. Langford, F. Assah, A. Mohammad, I. C. da Silva, M. I. Trenell, T. White, N. J. Wareham, and S. Brage. 2014. 'Autocalibration of accelerometer data for free-living physical activity assessment using local gravity and temperature: an evaluation on four continents', *J Appl Physiol (1985)*, 117: 738–44.

van Hees, V. T., L. Gorzelniak, E. C. Dean Leon, M. Eder, M. Pias, S. Taherian, U. Ekelund, F. Renstrom, P. W. Franks, A. Horsch, and S. Brage. 2013. 'Separating movement and gravity components in an acceleration signal and implications for the assessment of human daily physical activity', *PLOS ONE*, 8: e61691.

van Hees, V. T., F. Renstrom, A. Wright, A. Gradmark, M. Catt, K. Y. Chen, M. Lof, L. Bluck, J. Pomeroy, N. J. Wareham, U. Ekelund, S. Brage, and P. W. Franks. 2011. 'Estimation of daily energy expenditure in pregnant and non-pregnant women using a wrist-worn tri-axial accelerometer', *PLOS ONE*, 6: e22922.

van Hees, V. T., S. Sabia, K. N. Anderson, S. J. Denton, J. Oliver, M. Catt, J. G. Abell, M. Kivimaki, M. I. Trenell, and A. Singh-Manoux. 2015. 'A novel, open access method to assess sleep duration using a wrist-worn accelerometer', *PLOS ONE*, 10: e0142533.

van Hees, V. T., R. C. van Lummel, and K. R. Westerterp. 2009. 'Estimating activity-related energy expenditure under sedentary conditions using a tri-axial seismic accelerometer', *Obesity (Silver Spring)*, 17: 1287–92.

van Remoortel, H., S. Giavedoni, Y. Raste, C. Burtin, Z. Louvaris, E. Gimeno-Santos, D. Langer, A. Glendenning, N. S. Hopkinson, I. Vogiatzis, B. T. Peterson, F. Wilson, B. Mann, R. Rabinovich, M. A. Puhan, and T. Troosters. 2012. 'Validity of activity monitors in health and chronic disease: a systematic review', *Int J Behav Nutr Phys Act*, 9: 84.

Ward, D. S., K. R. Evenson, A. Vaughn, A. B. Rodgers, and R. P. Troiano. 2005. 'Accelerometer use in physical activity: best practices and research recommendations', *Med Sci Sports Exerc*, 37: S582–8.

Wijndaele, K., K. Westgate, S. K. Stephens, S. N. Blair, F. C. Bull, S. F. Chastin, D. W. Dunstan, U. Ekelund, D. W. Esliger, P. S. Freedson, M. H. Granat, C. E. Matthews, N. Owen, A. V. Rowlands, L. B. Sherar, M. S. Tremblay, R. P. Troiano, S. Brage, and G. N. Healy. 2015. 'Utilization and harmonization of adult accelerometry data: review and expert consensus', *Med Sci Sports Exerc*, 47: 2129–39.

Willetts, M., S. Hollowell, L. Aslett, C. Holmes, and A. Doherty. 2018. 'Statistical machine learning of sleep and physical activity phenotypes from sensor data in 96,220 UK Biobank participants', *Sci Rep*, 8: 7961.

Zhang, S., P. Murray, R. Zillmer, R. G. Eston, M. Catt, and A. V. Rowlands. 2012a. 'Activity classification using the GENEA: optimum sampling frequency and number of axes', *Med Sci Sports Exerc*, 44: 2228–34.

Zhang, S., A. V. Rowlands, P. Murray, and T. L. Hurst. 2012b. 'Physical activity classification using the GENEA wrist-worn accelerometer', *Med Sci Sports Exerc*, 44: 742–8.

9

E-SCIENCE

Big data, management, processing and analysis

The increasing demands of wearable sensors, in terms of data storage, sharing and analysis already present logistical problems. However, no sooner are these uncovered than technology is able to tackle them. Computer technologies are needed to store and analyse raw accelerometer data. With data sets rapidly increasing in size and data analyses evolving at a rapid pace, ambitious plans to develop an International Activity Monitor Database look ever more feasible.

The increasing need for technology in physical activity assessment occurs in much the same way and same time as technology revolutions in other areas, such as medicine and healthcare.

This chapter will discuss areas of technology, already involved in other areas of science, that make progress in physical activity measurement more rapid and realistic. We will address four areas:

- E-science – a computationally intensive science focused on the development of new computational tools and infrastructures to support scientific discovery.
- Big data – data sets that exceed the capabilities of commonly used software tools for their storage, management and processing, and require advanced technological innovations.
- Cloud computing – 'cloud' refers to online infrastructure that provides storage services and can also provide data analytics. Unlike conventional physical storage space, cloud storage scales according to the needs of the user.
- Almost all aspects of modern life have been changed permanently by the omnipresent system linking technologies around the globe: the internet. 'Medical Internet of Things' refers to devices which can monitor health indicators, administer medication, provide lifestyle prompts and track real-time data, and can all connect and interact

Introduction

Technical advances in accelerometer-based devices are occurring rapidly and continuously. These include increasing memory and battery capacities, wider acceleration range, smaller size and lower costs. Raw acceleration signal data facilitates the use of numerous analytical methods to derive various measures from a single acceleration signal.

An ever-increasing number of studies are using accelerometers to obtain objective measures of physical activity, and the use of a large sample size often reveals new and original insights. The pooling of data across studies is one way to achieve this. The use of accelerometers in large-scale population-level surveillance over periods of the lifecourse results in growing amounts of stored acceleration data across the globe.

The combination of an online web platform with cloud computing has the potential to revolutionise physical activity research by giving scientists the computational resources they need on a cost-effective basis. Accompanying the enthusiasm regarding high-resolution raw acceleration signal capture are concerns related to storage and transmission of the high data volumes as well as appropriate data modelling methods.

Data transfer from the onboard memory of raw accelerometers (about 0.5 GB for each 7-day collection) can now be performed within minutes, and analysis in under 30 minutes. Such large accelerometer data sets (UK Biobank n = 100,000) are too large and complex for traditional statistical software to adequately deal with. Online applications overcome this. However, these resources need to be user-friendly and accessible to researchers of all backgrounds. Online applications represent a way for users to access network storage capacities on a large scale. These applications, shown schematically in Figure 9.1, not only offer data storage, but also the capacity for data governance and analysis.

The wave of new technologies sweeping across modern science enables data to be generated at unprecedented scales. Enthusiasm for the collection of raw, unprocessed accelerometer data supports efforts to standardise and harmonise procedures for data collection, processing and analysis. This overcomes problems caused by variation in monitor output (proprietary counts) and the inconsistent use of data analysis techniques. Expert consensus states that researchers should use raw accelerometer data routinely across all studies, and obtain important sociodemographic, anthropometric and health status data. In addition, it is recommended that methodological transparency of data collection procedures is preserved. Combined, this promotes the formation of an International Activity Monitor Database. However, strategies enabling comparisons of activity monitor data between studies/countries require the development of an online infrastructure.

The technology needed to build web-based services is readily available. In areas of science handling the largest amounts of data, such as genomics using genomic information about an individual as part of their clinical care (Halligan et al. 2009), cloud computing and open-source software have been used since 2010. This provides theoretically limitless storage capacity, the opportunity to pool data, and easier

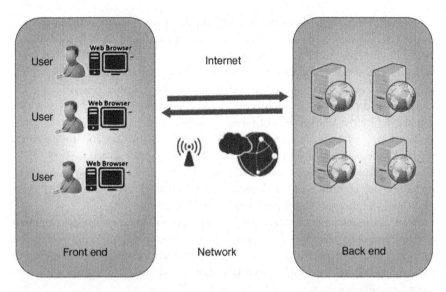

FIGURE 9.1   Cloud computing architecture. Users access the services using a computer and user interface (front end) connected to servers and storage (back end) on which their data is managed via the internet.

access to advanced analytics, where the cost of the service is the only expenditure. It makes sense to model future efforts on existing successes.

E-science applications often feature a graphic user interface (GUI) operated in a 'point and click' fashion. This allows researchers to process and analyse complex data, such as raw accelerometer, data without the need for specialist knowledge such as understanding and writing programming language specific to packages such as R, Python, C, Java and C++. The data from large-scale studies involving raw accelerometers taking place longitudinally is often measured in terabytes, and thus tests the limits of conventional desktop computing. Undoubtedly, the use of accelerometers in population surveillance will require network computing, or more often, cloud computing, which provides theoretically limitless storage capacity without the need for a physical hard drive. This quantity of data is called 'big data'

E-science applications

E-science is computationally intensive science which is carried out using a computer network. It represents the systems through which the user accesses and interacts with big data. Typically, the computer is part of a grid or network of computers which, combined, increases overall computing power: each computer shares its resources with every other system on the network. The increased computing power allows data collection, storage, data processing and analysis as well as the dissemination of research findings (Watson, Trefethen and Vander Meer 2010).

The UK, USA, Netherlands and Sweden have fully funded e-science infrastructures. In the UK, the first e-science programme was announced in 2000, funded mainly by the Engineering and Physical Sciences Research Council (EPSRC), a UK body that provides funding for research development in mathematics, artificial intelligence and computer science. The UK e-science programme comprises a wide range of resources in centres such as the National e-Science Centre (NeSC), which is managed by the Universities of Glasgow and Edinburgh. In the United States, e-science programmes are sometimes called cyberinfrastructure and are primarily funded by the National Science Foundation office of cyberinfrastructure (NSF OCI). The Netherlands eScience Centre in Amsterdam features a vast array of projects, including the continuation of sleep detection work by van Hees (2018), who pioneered so much developmental work in raw accelerometry.

Most of the research activities into e-science have focused on the development of new computational tools and infrastructures to support scientific discovery. The sheer cost and scale alone mean that e-science projects usually involve large teams managed and developed by research laboratories and large universities with substantial research income.

The UK-based e-Science Central is a cloud computing platform linked to over 25 research projects (Watson, Hiden and Woodman 2018). It provides storage and software as services to users who want to carry out management, analysis and sharing/collaboration. The use of cloud technology means that the storage available to users is theoretically limitless: Infrastructure as a Service (IaaS), which involves cloud storage and the option to organise and manage data how best suits them. However, potential users also want access to software. This is featured as applications such as Platform as a Service (PaaS), that can be combined to serve users' specific needs, and Software as a Service (SaaS), which makes several applications available to users. The type of software on offer depends on the needs of the user.

The creators of e-Science Central collaborated with physical activity researchers at the same institution, Newcastle University (Watson, Hiden and Woodman 2018). Together, they developed an accelerometer data capture application. The aim was to provide researchers with an application which facilitated upload and storage of accelerometer data and the facility to run an emulator algorithm to allow the use of older accelerometer models. However, the protocol involved a device wear time of 2 weeks. The authors suggest this is typical, but this is not the case. As a result, the processing time for one file was roughly 30 minutes. Here is a real-world example of the challenges involved with the use of raw accelerometer data.

As well as providing access to better resources regarding storage and data analysis, e-science platforms feature robust security mechanisms. For example, once uploaded, a data file is stored and duplicated so the original version is always accessible. The system maintains specific permissions for members of the study team. For example, some members of the team may have access to amend and run analyses on the data, whereas other users may have access to carry out visualisation and data cleaning. All user actions are tracked to ensure robust data governance.

The challenges presented by large, complex raw accelerometer data focus mainly on storage and analysis of the data. The use of web-based platforms theoretically overcomes these challenges. However, much more communication and collaboration is needed between researchers in physical activity epidemiology and the teams responsible for designing and developing e-science platforms. At present, there are no well-established, well-known research efforts using the services provided via e-science platforms. As studies such as UK Biobank and NHANES collect ever-greater quantities of data, the need to shift from desktop computing to e-science grows more pressing.

In addition to morbidity and premature mortality, physical inactivity is responsible for a substantial economic burden. This provides further justification to prioritise promotion of regular physical activity worldwide. Equally, the evidence underpinning this features important gaps. Physical activity, sedentary behaviour and health consequences have reached burdensome levels (Ding et al. 2016). Multidisciplinary, global collaborations are relatively new in physical activity research. As larger, more complex data sets such as those obtained using raw accelerometers accrue, they can be explored more thoroughly using e-science via data processing, data modelling and analysis.

Most organisations reach a trigger point where new data management options need to be explored; this is often when hundreds of gigabytes are being stored. A consensus amongst measurement experts is to use raw accelerometer data. The use of raw, unprocessed acceleration data facilitates the pooling of data from different studies and re-analysis using the same or newer analytical methods. Such large accelerometer data sets, for example UK Biobank (n = 100,000), are too large and complex for desktop-based data storage and traditional statistical software packages to adequately deal with (UK Biobank 2017). Here we enter the realms of 'big data'.

Big data: a new paradigm in scientific measurement

'Big data' refers to data sets that exceed the capabilities of commonly used software tools for their storage, management and processing (Bradley 2013). Big data does not have a standard definition, as the relative size of data is constantly changing. This growth is due in part to cheap yet omnipresent information-sensing devices such as mobile devices, cameras, microphones and wireless sensor networks. However, more is not always better. It is essential to maintain a high quality of data. As such, gatekeepers should be mindful of the importance of volume (the quantity of stored data – the size of the data determines its value), variety (type of data needs to be understood by the people who analyse it), velocity (the speed of transfer and processing must meet the demands of those who need it) and veracity (the quality of data may vary, which affects its accuracy) (Fung, Tse and Fu 2015).

Modern science is seeing the emergence of a completely new approach to the acquisition of knowledge from existing observational and empirical approaches. Big data research complements the more conventional, constrained hypothesis-driven approach in four significant ways: first, expanding the current approach to study sampling; second, providing objective measures, not just of physical activity, where conventional research relied on self-reported data; third, reaching populations that have proven difficult to access with conventional research methods; and finally, the potential for evaluating real-world interventions.

A second consensus amongst experts concerns the collection of sociodemographic, anthropometric and health-related data. This becomes ever more feasible as healthcare analytics attract the attention of researchers. The prevalence of data sources from numerous digital sensors in modern smartphones and wearable technologies is growing rapidly. Big data for health informatics presents opportunities to tackle disease, for example through more efficient prevention or treatment. The combination of raw accelerometer data with participant data creates opportunities to identify physical activity determinants. Combining data from studies in children, adults and older adults would fit in with a lifecourse approach and add greater insights into the determinants of physical activity and how they change as people age. However, good-quality data is needed to do this.

Maintaining the quality of raw accelerometer data requires clear reporting of device initialisation, and adherence to standardised data collection protocols where necessary. Good-quality data can more readily be combined to form larger data sets. Pooled accelerometer data was first published as part of the International Children's Accelerometry Database (ICAD) (www.mrc-epid.cam.ac.uk/research/studies/icad/). The ICAD pooled and harmonised data from ~26,000 children from 20 studies worldwide. However, there are lessons to be learned from the ICAD. First, studies used accelerometer data expressed in counts. This immediately raises concerns over the comparability of data pooled from different studies The device used, the ActiGraph, has demonstrated poor performance in children. Finally, investigators observed inter-study variability in physical activity. However, there was no way of determining the cause (Hansen et al. 2018). All things considered, the ICAD shows that methodological rigour is essential when attempting to develop an accelerometer database.

The pooling of raw accelerometry data is proposed in order to generate an International Activity Monitoring Database. Data pooled from studies as large as the UK Biobank and NHANES poses serious challenges. This data set would likely exceed the limits of physical data storage. The use of online repositories to store and combine raw accelerometer data from different studies makes this task feasible, similar to that carried out in line with the WHO STEPS chronic disease risk factor surveillance with IPAQ and GPAQ (www.who.int/ncds/surveillance/steps/en/). A global web-based dashboard would help researchers access the IAMD and assist in data governance, management and analysis.

The use of big data comes with big challenges. To fully exploit the technological advances made in the field of accelerometry, data storage and analysis need to be decentralised and move online. A structured approach to the use of big data has resulted in a new, web-based approach to the storage, management and analysis of big data using cloud technology.

Cloud computing

Web-based platforms in e-science typically feature a storage cloud, online infrastructure that provides storage services, often with data management and computational services. It is a means by which the user can access higher-level computer resources at a much-reduced cost without having to understand how to build and maintain them. Well-known cloud services are offered by Amazon, Microsoft and Google, to name but a few.

A storage cloud provides storage services (block- or file-based services), a data cloud provides data management services (record-based, column-based or object-based services), and a computing cloud provides computational services. Often, these are stacked together to serve as a computing platform for developing cloud-based applications. Cloud computing has the potential to revolutionise e-science. It offers scientists the computational resources needed for the storage, management and analysis of big data without the requirement for any specialist knowledge of cloud technology.

For the physical activity researcher, cloud computing offers a way of accessing an online platform with storage and software which far surpasses that which is available on a desktop computer setup. In general, there are three characteristics that are common among all cloud-computing platforms:

- The 'back end' (server, storage, hardware) is completely managed by the cloud vendor.
- The user only pays for services used, e.g. storage memory in terabytes, data processing time.
- Services are scalable,

Specifically, a cloud-based platform offers storage that scales according to the needs of the user. For example, say a study has 1.7 terabytes of data. Stored on the cloud, the user would only pay for 1.7 terabytes' worth of storage. Stored conventionally, the user might have to purchase a 2 terabyte hard disk drive. Other benefits of cloud computing are listed in Table 9.1.

The components required for cloud computing are referred to as its 'architecture'. This architecture typically consists of a front-end platform (computer, mobile device), back-end platforms (servers, storage), a cloud-based delivery system and a network (internet, intranet). Combined, these components make up the cloud computing architecture shown in Figure 9.1. The ability to pay on demand and scale quickly is largely a result of cloud computing vendors being able to pool resources that may be divided among multiple clients.

The aim of cloud computing is to allow users to take benefit from all of these technologies without the need for deep knowledge about or expertise of each one of them. Cloud computing reduces costs, and helps users focus on their study aims unimpeded by IT obstacles. The main strength of cloud technology is virtualisation: instead of conventional physical computing, software and computing are combined into one or more

TABLE 9.1 Comparison of traditional 'on-premises' data management versus cloud computing.

	On-premises	Cloud computing
Cost	User licences Hardware (storage) IT personnel	Subscription - fee

Performance	Influenced by many components
	    (machine spec, software updates)
		Single data centre
		Streamlined for specific needs
		    of the user

Security	User/site-specific	In line with vendor policies
Sharing	Data shared via email or online database	Users access centrally stored data
Scale	Site-specific	Global

User
    experience
	May need knowledge or IT support for
	    hardware/technology functions
		No need for specialist computer
		    knowledge
		On going training where needed

Maintenance	Dependent on IT upgrade	Carried out by vendor

'virtual' devices. Virtualisation provides important agility which speeds up IT operations, and reduces costs by increasing infrastructure utilisation. By minimising the extent to which the user is involved in standard processes, automation speeds these processes up, reduces labour costs and reduces the possibility of human errors.

On desktop applications, data would be downloaded from the device and stored on physical storage devices such as a hard disk drive or external memory. The user would select an analytical package and carry out the analysis to derive meaningful measures ready for entry into statistical tests. An online application could provide the following facilities. First, the user would upload data to a cloud server, which has theoretically limitless memory but scales with the needs of the user. Workflows can be automatically applied to the data to convert it into a desired format. Thereafter, data can be visualised, analysed and shared. Undoubtedly, online storage and processing of accelerometer data, such as shown in Figure 9.2, represents the next step in accelerometer-based assessment.

Online infrastructures increase user-friendliness, enhance data sharing opportunities and provide a service for researchers offering centralised data processing and data analysis. Other e-science platforms exist (Henriksen et al. 2017; Innerd et al. 2011). However, they need to be refined to fulfil the needs of the researcher who is keen to obtain the full spectrum of measures, physical activity to sleep, from raw accelerometer data.

The Medical Internet of Things

Almost all aspects of modern life have been changed permanently by the omnipresent system linking technologies around the globe: the internet. Strictly speaking, the internet is a broad array of electronic and wireless networking technologies. Connectivity was once only possible using specific devices such as desktops, laptops and tablets. However, we are now surrounded by internet connections in vehicles, home appliances, watches and other 'smart devices' which connect, interact and exchange data.

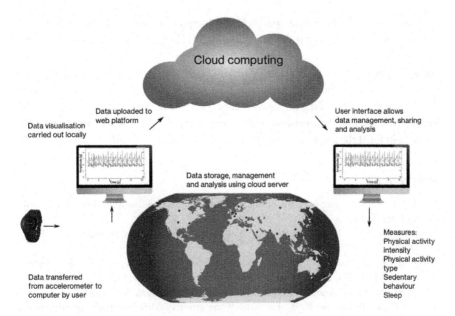

FIGURE 9.2 Storage, sharing and analysis of accelerometer data using cloud computing. Cloud computing allows the secure storage of data accessed via an online platform. Authorised users can access study data from anywhere across the globe.

The internet was created in the 1960s as a means of more effectively sending and receiving data between computers on a network. At the time, existing communication (telecommunication) occurred via circuit switching. This involved a connection, for example between the two telephones, through which data was sent for as long as the call lasted. In other words, a continuous wire circuit was occupied to send data, and if it was cut off, the data is lost. The improved version was packet switching, where the data is grouped or packed and sent in a way that ensures it arrives intact at its destination.

The Internet of Things has evolved due to multiple technologies such as the smart device. As the name suggests, this is an electronic gadget that is able to connect, share and interact with its user and other smart devices (smart devices were discussed as far back as the 1980s). Terms such as Smart Home or Smart Healthcare typically mean there is a level of automation involved.

The Medical Internet of things refers to devices which can monitor health indicators, administer medication, provide lifestyle prompts and track real-time data (Dimitrov 2016). Patients and the public already use a wealth of mobile applications to record and, in some cases, help manage their health needs. Wearable technologies being used in research, such as the accelerometer sensor, could be incorporated into healthcare. This could revolutionise data collection, where patients simply 'opt in' to share their data, in which case, e-science and cloud technology will be increasingly needed.

In fitting with a lifecourse approach, the Internet of Things can be used to track disease progression and promote early detection, and perhaps make decisions over critical situations for the improvement of the quality of life. At present, there is a significant focus on advancement of big data. The benefit for the public appears to be a better healthcare system to promote early detection and diagnosis of diseases. In the case of accelerometer sensors, the preventative effect of physical activity could be useful. For members of the public or patients needing treatment, 24-hour movement monitoring could help fulfil the assistive needs of the ageing population (Jagadeeswari et al. 2018).

References

Bradley, P. S. 2013. 'Implications of big data analytics on population health management', *Big Data*, 1: 152–9.

Dimitrov, D. V. 2016. 'Medical Internet of Things and big data in healthcare', *Healthc Inform Res*, 22: 156–63.

Ding, D., K. D. Lawson, T. L. Kolbe-Alexander, E. A. Finkelstein, P. T. Katzmarzyk, W. van Mechelen, and M. Pratt. 2016. 'The economic burden of physical inactivity: a global analysis of major non-communicable diseases', *Lancet*, 388: 1311–24.

Fung, I. C., Z. T. Tse, and K. W. Fu. 2015. 'Converting big data into public health', *Science*, 347: 620.

Halligan, B. D., J. F. Geiger, A. K. Vallejos, A. S. Greene, and S. N. Twigger. 2009. 'Low cost, scalable proteomics data analysis using Amazon's cloud computing services and open source search algorithms', *J Proteome Res*, 8: 3148–53.

Hansen, B. H., S. A. Anderssen, L. B. Andersen, M. Hildebrand, E. Kolle, J. Steene-Johannessen, S. Kriemler, A. S. Page, J. J. Puder, J. J. Reilly, L. B. Sardinha, E. M. F. van Sluijs, N. Wedderkopp, and U. Ekelund. 2018. 'Cross-Sectional associations of reallocating time between sedentary and active behaviours on cardiometabolic risk factors in young people: an International Children's Accelerometry Database (ICAD) analysis', *Sports Med*, 48: 2401–12.

Henriksen, A., L. A. Hopstock, G. Hartvigsen, and S. Grimsgaard. 2017. 'Using cloud-based physical activity data from Google Fit and Apple Healthkit to expand recording of physical activity data in a population study', *Stud Health Technol Inform*, 245: 108–12.

Innerd, P., V. van Hees, S. Woodman, H. Hiden, C. Turner, K. N. Anderson, M. Catt, M. Trenell, and P. Watson. 2011. 'MOVE eCloud: an open-source web platform for physical activity and sleep monitoring'. In *ICAMPAM (International Conference on Ambulatory Monitoring of Physical Activity and Movement)*, The Netherlands: Maastricht University.

Jagadeeswari, V., V. Subramaniyaswamy, R. Logesh, and V. Vijayakumar. 2018. 'A study on medical Internet of Things and big data in personalized healthcare system', *Health Inf Sci Syst*, 6: 14.

UK Biobank. 2017. 'Data Showcase'. Accessed 10 April 2019. www.ukbiobank.ac.uk/data-showcase/.

van Hees, V. 2018. 'Dr. Vincent van Hees'. Accessed 10 April 2019. www.esciencecenter.nl/profile/dr.-vincent-van-hees.

Watson, P., H. Hiden, and S. Woodman. 2018. 'e-Science Central'. Accessed 10 April 2019. www.esciencecentral.co.uk/.

Watson, P., A. Trefethen, and E. Vander Meer. 2010. 'E-science: past, present and future II', *Philos Trans A Math Phys Eng Sci*, 368: 4003.

10

PHYSICAL ACTIVITY ASSESSMENT IN LIFECOURSE EPIDEMIOLOGY

Future horizons

24-hour movement guidelines and knowledge gaps: a new research agenda

The assessment of physical activity across the lifecourse has evolved from an area of almost complete reliance on paper-based questionnaires to one of small, body-worn devices, housing advanced nanotechnology, with high-resolution data sampled at the sub-second level, continuous technological innovation and limitless opportunity. Continuous recording of week-long raw accelerometer data in large numbers of people has resulted in the profiling of physical activity, sedentary behaviour, sleep and circadian rhythm from a single acceleration signal, providing new insights into the interconnectedness of these behaviours and their effect on health across the whole lifecourse. The pace at which this field advances makes identifying the latest trends in measurement methodology largely redundant; instead we should recognise timeless recommendations that will remain unaffected by continuous innovation.

Physical activity assessment in population surveillance has evolved dramatically, from early devices, placed at the hip and removed before sleep, to wrist-worn technologies recording continuous acceleration data from which the whole movement spectrum of physical activity, sedentary behaviour and sleep can be derived. These technological innovations have led to changes in policy and framework in several countries across the globe.

Physical activity surveillance has traditionally focused on measuring and reporting on the most active end of the activity spectrum. Emerging research suggests that in addition to insufficient MVPA, sedentary behaviour and inadequate sleep are also important risk factors for chronic disease. In order to create effective public health policy and programme initiatives to target all levels of activity (MVPA, light physical activity, sedentary behaviour and sleep), the demand for reliable, nationally representative data and information on the patterns of all of these behaviours is required from across the whole lifecourse.

Current evidence from 24-hour activity monitoring increasingly highlights the importance of promoting sleep and physical activity and reducing sedentary time in the fight to reduce the global burden of the NCD crisis. In light of the available evidence, some countries have developed 24-hour movement guidelines for early years, including Canada (Tremblay et al. 2017), Australia (Okely et al. 2017), the UK and the USA. This focus on movement behaviours across the 24-hour period is a positive step, recognising that the whole day matters and individual movement behaviours such as physical activity, sedentary behaviour and sleep need to be considered in relation to each other when examining their associations with NCDs and other lifestyle risk factors.

From a lifecourse perspective, key steps need to be taken to improve lifelong health and well-being. High-quality 24-hour movement data are required across the whole lifecourse, including activity trends of pregnant women, to form an international surveillance database of movement behaviours. Such data can be mapped to changes in key determinants of physical activity, sedentary behaviour and sleep at key points of the lifecourse. The strength of this evidence will identify new key catalysts of change, and highlight where to start intervening and how.

There are several key areas of investigation that are critical to this new research area. These include identifying the interactions between breaking up sitting and sleep hours, determining the critical composition of breaking up prolonged sitting (e.g. type, intensity, frequency) and sleep (e.g. duration, quality, timing) required not only for health benefits, but also to prevent the accumulative effects of a poor 24-hour activity/sleep profile early in life.

There is still considerable debate concerning the optimal or minimum type, intensity, duration and frequency of physical activity necessary to replace sitting time and to benefit health. Individuals who engage in intense, structured exercise two to three times per week may still not be active enough to preserve health. Similarly, adherence to current physical activity guidelines in the presence of abundant sedentary behaviour and poor sleep creates similar concerns. Minimum physical activity requirements will likely be adjusted for individuals who routinely obtain insufficient sleep.

Changing behaviour requires an understanding of why people engage in unhealthy behaviours, such as sacrificing sleep and choosing sedentary leisure pursuits. Therefore, intervention studies targeting multiple health behaviours simultaneously, not just improving physical activity levels, but in this case breaking up time spent sedentary, and improving sleep, should be carried out. The development of these interventions could take advantage of the connectivity provided by online web applications linked to commercial technologies such as smartphones or even consumer activity/sleep trackers, such as the Fitbit or Apple iWatch, if not to provide objective measures of movement behaviours, perhaps to provide an indication of progress, but certainly to be used as tools to support and encourage behaviour change (Zhang et al. 2017). Research-grade accelerometers which do not provide participants with feedback (so as not to modify their behaviour) would still be used in large-scale population-based studies in the style of NHANES and UK Biobank.

Effective prevention strategies that target both movement and non-movement behaviours (Cassidy et al. 2016) such as physical activity, diet, sleep and sedentary behaviour in combination are needed to improve lifelong health (Collings et al. 2015). Since physical activity guidelines are established and appear to be effective, a next step would be breaking up prolonged sitting and promoting adequate sleep. Current assessment methods now make it possible to investigate interactions between behaviours. However, technological advances are rapid. It is important to implement long-lasting innovations (van Hees et al. 2016) which do not impede the long-term aims of the lifecourse assessments mentioned above.

Avoiding past digressions: the dichotomy of accelerometry

Looking forward, we should remember past digressions in the field, to ensure the same mistakes are not repeated. Large-scale assessments of human behaviour are underpinned by robust measurements: when new measurement methods are introduced, users should understand how they work and what factors influence the data produced. When accelerometers were first introduced, manufacturers produced numerous devices with varying technical specifications; accelerometers were used by researchers often with no understanding of how they worked, what factors influenced the data produced or whether the measures derived from them were usable. Seemingly, there emerged an imbalance between innovation and methodological rigour: a dichotomy of accelerometry.

Raw accelerometers provide complete methodological transparency. Similarly, they provide complete analytical freedom. Despite the reproducibility of results being a central tenet of the scientific method, few studies re-analyse existing accelerometer methods in laboratory conditions after the first validation, much less in free-living conditions. Consequently, researchers looking to track long-term trends across the lifecourse are dependent on claims made in existing laboratory-based validation studies. To avoid methods becoming popular without thorough evaluation, it is essential that methodologies are published in full, then reproduced and verified by other scientists in children, adults, older adults and the oldest old.

Certainly, the future is set to look very different from the past. The future of physical activity assessment will involve the pooling of data sets to form 'big data', centralised online storage and processing, and advanced computational analytics. Transparency is essential at all stages – and indeed, it is possible.

This collection and pooling of raw, unprocessed data may seem a monumental task. However, the rate of change seen in computer technology makes it increasingly realistic. Countless review papers, position statements and consensus reports have attempted to predict future trends in how physical activity will be assessed; few have proven accurate. Researchers from all fields interested in physical activity must recognise that the increasing involvement of technology in physical activity assessment – and indeed, all areas of life – means that predictions about the future are difficult to make, other than the fact that the future will be mind-blowingly different.

Technological change is exponential, although this is difficult to see, so let us use an example. The idea of smartphone technology, with direct interaction via a multi-touchscreen, came about in 2005. The first smartphones were manufactured in 2007. Less than two years after this, users were able to integrate technology from sensors such as built-in accelerometers with smartphone applications to track physical activity, sleep and various aspects of health-related behaviour. Only 8 years later, in 2015, all of this technology was miniaturised into a small device worn on the wrist.

Technological change is occurring at a pace faster than human innovation. Small human innovations result in significantly improved processes in data collection, storage and analysis. For example, an increase in the efficiency of a process typically results in an increase in output without any necessary increase in input from the user or researcher. Put simply, a human invents or improves a process, and as a result, bigger rewards are obtained for the same amount of work.

The accelerometer-based activity monitor has demonstrated a similar pace of evolution. In 2009, the technology was beginning to become small and cost-effective enough for use to monitor human movement and give measures of physical activity. By 2012, wrist-worn raw accelerometers were being used to collect raw movement data in roughly 100,000 adults as part of the UK Biobank. In under 10 years, there now exists a move to amass a global database featuring accelerometer-based movement data combined with sociodemographic and biological data from across the lifecourse.

Lifecourse physical activity assessment: focusing the picture

The increasing use of wrist-worn raw accelerometry represents the opportunity to capture and store continuous, high-resolution movement data over 7 or more days. The progress reported in these chapters provides researchers with the methods needed to derive measures of physical activity, activity intensity, activity type, sedentary behaviour and sleep from a single acceleration signal.

The wealth of information that can be derived from an acceleration signal is limited only by the rate of technological advances seen in analytical power. Therefore, researchers should aim to pool data in online repositories, such as the International Children's Accelerometry Database (Sherar et al. 2018). A key priority in lifecourse physical activity assessment is the development of an International Activity Monitor Database (Wijndaele et al. 2015). At the current rate of technology development, far more than a database is possible.

Technology advances at an increasingly rapid rate, making the future difficult to predict. Change is exponentially speeding up, so advances made in the past decade may begin to look trivial within a few years. Advanced computational methods such as 'deep learning' rely on a form of artificial intelligence that uses powerful microprocessor chips and algorithms to simulate neural networks that train and learn through experience, using massive data sets. Technologies like these close the gap between advanced analytics and measurements that can be used on a large scale.

Epidemiological research is becoming ever more information-driven, with sensor-based technologies generating terabytes of accelerometer data in months. A big data revolution in science is accompanied by high-performance computing that is available to all researchers. Therefore, large-scale data analysis, including data transfer, controlling access to the data, managing the data, standardising data formats and integrating data of multiple different types from different studies, represents the new frontier for experts to explore.

Cloud computing provides a highly flexible, low-cost computational environ-ment with capacity that scales with the needs of the user. It provides researchers with an online web platform incorporating cloud technology that facilitates the online storage, governance and analysis of raw accelerometry data. This also revo-lutionises current thinking about movement assessment, where desktop computing is likely to become redundant.

The researcher, the physician and the patient are surrounded by a network of tech-nology, devices embedded with electronics and sensors, all with network connectivity. Indeed, most areas of health are converging with technology, and all areas of healthcare are seeing reduced costs and increased efficiency. Mainly this has brought about two things done now better than ever before: measurement and communication. In the field of physical activity assessment, we are witnessing the importance of measuring only that which is useful and that can be communicated clearly (Figure 10.1).

The challenge of communicating the rich and plentiful data resulting from advanced sensor technology is evident throughout the whole of healthcare. As new technologies are created, the problems caused by manufacturers using their own proprietary protocols means sensors often talk in different languages and conse-quently cannot communicate with one another. This causes islands of information to develop, marooned behind bureaucracy, which undermines the whole concept of sensor-based measurement: this reduces benefits to the very individuals these technologies are aimed at helping.

Where big data is concerned, future developments must keep in mind common challenges, to avoid technology developments which do not help as intended. The rate of technological advance is too rapid to provide rigid guidelines. Future decisions should be informed by principles that are independent of temporal change. The principles guiding progress are focused on volume, velocity, variety, veracity and value.

The *volume* of data now generated is considerable. Before generating it, clear decisions must be made about how it is stored and how it is used. The speed or *velocity* at which we can analyse data is continuously increasing. Similarly, analytical procedures should be in place to provide the necessary velocity at which data can be rendered useful. This book has mainly discussed data arising from accelerometer-based devices. However, it is clear that these data alone are of little use without a variety of accompanying data to assist in understanding how and why physical activity changes across the lifecourse. We have discussed the effects of subjectivity

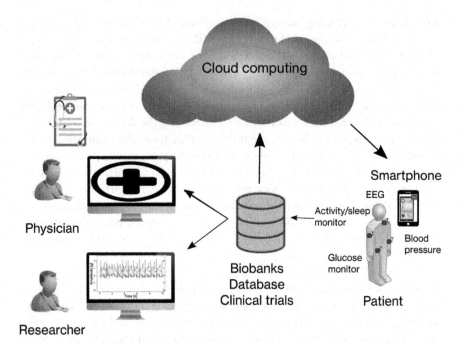

FIGURE 10.1 The future of big data in healthcare. Technology will allow patients to monitor themselves and to be monitored in real time by their physicians and consent to have their data stored in biobanks as research data.

on self-report assessment methods and the use of early accelerometers by researchers perhaps lacking an adequate understanding of how they should be used. The *veracity* of data is of principal importance, and combined with all the previous Vs, contributes directly to *value*. The aim of this book is to equip you with the knowledge and skills needed to comprehend and collect data that is of *value*. Research into the health of people across their lifecourse stands to benefit massively from the data described in this book.

For the models described above, it is easy to connect the data, the network and the computer: the human must develop and implement these tools correctly. WHO's STEPwise approach to chronic disease risk factor surveillance provides a good framework and practical ways to initiate physical activity surveillance. A key aim is to reduce physical inactivity by 10% by 2050. However, at the current rate of technology change, this target may well be surpassed. Ironically, the rate-limiting factor is no longer the technology we use, it is us. Looking forward, we must be careful to maintain the correct balance between robust scientific measurement and innovation. All researchers involved in the development, implementation and reporting of lifecourse physical activity should work together to achieve this and subsequent efforts to effectively tackle the burden of worldwide physical inactivity.

Summary

- The collection of continuous raw acceleration data over 24 hours gives rise to the opportunity to look at interactions between physical activity, sedentary behaviour and sleep.
- A new research agenda of 24-hour movement assessment has been proposed to more effectively tackle the NCD burden, with several countries developing 24-hour movement guidelines.
- From a lifecourse perspective, 24-hour movement assessment needs to be carried out from before childbirth, in pregnant mothers, during childhood, adulthood and in older adults.
- Whilst current technologies allow the interdependence of physical activity, sedentary behaviour and sleep to be explored, researchers should be careful to avoid repeating past errors in accelerometer-based movement monitoring and to make progress which maintains both innovation and methodological rigour.
- Future technologies look set to connect the patient/public, the clinician and researcher in the possible real-time monitoring of a wide range of variables from new and existing wearable sensor-based technologies.

References

Cassidy, S., J. Y. Chau, M. Catt, A. Bauman, and M. I. Trenell. 2016. 'Cross-sectional study of diet, physical activity, television viewing and sleep duration in 233,110 adults from the UK Biobank: the behavioural phenotype of cardiovascular disease and type 2 diabetes', *BMJ Open*, 6: e010038.

Collings, P. J., K. Wijndaele, K. Corder, K. Westgate, C. L. Ridgway, S. J. Sharp, V. Dunn, I. Goodyer, U. Ekelund, and S. Brage. 2015. 'Magnitude and determinants of change in objectively-measured physical activity, sedentary time and sleep duration from ages 15 to 17.5y in UK adolescents: the ROOTS Study', *Int J Behav Nutr Phys Act*, 12: 61.

Okely, A. D., D. Ghersi, K. D. Hesketh, R. Santos, S. P. Loughran, D. P. Cliff, T. Shilton, D. Grant, R. A. Jones, R. M. Stanley, J. Sherring, T. Hinkley, S. G. Trost, C. McHugh, S. Eckermann, K. Thorpe, K. Waters, T. S. Olds, T. Mackey, R. Livingstone, H. Christian, H. Carr, A. Verrender, J. R. Pereira, Z. Zhang, K. L. Downing, and M. S. Tremblay. 2017. 'A collaborative approach to adopting/adapting guidelines – the Australian 24-Hour Movement Guidelines for the early years (birth to 5 years): an integration of physical activity, sedentary behavior, and sleep', *BMC Public Health*, 17: 869.

Sherar, L. B., P. Griew, D. W. Esliger, A. R. Cooper, U. Ekelund, K. Judge, and C. Riddoch. 2018. 'International Children's Accelerometry Database (ICAD)'. Accessed 10 April 2019. www.mrc-epid.cam.ac.uk/research/studies/icad/.

Tremblay, M. S., J. P. Chaput, K. B. Adamo, S. Aubert, J. D. Barnes, L. Choquette, M. Duggan, G. Faulkner, G. S. Goldfield, C. E. Gray, R. Gruber, K. Janson, I. Janssen, X. Janssen, A. Jaramillo Garcia, N. Kuzik, C. LeBlanc, J. MacLean, A. D. Okely, V. J. Poitras, M. E. Rayner, J. J. Reilly, M. Sampson, J. C. Spence, B. W. Timmons, and V. Carson. 2017. 'Canadian 24-Hour Movement Guidelines for the Early Years (0–4 years): an integration of physical activity, sedentary behaviour, and sleep', *BMC Public Health*, 17: 874.

van Hees, V. T., K. Thaler-Kall, K. H. Wolf, J. C. Brond, A. Bonomi, M. Schulze, M. Vigl, B. Morseth, L. A. Hopstock, L. Gorzelniak, H. Schulz, S. Brage, and A. Horsch. 2016.

'Challenges and opportunities for harmonizing research methodology: raw accelerometry', *Methods Inf Med*, 55: 525–32.

Wijndaele, K., K. Westgate, S. K. Stephens, S. N. Blair, F. C. Bull, S. F. Chastin, D. W. Dunstan, U. Ekelund, D. W. Esliger, P. S. Freedson, M. H. Granat, C. E. Matthews, N. Owen, A. V. Rowlands, L. B. Sherar, M. S. Tremblay, R. P. Troiano, S. Brage, and G. N. Healy. 2015. 'Utilization and harmonization of adult accelerometry data: review and expert consensus', *Med Sci Sports Exerc*, 47: 2129–39.

Zhang, Q., X. Yang, D. Liu, and W. H. Zhao. 2017. 'Measurement and assessment of physical activity by information and communication technology', *Biomed Environ Sci*, 30: 465–72.

INDEX

Page numbers in bold indicate the location in the book where the term is defined, or where the primary discussion of it is located.